THE DICTIONARY OF
AMERICAN
BIRD NAMES

THE DICTIONARY OF
AMERICAN
BIRD NAMES
ERNEST A. CHOATE

Gambit
Boston

FIRST PRINTING

To Elaine and Shirley

Alison, "What's that, Granddaddy?"
Grandfather, "A robin."
Alison, "Why?"

(Adapted) *Punch*, January 17, 1906
From Ernest Weekley, *An Etymological
Dictionary of Modern English*

Preface

> And smale foweles maken melodye,
> Chaucer, *The Canterbury Tales*, Prologue

> This is to seyn, the foules of ravyne
> Were hyest set, and then the foules smale,
> That eten as hem nature wolde enclyne,
> As worm or thyng, of which I telle no tale;
> And water-fowl sat lowest in the dale,
> But foul that lyveth by seed sat on the grene
> And that so fele that wonder was to sene.
> Chaucer, *The Parlement of Foules*, The Proem

The writings of Chaucer are preeminent not only for their literary worth and their portrayal of the social life of the time, but also as a philological "monument." This is the term that language specialists attach to a noted body of writing in a given language from a specific period in the past, in this case the period of Middle English. At that time, quite evidently, a prominent member of the court of Edward III could use such spelling variations as *foweles* or *foul* and *yeer* or *yere* with no social penalty. The "monument" also shows that while the ways of letters in some words were already set, the spelling of others might vary until the custom of "correct" spelling became a matter of concern to school teachers and dictionary makers, as in our present period of Modern English. We can also note that *foul* (*foule, fowel, foghel*) in Chaucer's time meant all clothed in feathers, as *bird* does today. Chaucer's *briddes* was shifting away from its contemporary meaning of "young birds" and was gradually beginning to replace the then more inclusive *fowl*, which is now more commonly applied to the larger edible game birds and poultry, and likely to be found in combination with other words, as in waterfowl, wildfowl or wild fowl, or barnyard fowl.

The suggestion of a shift of meaning for *brid, briddes* in Chaucer's time is found in his "Parlement of Foules":

On every bough the *briddes* herde I synge,
With voys (voice) of aungel (angel) in her armonye (harmony);
Som besyede (beside) hem (them) hir (their) *briddes*
   forth to brynge.

The first *briddes* means adults in the present sense of the term, while the second evidently means the young, an older connotation. A few lines later, Chaucer with his inconsistent spelling has "every bryd cometh ther to chese (chase) his make (mate)," and "the goshawk that doth pyne (pain) to bryddes." The spelling *brid* and *byrd* both came into Middle English from Anglo-Saxon where the word was derived from *bredan*, "to breed." The transposition of the *r* changing *brid* to *bird* occurred first in the Northumbrian dialect, which gradually supplanted the older spelling. Although the new spelling prevailed in Shakespeare's time, the old meaning of young had not been dropped, as evidenced by:

And, being fed by us, you us'd us so
As that ungentle gull, the cuckoo's bird, (young)
Useth the sparrow;

which we find in *Henry IV*.

The gradual three-century-long change in the meaning of bird has at long last ended. Both spelling and meaning have attained a modicum of solitary distinctness when applied to a feathered animal. Its former meaning is archaic, and it is, from the linguist's historical viewpoint of language, quite a new word. What does the future hold? Doting grandmothers while supervising the photographing of their wriggling charges have been heard to say, "Look at the birdie" (spelling and meaning). Youth in our institutions of higher learning have been recorded as exclaiming, "College isn't what those old birds (meaning) say it is."

Contents

Cranes keep a watchful guard at night. They keep themselves awake for their sentry-go by holding stones in their claws,

When the stone is dropped through drowsiness, this wakes up the sentinel.

T. H. White, *The Bestiary*

I was always a lover of soft winged things.

Victor Hugo

Introduction

The purpose of this book is to promote an appreciation of the common and scientific names of North American birds. It aims to do this through an exploration of their origins and their meanings in the past, with the hope that that will give an understanding and in turn an added pleasurable dimension not only to the words themselves, but also to the recognition of the birds of which they are the voiced and written symbols. Thus we may become involved both in linguistics, the science of language, and in ornithology, the science of birds.

Modern linguistics looks upon a spoken language as a continually changing group of dialects which have enough in common for those using them to be able to understand one another. Attempts have been made to standardize a language by giving official sanction to a preeminent dialect, as Parisian for the French language, Castillian for Spanish, and Tuscan for Italian. No such thing has been attempted for the English language, although schools and mass media have had a strong unifying influence. We are here chiefly concerned with American English, a major dialect of the mother tongue. It contains words from many languages, ancient and modern. It is constantly adding new ones and dropping old ones. It carries not only an enormously rich cultural heritage, but also a tremendous body of scientific knowledge. This sumptuous and varied load is stored in and communicated through language.

In English the written word is not necessarily an exact reflection of the spoken one so far as the spelling is concerned. There is sometimes quite a gap between the two. More technically, the written language instead of being phonetically functional may use a spelled word as a recognized and conventional symbol of the spoken word, carrying a meaning rather than just a series of letters representing the exact sound of the spoken word. For example, *c* in English may be used for the sound of either *s* or *k*, as in *circus* or *concern*, or combined with *h* for still another sound, *ch*, as in *church*. *Ghoti* could spell *fish* if we use the *gh* sound in *enou(gh)*, the *o* sound in *w(o)men* and the *ti* sound in *mo(ti)on*. The point is that the phonetic inexactness of written English in recording words makes the task of working with their origins and meanings complicated and at times futile.

When dealing with the problem of transliteration, words passing through more than one language compound the difficulty. Greek has no *c*, but Latin does. Greek has *k* (kappa), but the Latin *k* was introduced only in later days when authors began using Greek words with Greek spellings. A hard-sounding Greek *k* generally became a hard *c* in Latin and passed into English as a sound which might or might not be the same as the original. Thus Greek *kuklos* becomes Latin *cyclus* and then English *cycle*. As our aim is to enrich the background of meaning in American bird names rather than to trace the vagaries of philological transliteration, we have chosen the spellings which we hope make it easiest to see word relations. We thus avoid a pedantic overload of explanations of differences in words due to cases of nouns, irregularities and tenses of verbs, varied transliterations of letters from one language to another, and the occasional spelling errors in words from dead languages. Although this arbitrary and somewhat inexact way of handling things may result in such spelling variations as Progne, Prokne, and Procne, we hope that the young lady in question can be recognized although she at times appears in a different dress.

A work of this type is made possible only through the activities of a vast number of writers through a succession of milleniums, from the Egyptians, who first made paper from papyrus, to the authors of the latest field guides for birds. Wilson found and named new birds, Linnaeus invented a system of nomenclature that made possible a scientific organization in naming living organisms, and Darwin explained how life changes and evolves. A word of appreciation is also in order for the philologist, the linguist, and the lexicographer, whom Samuel Johnson defined as "a harmless drudge."

The black and white illustrations are from Thomas Bewick's *A History of British Birds*. The woodcuts illustrating his book for both their accuracy and artistry made the work an outstanding contribution to ornithological literature.

Among those who have given more immediate help and encouragement are the late J. d'Arcy Northwood, Floyd Oliver, Charles H. Rogers, James Reid, Lester S. Thomas, and C. Brooke Worth.

Language Abbreviations

The scheme used below follows in the main that used by Jaeger.

Ar.   Arabic
AS.   Anglo-Saxon, c.450–c.1200
D.   Danish
Du.   Dutch
E.   English
F.   French
G.   German
Gr.   Classical Greek
H.   Hebrew
HG.   High German, the language spoken in southern Germany before it evolved into modern German.
I.   Italian
Ic.   Icelandic
IE.   Indo-European, the ancestral language of most classical and modern European languages as well as classical Sanskrit.
L.   Latin, Classical Latin, the language of the Romans until about 200 A.D.

LG.   Low German, the dialect of the low countries of northern Germany, particularly along the coast. It was basically Saxon, but gradually gave way to High German.

LL.   Low Latin, the Latin of the early church fathers and the Middle Ages, c.200–c.1500.

ME.   Middle English, c.1200–c.1500

ML.   Modern Latin, c.1500, includes a host of scientific names, especially in biology. Words from many languages are Latinized by the addition of Latin endings.

Nor.   Norwegian

ON.   Old Norse

OE.   Old English, c.1200–c.1500

OF.   Old French, c.800–c.1500

Per.   Persian

Por.   Portuguese

Prov.   Provencal, an old southern French dialect which was the first French to contain a considerable amount of written material of literary worth. It was the language of the troubadors.

S.   Swedish

Sa.   Sanskrit

Sp.   Spanish

And out of the ground the Lord God formed every beast of the field, and every fowl of the air; and brought them unto Adam to see what he would call them, and whatsoever Adam called every living creature, that was the name thereof.

And Adam gave names to all cattle, and to the fowl of the air, and to every beast of the field . . .

Gen. 2:17

Common Names

Background

Just to contemplate the sheer number of common names for all birds is overwhelming. Kalmbach, in "An Ornithological Treasure Awaits Resurrection" (*The Auk*, vol. 85, no. 4, October 1968), tells of Waldo Lee McAtee's work, *American Bird Names and Their Histories and Meanings*. The unpublished data consist of 1,697 manuscript pages for volume one. The material for volume two is "recorded on about 153,000 slips and 4,100 bibliography cards in 90 file drawers." The grand total of names is estimated to be about half a million, and McAtee admitted it was by no means complete. It would seem possible for a reader to become completely befuddled by an article in which only the rarer bird names were used. In actual practice there was some confusion in understanding, as different common names for the same bird were widely used in different parts of the country. The problem was particularly vexing as local and state bird organizations were prone to use only the common names. As the interest in birds developed beyond the local level, the need for a widely acceptable list of common names of North American birds became apparent. The American Ornithologists' Union went a long way toward filling this need by including in its latest (1957) *Check-list of North American Birds* one common name for each species.

If there is a difference in the common names of birds in both countries, the British Ornithologists' Union *Check-list* places the common American name under the British. The American Ornithologists' Union *Check-list* does not do this. In this work the common British name follows the American one in the list of scientific names thus: Common Loon–Great Northern Diver; Common Teal–Teal.

The task of selecting one common name for each bird was a formidable one. From the sidelines it would seem less difficult to choose a name for a rare bird than for one that was widespread and abundant. There would be on the surface fewer names to choose from. A very rare species might be more familiar to professional ornithologists than to bird watchers. In such cases the scientific name would be better known and its reflection in the common name justified. This process is by no means limited to rarer species, and may come about independent of scientific influence. For example, vireo, which might be considered a scientific name, has crowded out greenlet, which was in vogue to some extent in the last century. Pyrrhuloxia seems to have come from the genus end of *Pyrrhuloxia sinuata* while Common Merganser after adding Common may likely have been generated from the specific portion of *Mergus merganser*. So even the common names with a scientific name in their ancestry, like Topsy, just grew up.

At the other end of the philological spectrum are the names of the familiar, abundant, and widely distributed species. Many, local in origin, have either remained so or have fallen into disuse. The use of some names has spread and become widely accepted. Other names have changed both in their degree of usage as well as in their form. Some appellations, reflecting a fond intimacy, originated as pet names. We have quite a few: Jackdaw, Jay, Jenny Wren, Magpie, Martin, Parakeet (little Peter), Philip Sparrow, Robin, and Tom Tit. Several of these still remain in the realm of the nickname while others have attained the status of preferred acceptance. Jay came into English from French, beyond which the derivation is obscure. It is remotely possible that the word in French is derived from the Latin, *gaius,* which carries the implication that it was a "joy" about the Roman home. Magpie was Shakespeare's Magot-pie. Magot along with Maggot, Margot, Mag, Maggie, and Peg were all nicknames for Margaret. Robin, a common pet name, first preceded Redbreast as a mark of endearing familiarity and gradually took over; Redbreast, then Robin Redbreast, and finally Robin. The more literate the speakers of a language and the more general and widespread their education, the slower are the changes in their language. Thus whatever tendency there might be for Jenny to gradually supplant wren, the present state of our culture suggests that it will take a long, long time.

Aside from their use as names for species, vernacular terms and words have other important functions in ornithology. They are useful in describing variations and aberrations which do not warrant categorical scientific attention. We use the terms red-brown phase or gray phase for the plumages of the Screech Owl. We use light and dark phase for the different plumages of the Rough-legged Hawk. Common terms may well be used for variations in a species whose particular segments of population do not warrant scientific subspecific status. Vernacular words used correctly are just as accurate in conveying meaning as scientific terms and are, of course, indispensible. Without common names familiar to most people, communication about birds would be nonexistent.

Common names are used not only to identify individual species, but also to show relationships in a kind of vernacular binomial nomenclature. Although they belong to different genera, all three members of the

scientifically termed family Phalaropodidae have the
same common name, phalarope. Our three American
jaegars, which belong to the same genus, have the same
second common name. Showing the relationships in
such common names as duck, gull, swallow, hawk, or
sparrow is not so much or at all the expression of a need
for terms of this type, but rather a reflection of the
degree of most people's interest in birds. Only bird
watchers, who are rather a unique minority, require a
more specific vocabulary for their esoteric communication.

List of Common Names

ACCENTOR   A local name for the Ovenbird. For the
penetrating song in which the first note of each
two-syllable phrase is accented as it calls,
"TEACHer, TEACHer, TEACHer."

ALBATROSS   In its present form since the seventeenth
century. Obsolete E. *alcatras* (Hawkin's voyage,
1564), *alca* changing to *alba* possibly by the influence
of L. *alba*. Por. *alcatraz,* "sea fowl, cormorant,
albatross, but most frequently a pelican"; Por.
alcatrus, "bucket, bucket or trough on a waterwheel," with a second meaning, "pelican," for the
shape of the bill in which it was believed to carry
water for its young. Ar. *alquadus,* also primarily a
"bucket on a waterwheel" and secondarily a "pelican"; *al* is the Ar. definite article and *quadus,*
"bucket." Gr. *kados,* "jar," possibly of Semitic
origin, cf. H. *kad,* "bucket." Newton says that the
name was spelled *albitross* in *Shelvache's Voyage*
(London: 1726), wherein (pp. 72, 73) is recorded the
incident that, on Wordsworth's suggestion, Coleridge
immortalized in the "Ancient Mariner." **Black-
browed A.** for the dark line over its eye. **Black-footed
A.** for the black color of its feet. **Laysan A.** for the

island where the first specimen was obtained. **Short-tailed A.** for its short tail. **White-capped A.** for its white crown. **Yellow-nosed A.** for its yellow beak.

ALTA MIRA A name in general use for Lichtenstein's Oriole. Sp. *alta*, "high"; Sp. *mira*, "lookout." Called Alta Mira by Ridgway because his subspecies, *tanaulitensis*, has its type locality in Alta Mira, Tanaulipas, Mexico.

ANHINGA Same as the scientific name. A South American (Tupi) native name for the Water Turkey.

ANI Brazilian name for the bird. **Smooth-billed A.** for its smooth-surfaced bill in contrast with the **Groove-billed A.**

AUK Occurs also as alk, ON. *alka*. A name given to several northern sea birds. **Great A.** extinct. The largest of the auks, not a name of great antiquity in English, is referred to by Willughby (1678) as, "the bird called penguin by our seamen." **Little A.** British and occasional American name for the Dovekie, one of the smallest sea birds.

AUKLET For auk (see above) plus *-let,* diminutive suffix, hence "little auk." **Cassin's A.** for John Cassin (see Appendix). **Crested A.** OF. *creste,* L. *crista,* "crest on a rooster or plume on a helmet." E. *crestfallen* is a cockfighting term. When applied to horses the word slips from the top of the head to the ridge of the neck. **Least A.** for its small size. **Parakeet A.** for the almost circular bright red bill of its breeding period which suggests the bill of a Parakeet (see Parakeet). **Rhinoceros A.** for the pointed growth on its bill during summer. **Whiskered A.** for the facial plumes. Whisker from the likeness to a small brush, a whisk.

AVOCET F. *avocette,* I. *avosetta,* "avocet." Quite possibly from L. *avis,* the suffix suggesting small and graceful. American, a different species from the European.

BALDPATE A popular name for the American Wigeon. (For bald, see Eagle, Bald E.) Pate, origin unknown. The white feathers on the crown suggest a bald head or pate. The name is also used, according to Newton, by the English in the West Indies for a dove with a white head.

BANANAQUIT Another name for the Bahama Honey-creeper. Banana, possibly a Carib name; no connection with the banana tree or fruit. *Quit,* likely for the note of the bird.

BASKETBIRD The Orchard or Baltimore Oriole. From the resemblance of the woven nest to a basket.

BECARD F. *bec,* "beak"; *-ard,* HG. *hart,* "bold, hardy," an intensifying suffix, hence "big beak." **Rose-throated B.** for the rosy throat of the male.

BEE-BIRD The Kingbird. For taking bees near their hive.

BEE-MARTIN Another name for the Kingbird.

BELLBIRD The Wood Thrush. For its clear and ringing song.

BIG CRANKY The Great Blue Heron. Possibly for its rather aloof habit of fishing, suggesting by its pose a dour disposition.

BILL-WILLIE The Willet. For its call.

BIRD The earliest ancestor of our word "bird" is unknown. We first meet it in Old English as *brid,* meaning generally the young of animals. Newton gives as early illustrations Wycliff's *Translation of Matthew XXIII*, "eddris and eddris briddis," which in the King James version is rendered, "ye serpents, and generation of vipers." We find in other quotes from Newton: "In temperat yeres ben fewe byrdes of been (bees)," "All fysshe (fish) fede and keep theyr byrdes," and "The Woolfe and Woolfe-birdes (cubs) suld (should) be slaine." Thus it seems that *brid,* in one form or another, could mean the young of reptiles, insects, fish, or animals. For a fuller understanding of the word's evolution we are fortunate to have a comparative wealth of material in the writings of Chaucer (see Preface).

BITTERN A variety of OE. forms: *bitoyre, bittour, bytoure, botor, buttour;* became crystallized into *bittern* soon after the English translation of Willughby's *Ornithology* appeared in 1678. He says, "It is called by later writers Butorius or Botaurus because it seems to imitate *boatum tauri,* the bellowing of a bull. The common people are of the opinion that it thrusts its bill into a reed, by the help whereof it makes that lowing and drumming noise." **American B.**, smaller and slightly different in appearance from the European B., a different species. **Least B.** for its small size.

BLACKBIRD For the predominant color. **Brewer's B.** for Thomas M. Brewer (see Appendix). Retained as the common name although dropped from the scientific one originally given by Audubon. **Red-winged B.** for the red and yellow epaulets of the male. **Rusty B.** for the rusty tinge of the fall plumage. **Tricolored B.** as the red and white epaulets of the male add two colors to the bird. **Yellow-headed B.** for the bright yellow head of the male.

BLUEBILL A secondary name for the Ring-necked Duck and the Ruddy Duck both scaups, their blue and whitish bills.

BLUEBIRD For the predominant color. **Eastern B.** for its range. **Mountain B.** for its habitat at high elevations. **Western B.** for its range.

BLUE CRANE A colloquial name for the Great Blue Heron.

BLUE DARTER Either the Sharp-shinned or Cooper's Hawk. For the slate-blue color of the male.

BLUE PETER Either Coot or Purple Gallinule, for the dark gray-blue color.

BOBOLINK Bent suggests that the name is an abbreviation of "Robert O'Lincoln" from the poem by William Cullen Bryant. This is hardly creditable. It likely originated in imitation of the bird's unpatterned bubbling song, and is certainly preferable to Skunk Blackbird suggested by the color pattern of its back.

BOBWHITE   In imitation of its call.

BOGBUMPER   American Bittern. Probably for its call (see Stake Driver).

BONXIE   A Shetland name for the bird which the British call the Great Skua, and the Americans, the Skua.

BOOBY   Sp. *bobo*, "stupid"; L. *balbus*, "stammering," hence by Roman logic "stupid." Being unfamiliar with men on its isolated nesting sites, it was unaware that the intrusion was a threat to its safety and therefore acted indifferently. This was considered stupid by the seamen, who quite correctly deemed any living thing that trusted them foolish, and so named the birds boobies or fools. **Blue-faced B.** for the slate-blue color of the exposed skin near its bill. **Blue-footed B.** for its bright blue feet. **Brown B.** for the dark brown upper parts and head. **Masked B.** another name for the Blue-faced B. **White-bellied B.** another name for the Brown B.

BOTTLE-HEAD   Local name for the Black-bellied Plover. For its comparatively large round head.

BRANT   Other species in England were called *brent goose* or *brand goose;* cf. G. *brand gans*, literally *"burnt goose."* Possibly from AS. *bernan, brennan,* "burned," referring to the dark brown color of the plumage. **Black B.** for the western species which has a dark belly.

BRISTLE TAIL   A hunter's name for the Ruddy Duck. For its stiff upright tail.

BROAD-BILL   A hunter's name used indiscriminantly for

the Shoveler, Redhead, both scaups, and the Ruddy Duck.

BUFFALO-BIRD A name, alas, no longer appropriate for the cowbird. Por. *bufalo,* L. and Gr. *boubalos,* "a kind of antelope," incorrectly given to the American bison.

BUFFLEHEAD For the shape of the bird's head suggesting that of a buffalo (see Buffalo Bird).

BULBUL Per. *bulbul.* In imitation of its note. The name was applied to various species by the English in India, one of which, below, has been introduced into the United States. **Red-whiskered B.** for the red mark below the eye.

BULLBAT Nighthawk. For its crepuscular habit which it shares with bats. Bull, for its comparatively large size and noisy habit.

BUNTING An early name for the British Corn Bunting and now given to several sparrow-like birds in Britain and in America. The origin is obscure. MacLeod suggests it may be cognate with G. *bunt,* "mottled," and apply to the Corn Bunting. Weekley thinks it is possibly derived from a double diminutive of F. *bon-et-on,* and a pet name, as for a child in the old nursery rhyme, "Bye, Baby Bunting." **Indigo B.** L. *indicum,* Gr. *indicon,* "Indian," for the country of origin of indigo dye, a bluish powder obtained from plants. For the color of the male's plumage. **Lark B.** as it sings on the wing like a lark. **Lazuli B.** ML. *azulus,* "azure," a term generally used in connection with the semiprecious stone, lapis lazuli. For the blue color of the male's plumage. **McKay's B.** for Charles McKay (see Appendix). **Painted B.** as it appears to be painted in a variety of colors. **Snow B.** for the color of the plumage with wintry associations. **Varied B.** for the different shades of the male's plumage.

BURGOMASTER A name for both the Glaucous and Great Black-backed Gull. Du. *burge-moester*, "town master," possibly suggested by the manner in which these large gulls dominate their lesser associates.

BUSHTIT ME. *bush*, "a thicket," for the bird's habitat; *tit* (see Titmouse). Both **Black-eared B.** and **Common B.** have been dropped as both are considered belonging to one species with the name **Bushtit.**

BUTCHER-BIRD A name for the shrike. For its habit of impaling its food.

BUZZARD L. *buteo* through F. *busard.* In Britain a common name for the larger soaring hawks. The early colonists coming from a country devoid of vultures bestowed the name on the large soaring American vultures, giving us Turkey Buzzard, Black Buzzard and even Mexican Buzzard for the Caracara.

CALICO-BACK Hunter's name for the Ruddy Turnstone. This name still persists along the sandy coasts where there are no stones to turn, although hunting of the shore birds is now a thing of the past. For the striking and colorful pattern of the back, especially in flight. E. *calico* formerly *calicut* from the dappled pattern of the cloth imported from Calicut (now Kozhikode), a port of the southwest coast of India. Cf. calico cat.

CAMP ROBBER One of a variety of common names used by the hunter, trapper and backwoodsman of the north for the Gray Jay, the term most familiar to the ornithologist. According to Bent, "the 'camp robber' will eat anything from soap to plug tobacco, for it will, at least, steal and carry off such unsavory morsels; some Indians have said: 'Him eat moccasins, fur cap, matches, anytink.' " He goes on to quote William Brewster's journal (1937), ". . . they spend the greater part of each day carrying food back into the woods. They seemed to prefer baked beans to any other kind of food . . . and next to beans, oatmeal. . . . Of baked beans they regularly took four at one load, three in the throat and one held in the bill." Bent goes on to quote a letter from Manly Hardy: "I know of nothing that can be eaten that they will not take, and I had one steal all my candles, pulling them out endwise one by one from a piece of birch bark they were rolled in, and another pecked a large hole in a cake of castile soap. A duck which I had picked and laid down for a few minutes had the entire breast eaten out by one of these birds. I have seen one alight in the middle of my canoe and peck away at the carcass of a beaver I had skinned. They often spoil deer saddles by pecking into them near the kidneys. They do great damage to the trappers by stealing the bait from traps set for martins and minks and by eating the trapped game; they will spoil a martin in a short time. They will sit quietly and see you build a trap and bait it, and then, almost before your back is turned, you hear their hateful "ca-ca-ca" as they glide down and peer into it."

CANARY Our wild birds get the name from their resemblance to the caged birds first introduced into Italy from the Canary Islands in the sixteenth century. F. *Canarie*, Sp. *Canaria*, L. *insula Canaria*; L. *canis*, "dog," the islands being so named, according to Pliny, for the dogs found there. **Wild C.** for either the Goldfinch or the Yellow Warbler. **Blue C.** for the Indigo Bunting.

CANVASBACK For its whitish back.

CARACARA Probably a South American native name in imitation of its call, a low rattle.

CARDINAL L. *cardinalis*, "important," from L. *cardo, cardin-*, "hinge," which came to mean important as it was something on which an object or idea depended or hinged. Cf. Gr. *cardan*, "to swing." LL. *episcopus cardinalis*, originally the designation of one in charge of an important (cardinal) church in Rome and member of the council electing the Pope. Now a name for high church officials whose robes and hats are red. Hence a name for the bird whose plumage is that color.

CATBIRD For one of its notes which resembles the mewing of a cat.

CEDAR BIRD The Cedar Waxwing. For one of its favorite habitats.

CHACHALACA In imitation of the bird's call.

CHAPARRAL COCK A name in general use for the Roadrunner over most of its range. Sp. *chaparra,* "evergreen oak," which has evolved in southwestern United States into a name for dense scrub made up of a variety of plants. The "chaps" of a cowboy, the tough overtrousers worn to protect his legs from thorny undergrowth, are a shortening of chaparral. This name for the bird comes from its habitat. A modern dictionary states that the female is called the chaparral hen; not so, as the sexes are alike in plumage. Cock, AS. *cocc,* "adult male chicken, rooster," probably imitative of its cry, a shortening of cock-a-doodle-do. The name became associated with other birds with or without reference to the sex and for no apparent reason, as in Cock Robin. The aggressive and jaunty character of the cock has given us "cocky," and the jauntiness implied in cocked hat for the tilt, which, if happening to the eye, is rendered "cockeyed."

CHAT In England used with a prefix for bird names, as in *Stonechat, Whinchat.* The Stonechat gets its name from its persistent call of harsh notes resembling, according to Newton, the clicking of stones together. Although the American Chat resembles the European bird in size only, some of its notes may have suggested to the colonists the bird of the Old World. On the other hand, the American name may have come about independently, as chat for chatterer, which the bird surely is, with its unique and amazing conglomerations of whistles, squeaks, squeals, musical single notes and phrases, and harsh chattering in varied sequence and timing, poured out in unpremeditated artlessness. Stone claims he identified in the song, "the rasped call of the kingfisher, . . . trill of the tree toad, call of the yellowlegs, and a distant auto horn." **Yellow-breasted C.** for its bright yellow breast. **Long-tailed C.** another name for the Yellow-Breasted, for its long tail.

CHEBEC For its call, which is one of the surest means of identifying the Least Flycatcher.

CHERRY BIRD The Cedar Waxwing. For one of its favorite foods, the wild cherry. It has been observed squeezing the juice into the open mouths of its nestlings for their first feedings.

CHEWINK An alternative name for the Towhee, also imitative of its call.

CHICKADEE Onomatopoeic. **Black-capped C.** for the black crown. **Boreal C.** L. *borealis, Boreas;* Gr. *Boreas,* "god of the north wind." Boreas fell in love with the nymph Crithyia, but his breathing was so harsh that it repelled her, not being in concordance with her maidenly ideas of a lover's sighs. True to his rough-and-ready character, Boreas soon lost his patience and carried her off. This name for the chickadee does not imply a virile harshness but a northern range. **Carolina C.** A place name first used for the colonies when Charles II was king of England. L. *Carolus,* "Charles." Also a loose term of the naturalists meaning "southern," for the range of the bird. **Chestnut-backed C.** for the rich brown color of the back. **Gray-headed C.** for its gray cap. **Mexican C.** for its southern range. **Mountain C.** for its range in the Rocky Mountains.

CHICKEN ME. *chiken,* AS. *cicen,* "chicken," related to the work cock. **Greater Prairie C.** F: *prairie,* "meadow," a name given by the early French explorers to the great central plains; L. *pratum,* "meadow"; Greater as it is slightly larger than the · **Lesser Prairie C.** Prairie is a habitat name for both birds.

CHIPPY   A familiar name for the Chipping Sparrow (see Sparrow, Chipping S.).

CHUCK-WILL'S-WIDOW   In imitation of the bird's call.

CHUKAR   Hindu *chakar,* "the Indian Hill Partridge," a range name for one of the twenty geographic races of the species whose total range extends from the Alps to the Himalayas. It is used in America for the racially mixed introduced species.

CLAM BIRD   For the food preference of the Oyster Catcher. It could easily be called Mussel Bird as it also feeds on mussels.

COCK OF THE WOODS   The Pileated Woodpecker. For its red crest resembling a comb, and its habitat.

COFFIN-BEARER   For the Great Black-backed Gull or Burgomaster who, indeed, seems to walk at a deliberate and mournful pace.

COLLECTIVE NAMES

Bevy: In late ME. *bevy,* "a company of roes (deer), larks, quails or ladies"; as in a bevy of beauties.

Brace: As in a brace of partridges. L. *brachio* (pl.), "two arms," came to mean that which held things together as by a string, hence two birds tied together. We find another use of the term in embrace.

Brood: AS. *brod,* "the hatching and the care of the young," hence a number of birds from one nest.

Clutch: Used for the young hatched from one set of eggs or for the number of eggs in one nest; formerly also a number of chickens. From Scottish and Provincial E. *cleck,* "to hatch," allied to "cluck" of a hen.

Colony: For birds breeding together. It may be

refined to denote the breeding sites for some species, as in heronry or rookery. L. *colonia,* "a farm or settlement."

Congregation: L. pp. of *congregare,* to collect in a flock," more commonly used in Britain for an assemblage of Rooks.

Covey: F. *couvée,* "brood"; pp. of F. *couver,* "to brood, to hatch." Now a sport term for a foraging flock of partridges, Bobwhite or pheasants.

Creche: F. *crêche,* "A hospital for foundlings, or public nursery where working mothers can leave their children." The term has been adopted by ornithologists for aggregations of young birds such as the Flamingo and the Emperor Penguin of the Antarctic.

Flock: AS. *flocc,* "a company of sheep, and other animals as in a flock of geese or teal." AS. also used the word for a gathering of men, but not as in E. where usage is generally limited to members of a church. The most usual term for a number of birds of the same kind.

Murmuration: A falconry term for a flock of Starlings, an echoic word. F. *murmurer,* L. *murmurare,* "to murmur."

Raft: A large and rather closely packed number of ducks on water.

Skein: For the resemblance of a line of geese in flight to a length of thread.

Spring: For a number of teal, possibly from the impression given by their quick takeoff as they spring into flight.

Wisp: For the resemblance of a wavering line of shorebirds in flight to a thin column of smoke.

CONDOR Sp. *condor,* from Peruvian *cuntur,* "condor."

California C. for the state where the bird is found. It is not the same species as the Andean Condor.

COOT Of uncertain origin and perhaps cognate with

scout and scoter. Used in ME. for various waterfowl and still in general use for all three scoters. **American C.** as it is a different species from the European.

CORMORANT F. *cormoran,* "cormorant," (in some patois, *cor marin*); L. *corvus,* "crow." L. *marinus,* "pertaining to the sea." As the final *t* is not found in any source of the word, it is labeled spurious by etymologists. **Brandt's C.** for J. F. Brandt (see Appendix). **Double-crested C.** for the almost invisible crests. **Great C.** is the cormorant common in Europe. Americans add the adjective to differentiate it from the Double-crested C. **Olivaceous C.** alludes to the dull green color which is not distinctive. **Pelagic C.** Gr. *pelagious,* "of the sea," but not more so than other cormorants. **Red-faced C.** has more and brighter red in the face than the Pelagic C.

CORN CRAKE Corn is the British word for grain. AS. *corn,* "corn," a habitat word for the grain fields frequented by the birds. Crake imitates the bird's call, probably from AS. *cracian,* "to make a noise"; cf. crack, creak.

COWBIRD In England, the Yellow Wagtail. In America, the bird which associates with cattle. Catesby says it is an abbreviation of Cowpen-bird. "They delight much to feed in the pens of cattle, which has given them their name." The plumage of both sexes has a light bronze sheen. **Bronzed C.** for the metallic sheen of its plumage. **Brown-headed C.** for the male's brownish head. **Common C.** another name for the Brown-headed C. **Red-eyed C.** alternative name for the Bronzed C.

COWCOW Onomatopoeic name for the cuckoos.

CRANE AS. *cran,* "crane," ultimately from an ancestral Indo-European root, *gar, ker,* "to cry out." That such a word once existed is inferred from the number of words similar in form and meaning in the same language family. Thus, besides the parental

relation in AS. *cran,* we find its first cousins in other
Teutonic languages: Du. *krean,* G. *kranich,* "crane,"
and among second cousins in the Romance languages, the descendents of Latin, F. *grue,* I. *gru,* from
L. *grus,* all meaning "crane." Another second cousin,
Greek, has *geranos,* "crane." We call these cousin
words cognates to denote common ancestry. E.
geranium, so-called because its seed pod resembles a
crane's bill, comes directly from Greek with only the
last syllable undergoing a Latin change. E. *pedigree*
comes from L. *ped,* "foot," and L. *grus,* "crane," with
maybe a brief stop in France where we find it in
old Anglo-French as *pe de gru* and in French, *pied de
grue.* The meaning comes from the sign, the foot of
the crane, used to indicate relationships in the family
tree. The number of the bird's toes depended on the
number of children in the family. Words develop
figurative meanings which are paralleled, as Gr.
geranos means a lifting machine, which *crane* does in
English. L. *grus* also means battering ram, as its long
pole suggests a crane's neck. We crane our necks,
have a crane fly for its birdlike silhouette, and a
crane-fly orchid for its crane-fly-like appearance.
Sandhill C. probably from its congregating on a low
hill for its courtship dance. **Whooping C.** from the
bird's note. F. *houper* from the cry *houp* used to
command dogs and horses as *hup* was used to get
horses moving. The original form was *hoop.* And a
child with the whooping cough does sound like the
Whooping Crane and vice versa.

CREEPER From its habit of moving up tree trunks.
Brown C. for the predominating color of the back.
Tree C. the British name for the same species,
possibly to differentiate the bird from a nuthatch,
which is also called creeper.

CROSSBILL OE. *cros,* L. *crucem,* "cross." After the
Roman gallows became a religious symbol, the Latin

word for it spread in various forms over Europe,
making it difficult to trace the direct route from one
language to another. Preoccupation with the word as
a religious symbol accounts for the legend that the
bird acquired the shape of its bill while attempting to
withdraw the nails that held Christ to the cross; and
in so doing the bird became so splattered with blood
that its plumage became ever after generously hued
with red. The name for the bird comes from the
overlapping ends of the beak, which make it appear
crossed. This shape makes it a specialized tool for
extracting seeds from cones. AS. *bile,* "a bird's
beak"; allied to AS. *bill,* "sword, axe." **Crossbill**
British name for the American **Red Crossbill,** which
is red with the exception of the dark brown wings
and tail. **Two-barred C.** British name for the American **White-winged C.** whose wings are dark brown
with two white wing bars.

CROW AS. *crawe,* "crow," in imitation of the call,
although we find it comfortable to say "a crow caws"
and "a rooster crows." An individual "crows" when
unduly bragging and "eats crow" when he finds it
necessary to retract an ill-considered assumption.
Age puts "crow's feet" beside the eyes. We have
"crow berry" for the evergreen plant with black fruit
and the "crow-foot violet" from the shape of its
leaves. "Jim Crowism" is a term for the doctrine and
practice of discrimination against blacks. The crow's
habit of flying rather directly to its roosts seems to
account for the expression "straight as the crow
flies." **Carrion C.** A local name for the Black Vulture
in America but a species of crow in Britain. **Common
C.** a good name for this widely distributed American
bird. **Fish C.** generally found near the seashore where
it scavenges for many kinds of food. **Northwestern C.**
for its range in northwestern United States.

CUCKOO An imitative name so appropriate that there

are practically no others in English or foreign languages which have kindred words: F. *coucou,* G. *kuckuck,* Gr. *kokkus,* Sa., *kokila;* in OE. and ME. we find *coccou, cuccu, cukkow, cocow.* The European Cuckoo of parasitic fame is a different species from the American birds. **Black-billed C.** for the color of its bill. **Black-eared C.** another name for the Mangrove Cuckoo, for the black feathers behind the eye, an excellent field mark. **Ground C.** the Roadrunner which is closely related to the cuckoo. **Mangrove C.** for one of its favorite habitats, the mangrove thickets. **Yellow-billed C.** for the bill's color.

CURLEW F. *corlieu,* "curlew," in imitation of the call. **Bristle-thighed C.** for the barbless feather shafts projecting from its flanks. **Eskimo C.** from the name of its human cohabitants. **Hudsonian C.** once in general use for the Whimbrel. **Long-billed C.** for the bill which is about a third of the bird's length. **Spanish C.** for the White Ibis, as the bill is shaped somewhat like a curlew's.

CUTWATER A local name for the Black Skimmer. For its manner of flying with its bill in the water. Also used for the shearwaters.

CYGNET L. *cygnus,* "swan," plus the diminutive *-et,* hence "little swan." For the young of the swan, generally the Mute Swan.

DABCHICK Formerly dap or dopchick. AS. *dop-snid,* "dipping duck," a name in Britain for the Moorhen as well as the sanctioned name for the Little Grebe. In America it is a local name for the Pied-billed Grebe.

DADDY-LONG-LEGS The Black-necked Stilt whose legs, excepting the flamingo's, are the longest in proportion to the size of its body than those of any other bird.

DARTER Local name for the Anhinga. **Blue D.** Cooper's Hawk. **Little Blue D.** Sharp-skinned Hawk.

DEVIL DOWNHEAD Local name for the nuthatches. For its going head first down tree trunks, in the sense of a daredevil.

DICKCISSEL In imitation of its song.

DIPPER Quite possibly not from its dipping into the water to feed, but from its dipping motion when perched on a stone in a stream. Suffix -er, "one who," hence, "one who teeters."

DOTTEREL The diminutive of "dolt," ME. *dote,* "to be foolish," especially in old age as in dotage. Swann quotes Ray as saying, "It is a very foolish bird, and is taken in the night time, by the light of a candle, by imitating the gestures of the fowler, for if he stretches out an arm the bird stretches out a wing, if a foot, the bird likewise a foot; in brief, whatever the fowler does, the bird does the same, and so being intent upon the man's gestures it is deceived, and covered with the net spread for it." This is, of course, nonsense to anyone who has observed the birds. Newton points out that it is the fowlers imitating the birds and not vice versa. "We call a foolish, dull person a Dotterel, and on this account our people also call it Dotterel, as if they were to say doting with folly."

DOVE Probably from AS. *dufan,* "to dive." From the bird's swift and irregular flight. In the past in England a general term for "wild pigeon." **Ground D.** where it is generally seen. **Inca D.** found from southwestern United States to northwestern Costa Rica. In Mexico it is called *coquito common,* which suggests that it is fairly abundant in the land of the ancient Aztecs. The common name of the bird reflects the scientific name given it by Larson. It appears that he confused the land of the Aztecs with the land of the Incas in Peru. **Mourning D.** for its forlorn call. **Ringed Turtle D.** for the dark line of feathers on the back of the neck; turtle from AS. *turtla*, "turtle dove," imitating the cooing of the bird. Chaucer tells us of "the wedded turtil with her hearte trewe." To the confusion of the nonliterary, the bible reminds us that "the voice of the turtle was heard in the land." Beginning in the sixteenth century and increasingly in the seventeenth, we find the name of the bird appearing as turtle dove. Although this marriage of words enlarged the meaning to show the relationship with the larger doves, the more potent reason was that another meaning for turtle came into the language. English sailors of the period became acquainted with the large sea tortoises of the Caribbean. This animal became known to them as turtle, possibly from their corruption of F. *tortue* or from their idea that the neck of the turtle resembled that of the turkey. Gradually the word turtle by itself came to be used for the creatures having shells and the name for the small dove became the two word turtle dove. **Rock D.** is the progenitor of the domestic pigeon, which got its name from nesting in rocky cliffs. **Spotted D.** most likely for the lacy pattern of the neck. **White-fronted D.** F. and L. *frons, front,* "forehead" which was its original sense in English, here retained for the white forehead of the bird. **White-winged D.** for the large white wing patches on the secondaries. **Zenaida D.** Charles L. J. L. Bonaparte (see Appendix), the nephew of Napoleon, came to America with his wife, Zenaide, a niece of Napoleon, and her father, Joseph Napoleon, following the decline of the family fortunes after Waterloo. Charles, an eminent ornithologist, was employed by the Academy of Natural Sciences in Philadelphia, Pennsylvania. In reorganizing the classification of American birds, he gave his wife's name, Zenaide, to the genus of doves in which he placed this one. Latinized to Zenaida, it has become, in addition to the genus name, the common name for this species (see Appendix under Zenaide).

DOVEKIE As in "dove" plus *-kie,* a diminutive suffix giving us "little diver."

DOWITCHER Before crystallized into its present spelling, it was dowitchee, doewitch, and dowitch from Deutsher (German) or Duitsch (Dutch) snipe to distinguish it from the English (common) snipe. Coues says the name was associated with Dutch traditions in New York. In Stroud we find "its odd name 'Deutacher snipe' may derive from its popularity as a food in Revolutionary times with the Hessians." While this is possible, it seems unlikely that the Hessians stayed long enough in one place to establish a lasting impression on the language from an item on their menu. The Dutch, on the other hand, played an important role for a considerable period of time in colonial New York and may have contributed to the name. Maybe both played a part or neither, as the name may be of Indian origin. The British name, Red-breasted Snipe, is much simpler. **Long-billed D.** Its bill is on the average longer than that of the Short-billed D. with considerable overlapping in size. Competent bird watchers (and listeners) find that the weak crisp notes of the Long-billed D. distinguish it from the two- or three-syllabled liquid call of the **Short-billed D.**

DUCK AS. *duce,* "diver." Also a female duck with drake as the male. With *-ling,* the diminutive suffix, *duckling,* "a young duck." **Black D.** for the very dark brown plumage. **Black-bellied Tree D.** for the black underparts. Often perches in trees and sometimes nests in them. **Fulvous Tree D.** L. *fulvus,* "reddish-yellow," for the color of its plumage; tree, not because it is at all partial to trees but because it is much like the duck above, being in the same genus.

Dusky D. another name for the Mottled Duck. **Gray D.** a name for the Gadwall. **Harlequin D.** for the variegated plumage which recalls the pantomime costume of the Italian stage. **Labrador D.** for the breeding area of this extinct bird. **Masked D.** for the pattern of the male's face. **Mexican D.** for the main area of its range. **Mottled D.** for its streaked and speckled plumage. **Ring-necked D.** for the faint line of lighter color at the base of the neck. **Rock D.** another name for the Harlequin Duck for its frequenting of rocky shores. **Ruddy D.** for the striking color of the male's breeding plumage. **Whistling D.,** or Whistler, a popular name for the Goldeneye and both wigeons. **Wood D.** for its nesting in hollows of trees.

DUNLIN AS. *dunn,* "dark"; *-lin* (having dropped a terminal *g*) the diminutive suffix, giving us "the little dark one" for the bird in the breeding plumage.

EAGLE F. *aigle,* L. *aguila,* "eagle," originally black eagle from L. *aguilus,* "dark"; also L. *aquilo,* "the north wind," which darkened the sky; used by imperial Rome as a military standard. Aquiline describes a rather large and somewhat hooked nose which suggests the beak of the bird. **Bald E.** Although *bald* now means bare and hairless, in ME. *balled* meant "shining white." The present meaning is the one used for this bird in describing its head, although the bald appearance is due to the white feathers rather than to a lack of them. This bird is the official symbol of the United States, appearing on its seal. The choice of this bird was deplored by Benjamin Franklin who was familiar with its robbing the Osprey and termed it a bird of "bad moral character." His choice of bird was the Turkey. **Golden E.** from the color of the feathers of the neck and head.

EGRET F. *aigrette,* "egrett"; Old High German *heigir,*

"heron," the -ir was replaced by the suffix -ette, a diminutive which suggests that the name originally meant the Little Egret of the eastern hemisphere. **Cattle E.** for its associating with cattle. **Common E.,** the American name for the bird; called in Britain the Large Egret. The British Ornithologists' Union says this more appropriate name, used in India and elsewhere in the Old World normal range for this species, is preferred to the Great White Heron of British bird books. The choice for the American name may have been because it is widespread. The American Ornithologists' Union now prefers **Great Egret. Reddish E.** for the color of the neck plumage. **Snowy E.** for the white plumage.

EIDER   Ic. and ON. *aedr,* "eider." The "down" in eiderdown is also from Old Norse *dunn.* **Common E.** The British call this bird the Eider Duck. The American Ornithologists' Union dropped "Duck" from the name, which was established in English, and added the innocuous adjective "Common," apparently for its presence locally in large numbers off the New England coast in winter. It is rare elsewhere. **King E.** as it has raiment fit for a king. **Spectacled E.** for the white patch bordered by a black rim, around the eye of the male. **Steller's E.** for George W. Steller (see Appendix).

EYAS   A falconer's term for a young hawk obtained from the nest, generally the female. F. *niais,* "nestling"; L. *nidus,* "nest." The *n* was lost and the ME. *ey,* "egg," mistakenly added. The spelling may also have been influenced by a mistaken association with *eyry.* The name for the male bird taken from the nest was eyas tiercel. Some say it was so-called because it was a third smaller than the female, while others maintain the reason was that every third bird in the nest was a male. OF. *tierce,* L. *tertius,* "a third." The superstition that the third egg laid in a clutch

produced a male is also found as a justification for
the name.

EYRIE, EYRY, AERIE Nest of an eagle or other large bird
in a high place. No one derivation seems certain.
Several words may have been contributed as
sources: L. *ager,* "field," with the connotation of
birthplace; L. *aer,* "air," and ME. *ei,* "eggs."

FALCON L. *falx, falcis,* "sickle," for the curved beak
and talons. The name is now used for the swift flying
hawks with long and pointed wings, in the genus
Falco. In falconry the female peregrine was called the
"falcon gentle" while the male was the "tiercel
gentle." **Aplomado F.** Sp. *aplomar, plomado,* "to
plumb"; L. *plumbum,* "lead." As a lead weight on a
string was used to obtain an accurate perpendicular
line, the term "plumb" came to mean this method of
obtaining such a line. The stoop of this falcon after
prey in almost straight vertical descent suggests
the derivation of its name. Sp. *plomo,* "lead"; L.
plumbum, "lead," for its lead-colored plumage or its
vertical stoop, the bird plummeting on its prey.
Peregrine F. L. *per-,* "through"; L. *ager, agri,* "field";
L. *-inus,* "having to do with." The word peregrine,
which to the Romans meant "foreign, wandering,"
evolved into E. *pilgrim.* Ray, writing in 1713, is
quoted by Swann: "It took its name either from
passing out of one country into another, or because
it is not known where it builds." **Prairie F.** for its
habitat.

FINCH AS. *finc,* "finch" which it has been called since
the ME. period. It has a Teutonic ancestor as
evidence in Du. *vink,* G. *fink,* S. *fink* and D. *finke.* Its
most likely origin is onomatopoeic. **Black Rosy F.** for
its two predominant colors. **Brown-capped Rosy F.**
for the male's plumage. **Cassin's F.** for John Cassin
(see Appendix). **Gray-crowned Rosy F.** for the male's
plumage. **House F.** as it is commonly found around

dwellings. **McGregor's House F.** for R. C. McGregor (see Appendix). It is now considered a subspecies. **Purple F.** L. *purpureus,* "crimson" or other reddish color; Gr. *porphura,* "a shellfish," from which the Tyrean purple dye was obtained. This was the imperial purple of the Romans, and to them it meant either the color or the cloth so colored. The togas of their senators were bordered with it. In ancient times wearing crimson signified royal rank. So in the classical sense of the word, the name of the color is correct for the bird's plumage. Now E. *purple* means a color obtained by mixing red and blue and indicates a color less reddish.

FLAMECREST Local name for the Golden-crowned Kinglet.

FLAMINGO, American Sp. *flamenco,* Por. *flamingo,* "flamingo"; L. *flamma,* "flame," for the bright red plumage.

FLICKER AS. *flicerian,* "fluttering of birds." This seems to have been the original meaning of the word, which persisted at least until the time of Chaucer, who observed, "Above hir heed hir dowves flikernge." Cf. AS. *flacor,* "a flight of arrows," in some semblance of its original form. Later the meaning applied to a wavering light such as that of a candle in a draft and then to a passing feeling as in a "flicker of fear." The name Flicker for a bird seems to have been pre-empted solely by this bird. While the bird, being common, noisy, and conspicuous, has local names numbering in the hundreds, none rival Flicker in popularity. **Common F.** is now the specific name which includes the three following that are now classified as subspecies. **Gilded F.** for the yellow in its wings and tail. **Red-shafted F.** for the color of the shafts of feathers which show in flight and which distinguish it from the **Yellow-shafted F.**

FLINTHEAD For the dark, featherless scaly head and

neck of the Wood Ibis, which is not an ibis but a stork. (See Ibis, Wood I.)

FLYCATCHER A name for a number of birds that prey on insects in the air. **Acadian F.** The name suggests a northern breeding range, Acadia being the old French name for Nova Scotia, the scene of the beginning of Longfellow's "Evangeline." This is singularly inappropriate for a range name as the bird's range is the most southern of the three empidonax flycatchers, the Mason-Dixon line being a rough northern boundary. The name is also inappropriate if it is meant to suggest a habitat of "murmuring pines and hemlock." The bird prefers thickets along streams in swampy hardwood areas. Its name may be accounted for by the confusion of early ornithologists in identifying the three small similar flycatchers. **Alder F.** for its habitat. Formerly another name for Traill's F., it is now considered a full species. Its members sing, "fee-bee-o." **Ash-throated F.** for its whitish-gray throat. **Beardless F.** for the absence of bristles about the base of the bill common to flycatchers. **Buff-breasted F.** just a shade more so than others of the group. **Coues F.** for Elliott Coues (see Appendix). **Dusky F.** not particularly so when compared with the other empidonax. **Fork-tailed F.** for the tail. **Gray F.** about as helpful as the name for the Dusky F. **Great Crested F.** one of the larger flycatchers with a crest. **Hammond's F.** for William A. Hammond (see Appendix). **Kiskadee F.** for its call. **Least F.** as it is the smallest flycatcher in the eastern U.S. **Olivaceous F.** As most flycatchers are dark olive-gray, the name is no more distinctive than the plumage. **Olive-sided F.** for the dark streaks on the side of the belly. **Scissor-tailed F.** for the long outer tail feathers which suggest scissor blades. **Sulphur-bellied F.** for the rather dull yellow, heavily streaked underparts. **Traill's F.** for Thomas S. Traill (see Appendix). This name may still be used for this bird and the **Alder F.** where circumstances do not permit specific identification. This practically means all the time that either one is not singing. **Vermillion F.** for the brilliant plumage of the male. **Western F.** for its breeding range in North America. **Wied's Crested F.** for Prince Maximilian zu Wied (see Appendix). **Willow F.** This is a new common name for "fitz-bew" singing members of the former Traill's F. **Yellow-bellied F.** for its dull yellow underparts.

FLY-UP-THE-CREEK For the Green Heron's habit of flying along a water course with a squawk when startled.

FOREST CHIPPY For the habitat of the Worm-eating Warbler and the resemblance of its song to that of the Chipping Sparrow, which is not a bird of the woods.

FRIGATEBIRD A shortened version of the official name, Magnificent Frigatebird. The name was originally given to the bird by seamen for its habit of pursuing and robbing other birds.

FULMAR Swann says, "The name is said to be derived from the Gaelic, *fulmair,* but Mr. Harvie-Brown decides that the Gaelic is derived from the English and not the English from the Gaelic. The English name is of uncertain derivation: Swainson thought it akin to *foumart,* a polecat, meaning a foul martin, from the peculiar and disagreeable odor of the bird, owing to the oil which it emits and the rankness of its food. The oil vomited by this bird when caught is highly valued by the natives of St. Kilda as a cure for all diseases (Gray). Most authorities agree on ON. *ful,* "foul"; ON. *mar,* "maw," "gull." Noteworthy is the medicinal fortitude of the natives of the Outer Hebrides.

GADWALL Coues says: "The name Gadwall was formerly Gaddel, Gadwall, Gadwale, Gadwell;

origin obscure and etymology unknown." MacLeod agrees and then ventures, "Perhaps it is connected with AS. *gad,* a point, with reference to the fine tooth-like projections on the edges of the bird's mandible."

GALLINULE L. *gallinula,* "little hen." **Common G.** more numerous in the United States than the brighter colored **Purple G.** The British name for the Common G. is Moorhen.

GANNET AS. *ganot,* "little goose," which it was thought to be not only popularly but scientifically, being classed with the geese. An old name for the bird was solan goose, probably from ON. *sula,* "gannet"; ON., *ond, and,* "duck"; and E. *goose.* This gives us three bird names for one bird (see Goose).

GNATCATCHER AS. *gnatt,* "a small insect," in imitation of the buzzing of the wings of the insect. OF. *chasier,* "hunt"; L. *capio, captum,* "take," for the birds habit of catching insects. **Black-tailed G.** for the color of its tail. **Blue-gray G.** for the color of its plumage.

GOATSUCKER A name for the Whip-poor-will and its relatives from a superstition going back at least to Aristotle, who said: "Flying to the udders of she-goats, it sucks them, and thus gets its name. They say that the udder withers when it has sucked at it, and that the goat goes blind." Pliny gives us his version: "Caprimulgi, as they are called, look bigger than a Merula (thrush), and act as thieves by night; by day they even lack the power of sight. When I was in Switzerland I saw an aged man, who fed his goats upon the mountain, which I had gone up in search for plants: I asked him whether he knew of a bird the size of a Merula, blind in the day-time, keen of sight at night, which in the dark is wont to suck goats udders, so that afterwards the animals go blind. Now he replied . . . that he had suffered many losses from those very birds; so that he had once had six

she-goats blinded . . . but they now had flown away
. . . to Lower Germany. . . . But possibly that aged
man was jesting with me." Swann in 1912 felt called
upon to tell us, "the story has long been refuted."

GOBBLER The male Turkey, in imitation of its call.

GODWIT Origin uncertain. It may be from AS. *god,*
"good"; AS. *whita,* "animal," "bird," and more
literally "good eating," although Coues says this is
too easy to be true. **Bar-tailed G.** for the black and
white bars on the tail. **Hudsonian G.** The original
specimen came from the Hudson Bay region. **Marbled G.** for the mottled back.

GOLDCREST A popular name for the Golden-crowned
Kinglet. A British bird of the same name in the same
genus is not the same species.

GOLDENEYE For the bright yellow iris. **Barrow's G.** for
Sir John Barrow (see Appendix). **Common G.** as it is
more widely distributed than Barrow's G.

GOLDFINCH For the bright yellow plumage. The British
have the same name for a yellowish finch of a
different species. **American G.** to distinguish it in
name from the European G., and put on the
American Ornithologists' Union *Check-list* for a
colony on Long Island which was once thought to be
permanently established but has since disappeared.
Lawrence's G. for George N. Lawrence (see Appendix). **Lesser G.** for the smallest goldfinch.

GOOSANDER The British name for the Common Merganser, rarely used in the United States.

GOOSE, GEESE AS. *gos, ges,* "goose." Cf. Du. *gans,* G.
gans, ON. *gas,* Sp. *ganso,* cognate with L. *anser,* Gr.
ken, E. *gander* (the male goose) and *gannet* are all
derived from the same root, one of the few such for
bird names. The Aryan root has been given as *gha,*
"to gape or yawn," and may be the remote ancestor
of such words as chasm, chaos. The vigorous old
root is still producing a variety of descendants, albeit

with a taint of slang: goose flesh or bumps, take a gander, cook one's goose, a goose egg (a zero score). **Barnacle G.** The name for the bird seems to have come from an old superstition that it hatched from the shellfish, called barnacles, *Lepas anatifera,* the scientific name also originating in the tale. Turner (1544) says: "When after a certain time the firwood masts or planks or yard-arms of a ship have rotted on the sea, then fungi, as it were, break out upon them first, in which in course of time one may discern evident forms of birds, which afterwards are clothed with feathers, and at last become alive and fly." He cites Gyraldus (1175) as bearing witness to the phenomena and goes on to say, "by reason of the rarity of the thing I did not quite credit Gyraldus. . . . I took counsel of a certain man, whose upright conduct, often proved by me, had justified my trust, a theologian by profession and an Irishman by birth, Octavian by name, whether he thought Gyraldus worthy of belief in this affair. Who, taking oath on the very gospel which he taught, answered that what Gyraldus had reported of the generation of this bird was absolutely true, and that with his own eyes he had beholden the young." This seemed to satisfy Turner, who goes on to say that "the generation of the Bernicle will not appear so very marvellous to those who may have read what Aristotle wrote about the flying creature called Ephemerus." It seems it did not enter Turner's head to ask his Irish friend about the validity of Aristotle. Gerard in his *Herball,* or *Generall Historie of Plantes* (1597) not only goes into detail but also gives an illustration entitled, "The Barnacle Goose Tree." An excellent account of the fable may be found in Harting's *The Birds of Shakespeare* (1871). **Blue G.** for the dark-bluish hue of the back. **Cackling G.** a name for the smallest race of the Canada G., for its distinctive call. **Canada G.**

for the breeding range. **Emperor G.** Although considered our "handsomest" goose, the reason for the name is obscure. **Ross' G.** for Bernard R. Ross (see Appendix). **Snow G.** as it is white. It is now classified as a morph of the Blue Goose. **Tule G.** a common name for the White-fronted G., from its habitat. **White-fronted G.** for the white forehead.

GOSHAWK AS. *gos,* "goose"; AS. *havoc,* "hawk," for one of the birds on which the bird might prey. Cf. ON. *gas-haukr.* **Mexican G.** also called Grey Hawk.

GOSLING AS. *gos,* "goose"; plus the diminutive suffix *-ling,* "little." For the young goose.

GRACKLE ML. *gracula,* L. *graculus,* "jackdaw," "chough," also "cormorant." Adapted from a former scientific name for the genus in America but now for a genus found in southern Asia of which the best-known member is the Hill Myna. Fairly common, it is popular as a pet, being an exceptional mimic. **Boat-tailed G.** In flight the middle of the large tail is depressed, giving it a resemblance to the keel of a boat. **Bronzed G.** formerly a separate species but now classified as a race of the **Common G.** which includes the **Purple G.** formerly also classified as a distinct species. **Great-tailed G.** a new name for a former subspecies of the Boat-tailed G.

GREBE F. *grebe,* which MacLeod suggests may come from Breton *krib,* "crest," which some grebes have. **Eared G.** for the light-colored tufts on the side of the head in its breeding plumage. **Holboell's G.** another name for the Red-necked G.; for Carl Peter Holboell (see Appendix). **Horned G.** for the buffy tufts on the side of its head. **Least G.** for its small size. **Mexican G.** for the Least Grebe's range. **Pied-billed G.** for the parti-colored bill. **Red-necked G.** for the color of the neck in its breeding plumage. **Western G.** for its range in western North America.

GREENLET An old name which is losing ground to the more popular Vireo.

GROSBEAK F. *grosbec,* "grosbeak"; F. *gros,* "large"; F. *bec,* "beak." We might eliminate the French from the word and call the bird Grossbeak. **Black-headed G.** for the head coloring of the male. **Blue G.** for the male's bluish plumage. **Evening G.** a reflection of the scientific name, *vespertina,* which may mean either "western," the bird's range, or "evening" or "evening song" for its song in the evening. **Pine G.** for its habitat. **Rose-breasted G.** for the male's plumage.

GROUND-CHAT As it favors low vegetation and resembles the Yellow-breasted Chat in color.

GROUSE The ancestry of the word is vague, complicated by the confusion as to what bird was meant: bustard, godwit, crane, or grouse. Newton says: "The most likely derivation seems to be from the old French word *griershe, greoche* or *griais* (meaning speckled, and cognate with *grisius,* "grey") which was applied to some kind of partridge." **Blue G.** as it has a hint of blue on its underparts. **Ruffed G.** for the tufts on its neck resembling the neckware in vogue in the sixteenth century, which began as a ruffle on the wrist and gradually worked its way up. From *ruffle,* "to wrinkle," as the wind ruffles the water. It also seems to be related to the last syllable in dandruff, from ON. *hrufle,* "to scratch," an activity which ruffled (wrinkled) the skin. **Sage G.** for its habitat, the sage brush. **Sharp-tailed G.** for its pointed tail. **Spruce G.** for its habitat in spruce woods.

GUILLEMOT F. *Guillaume,* "William." A nickname with the transformed last syllable acquiring a *t,* suggesting a rendering of "little William" for the whole word. **Black G.** for the breeding plumage. **Pigeon G.** for its resemblance in size and shape to the domestic pigeon.

GULL OF. Celtic origin: Cornish, *gullan*; Welsh, *gwylan*; Breton, *gwelan*; "a gull." Breton, one of the Celtic dialects, had the word, *goelaff,* "weep," which suggested to one etymologist that the word might originally have been imitative. Welsh *gwylan* also means "throat" as does L. *gula.* From the latter via OF. *goule,* "throat," we have gotten such words as gulp, gullet, and gullible. This suggests that "gull" might be related to the bird's indiscriminate scavenging; it appears willing to swallow almost anything. **Black-headed G.** Chocolate-brown would be closer to the color of the head. **Bonaparte's G.** for C. L. J. L. Bonaparte (see Appendix). **California G.** for the locality of the type specimen which came from around Stockton, California. **Franklin's G.** for Sir John Franklin (see Appendix). **Glaucous G.** for its silvery-blue plumage. **Glaucous-winged G.** for the color of its plumage. **Great Black-backed G.** from its size and plumage. **Heermann's G.** for A. L. Heermann (see Appendix). **Herring G.** This scavenger might occasionally eat a herring. **Iceland G.** breeds in Iceland whence came the original specimen in 1822. **Ivory G.** for its all-white plumage. **Laughing G.** for the resemblance of its cry to derisive human laughter. **Little G.** for its small size. **Mew G.** OE. *mew,* "a gull"; the bird the British call the Common Gull. **Ring-billed G.** for the dark ring on the bill of the mature bird. **Ross' G.** for Sir James C. Ross (see Appendix). **Sabine's G.** for Sir Edward Sabine (see Appendix). **Thayer's G.** for John E. Thayer (see Appendix). Formerly classified as a subspecies of the Herring Gull; it is now a valid species. **Western G.** for its range on the west coast of the United States.

GYRFALCON The first syllable, the root *gyr,* seems to have caused a great diversity of opinions among etymologists. Here are some: (1) *Webster's New World Dictionary*, Germanic, *ger,* "spear"; (2) Albertus Magnus, L. *gyro,* "to circle," from the bird's habit of circling; (3) *Funk and Wagnalls New Standard Dictionary*, Gr. *hieros,* "sacred," as only royalty might hunt with them; (4) Skeat traces the word after several steps back to HG. *gir-* for *giri,* "greedy" (whence also G. *geier,* "a vulture"); (5) Coues quotes the *Century Dictionary*, "not connected with L. *gyrus,* 'a circle' but with G. *geier,* 'greedy' "; (6) The *Oxford Dictionary of English Etymology* says, "The first element (of gyrfalcon) is obscure." Various forms "have led to unjustifiable attempts to relate the first syllable to L. *gyrare,* 'gyrate,' and Gr. *hieros,* 'sacred'." In spite of the fact that the term *Hierofalco,* for the subgenus in the American Ornithologists' Union *Check-list* seems to lend some sanction to the Greek origin, it is most likely that the first element in the word is related to the G. *geier,* "greedy." (7) Weekley suggests ON. *verthr,* "worthy," and that *gyr* is due to wrong etymology, confused with gyrate. Various spellings of the word have not contributed to its etymological clarity, as Coues notes that we have in English, "gerfaulcon, gerfaucon, gerfawcon, jerfaucon, gierfalcon, girefaucon, gyrfacoun, and gerfauk among others with many identical or similar forms in other European languages." He remarks on the spelling as follows: "*Gyrfalcon* is the worst, *gerfalcon,* the better, *jerfalcon* the best spelling of the name, if we regard the etymology of the word." It is quite possible Coues was not overfamiliar with the terms used in falconry which differentiated between the male and the female. Despite the welter of words, *gyrfalcon* was commonly the proper name for the female, as Swann states: "The male being formerly called the Jerkin (either diminutive of Jer or else from Jerkin, a short coat, hence indicating inferior size)." With Dr. Coues thus disregarded we can appreciate the contribution of the American Ornithologists' Union *Check-list* for standardizing the common bird names.

HAG, HAGDON, HAGDOWN, HAGLET   Local names for the bird called Greater Shearwater by Americans and Great Shearwater by the British.

HAGGARD   A falconer's term for a hawk caught wild in adult plumage.

HANDSAW   See Heron.

HANGNEST   The orioles, as several species have distinctive hanging nests.

HARRIER   A British name for the hawks which usually hunt by flying low over the ground. The English names of *harnier* or *hen-harnier* came from the bird's harrying of poultry. The name appears first used for birds, in the sixteenth century. While there are four European species, there is only one American, the **Marsh Harrier,** a secondary name for the Marsh Hawk.

HAWK   AS. *hafoc,* "a hawk," cognate with *have* in the sense of grasp or seize. **Black H.** for its color. **Broad-winged H.** for its wide wings. **Cooper's H.** for William Cooper (see Appendix). **Duck H.** for the bird on which it is supposed to prey. A name in general use for the Peregrine Falcon. **Ferruginous H.** for its reddish color. **Fish H.** a very popular name for the Osprey. **Gray H.** for its color. **Harlan's H.** for Richard Harlan (see Appendix). This is now a subspecies of the Red-tailed H. **Harris' H.** for Edward Harris (see Appendix). **Marsh H.** for its habitat. **Pigeon H.** Primarily a bird eater, it is named after one of the many species on which it preys. This is the same species called the Merlin in Britain and now the approved American name. **Red-shouldered H.** for the coloring on the bend of the wing. **Red-tailed H.** for the adult's red tail. **Rough-legged H.** for the feathered tarsi. **Sharp-shinned H.** The long, thin front of the lower leg of a man is a shin.

The long, thin part of the lower leg of this bird suggests a shin, although it is below rather than above the ankle. The raised ridge on the front of the bird's tarsus (shin) is rather unique as the cross-section of the tarsus of most land birds is rounded. It is the reason for calling the shin sharp. **Short-tailed H.** for its short tail. **Sparrow H.** for its occasional prey. It is in the same subgenus as the Kestrel of Europe. The European Sparrow Hawk is an accipiter and not a falcon as the American. It would be a comfort to those with orderly minds if the English and Americans could have more uniformity with ornithological nomenclature. A beginning could be made by calling all eagles, eagles; falcons, falcons; buteos, buzzards; accipiters, hawks; and harriers, harriers. **Swainson's H.** for William Swainson (see Appendix). **White-tailed H.** for the white tail. **Zone-tailed H.** for the wide tail band.

HEATH HEN   A name for the eastern race, now extinct, of the Greater Prairie Chicken.

HELL-DIVER   A name for grebes, particularly the Pied-billed Grebe.

HERON   ME. *heroun, heiron, harn,* OF. *hairon,* HG. heiger, "heron." I. *aghirone,* "heron," is credited with contributing to the final syllable. *Hern* is found in place names, surnames, crossword puzzles and in poetry. *Heronshaw* or *hernshaw* according to Skeat should mean a young heron and by confusion a heronry. This is due to a false popular etymology: E. *heron,* "a heron" and *shaw,* "a wood." We are now able to understand the old taunt, "not able to tell a hawk from a handsaw" (*Hamlet,* Act II, Scene 2). A handsaw was not a tool for cutting wood but an end product of linguistic mutilation from OF. *herounceau* from older *herouncel,* the *-ceau* and *-cel* being diminutive, "a young heron." So it seems reasonable in the days when falconry was a popular sport to consider anyone who confused a hawk with a heron to be rather dimwitted. **Black-crowned Night H.** For the feature which differentiates it from the Yellow-crowned, and Night for its nocturnal habits, especially its loud cries which advertise its presence while flying in the darkness. **Great Blue H.** for its size and color. **Great White H.** The former bird and this one are the largest American herons, differing almost wholly in color. **Green H.** Some have remarked that it is also called the Little Green Heron because it has so little green in its plumage, but it does have some. **Little Blue H.** for its size and color. **Louisiana H.** so-called by Wilson who had a penchant for naming birds after the place where they were first collected. In describing the birds, of which this was one, collected on the Lewis and Clark expedition, Wilson named the bird for the vast area of the Louisiana Purchase and not for the state of Louisiana. **Tricolored H.** sometimes used for the Louisiana Heron. **Yellow-crowned Night H.** for its distinctive yellow crown.

HIGH-HOLE Another of the many common names for the Flicker.

HONEYCREEPER AS. *hunig,* "honey," for the bird's fondness for sweets; AS. *creepen,* "to crawl," for its ability to move along tree trunks as though it were creeping. **Bahama H.** for its range; now officially the Bananaquit.

HUMMINGBIRD For the sound of the buzzing wings. **Allen's H.** for C. A. Allen (see Appendix). **Anna's H.** for Anna, Duchess of Rivoli (see Appendix under Anna). **Black-chinned H.** for the dark chin. **Blue-throated H.** for the male's blue throat. **Broad-billed H.** maybe in comparison with another three-inch hummingbird. **Broad-tailed H.** As Coues says, the tail is "ample." **Buff-bellied H.** for the tawny color of the male's underparts. **Calliope H.** for Calliope, one of the nine muses, each of whom was head of some particular department in literature, science or the arts. Calliope was the muse of epic poetry. Any way you look at it, epic means big. But the Calliope is the smallest of the hummingbirds. From tip of bill to end of tail, it averages about two and three quarters of an inch. If Gould, who named the bird, admired the muses, why did he not choose Euterpe, the muse of lyric poetry? Lyrics are short and sweet. But maybe I am doing the namer of the bird an injustice. He could have had in mind the musical instrument, the calliope, which works by forcing steam through pipes. This interpretation is still more difficult to justify. **Costa's H.** for the Marquis de Costa (see Appendix). **Lucifer H.** meaning the torchbearer. **Rivoli's H.** for the Duc di Rivoli (see Appendix). **Ruby-throated H.** for its red gorget. **Rufous H.** for its rufous back. **Violet-crowned H.** for its distinctive violet crown. **White-eared H.** for the white patch behind its eye.

IBIS L. *ibis*, Gr. *ibis* "ibis," probably of Egyptian origin. It was mummified and also used in hieroglyphics. Thoth, the god of learning, had the head of an ibis. **Glossy I.** for the glimmering sheen on the dark plumage. **Scarlet I.** for the brilliant red color. **White I.** as only the wing tips are black. **White-faced I.** for the white lines on the face in breeding plumage. **Wood I.** for its nesting in woods. The bird is not an ibis but a stork. The name is sanctioned by usage as we call our red-breasted thrush a Robin. As **Wood Stork** avoids misleading taxonomic implications, the American Ornithologists Union now prefers it to Wood I.

JACANA A native South American name.

JAEGER G. *jager*, "hunter." E. *yacht* has the same origin, coming into the language from Holland. **Long-tailed J.** as it has the longest tail of these birds.

The British name is Long-tailed Skua. **Parasitic J.** no more a robber than the others. British name, Parasitic Skua. **Pomarine J.** Gr. *poma,* "a lid"; Gr. *rhynchos,* "beak"; for the growth at the base of the bill in the breeding season. British name, Pomatorhine Skua.

JAY F. *geai,* "jay." Although the origin is unknown, two possibilities are suggested. The first is that it was a Roman pet name from the name *Gaius.* The bird has such names as F. *Jacques,* "James," and G. *Wouter,* "Walter." The second is that the name is for the gay (bright) plumage. **Arizona J.** for the Mexican J. which is the better range name. **Blue J.** for its color. **California J.** formerly thought to be a separate species but now considered the Scrub J. **Canada J.** a name in general use for the Gray J. **Florida J.** like the California J., now a race of the Scrub J. **Gray J.** for the color of its plumage. **Green J.** for its color. **Mexican J.** for its main range. **Pinon J.** a Spanish name for the pine which the bird frequents. **Santa Cruz J.** for its locale; now considered a race of the Scrub J. **Scrub J.** for its habitat, scrubby growth. **Steller's J.** for George Steller (see Appendix).

JUNCO L. *juncus,* "a rush." Derived from the scientific name for the genus, which is certainly not partial to reeds. **Dark-eyed J.** This is the enlarged species name. **Gray-headed J.** for the color of its head. **Oregon J.** for its range. This is now a subspecies. **Mexican J.** for its range. **Slate-colored J.** for its dull color. ME. *slat, sclat,* from OF. *esclat,* "a splinter, a slice of wood," hence a slice or flake of stone, from the most common color of the stone. This is now a subspecies. **Pink-sided J.** another name for the Oregon J. **Red-backed J.** a local name for the Mexican J. **White-winged J.** for the two white wing bars.

KESTREL As it is of accidental occurrence in Greenland and Iceland, and since there is a Massachusetts record, this European cousin of our American Kestrel is on the American Ornithologists' Union *Checklist*. Weekley says, "F. *crecerelle,* dim. of *crecelle,* both used for kestrel. Originally a noisy bell or leper's clicket." He goes on to quote T. Cooper who in 1573 said, "Tinnunculus: a kinde of haukes; a kistrell or kastrell; a steyngall. They use to set them in pigeon houses, to make doves to love the place, because they fear away other haukes with their ringing voice." Thus it seems that the bird's name may come from its call. **American K.** Quite a few Americans prefer this name to Sparrow Hawk. The American Ornithologists' Union now sanctions this preference.

KILLDEER   In imitation of the call.

KINGBIRD   AS. *cyning,* "king." For the little crown, usually invisible like that of the Ruby-crowned Kinglet, of reddish gold feathers on the top of the head. **Arkansas K.** a popular name for the Western K. **Cassin's K.** for John Cassin (see Appendix). **Eastern K.** for its range in the eastern United States. **Gray K.** for its predominant color. **Tropical K.** for its southern range. **Western K.** for its range in western United States.

KINGFISHER   Literally chief of the fishers. AS. *cyning,* "king"; AS. *fisc,* "fish"; *-or,* suffix denoting "one who." **Belted K.** for the belt of colored feathers across the breast. **Green K.** for the greenish back. **Texas K.,** another name for the **Ringed K.,** for its white necklace.

KINGLET   AS. *cyning,* "king"; *-let,* diminutive suffix referring to the bright feathers of the bird's head and to its small size. **Golden-crowned K.** AS. *gold,* "gold"; ME. *corona* from OF. *corone,* from L. *corona,* "a wreath," from Gr. *coronis,* "a wreath," as the Greeks crowned their heroes with a garland of leaves.

> **Ruby-crowned K.** OF. *rubi,* from L. *rubinus,* "a ruby,"
> from L. *rubeus,* "red," the color of the stone which is
> the color of the feathers on the bird's crown.

KITE AS. *cyta,* "a kite." MacLeod suggests, "probably
from the Aryan root *skut,* to shoot, go swiftly, with
reference to the way in which the bird swoops on its
prey." *The Oxford Dictionary* points out that the
name corresponds to the G. *kauz,* "screech owl," and
suggests the name may come from an imitation of
the bird's plaintive voice. **Everglade K.** for its range
in Florida although it is a South American species.
Mississippi K. for the state where Alexander Wilson
found it. **Snail K.** another name for Everglade K.
Swallow-tailed K. for the shape of its tail. **White-
tailed K.** for the color of its tail.

KITTIWAKE Imitates the call. **Black-legged K.** for the
leg color. **Red-legged K.** for the leg color distinguishing it from the above.

KNOT See scientific name *Calidris canutus.* Drayton's
Poly-Olbion (1622) says, "The knot was called Canutus bird of old, of that great king of Danes, his
name that still doth hold, his appetite to please, that
farre and neare was sought, for him (as some have
said), from Denmark hither brought." Weekley says
the naming of the bird for Canute is baseless.

LANNER F. *lanier,* L. *laniare,* "to dissever." A falconer's term for the immature female peregrine. The
male was called the Lanneret.

LAPWING AS. *hleapewince,* "one who turns about in
running or flight," from AS. *hleapan,* "run," and
wincian, "wink"; for the bird's twisting flight.

LARK AS. *lawerce,* "lark," ME. *laverock,* "a lark."
Horned L. for the tufts of head feathers. **Shore L.** a
local name for the Horned Lark.

LIMPKIN Probably from *limp,* for the bird's odd gait,
and *-kin,* a diminutive suffix.

LINNET A name for a European finch in the same

genus as the American House Finch and incorrectly used for it. AS. *linete,* "flax," for the bird's fondness for flax seed.

LOG-COCK Local name for the Pileated Woodpecker.

LONGSPUR For the elongated rear claw. **Chestnut-collared L.** for the color of the back of the male's neck. **Lapland L.** whence came the first specimen. **McCown's L.** for J. P. McCown (see Appendix). **Smith's L.** for G. Smith (see Appendix).

LOON As the call of the bird suggests the wild laughter of a demented person, many are inclined to associate its name with lunatic, as in the phrase "crazy as a loon." Loon is a corruption of Shetland, *loom,* from Ic. *lomr* and D. or S. *lom,* "lame," for the awkward walk of the bird on land. **Arctic L.** OF. *artique,* from L. *ar(c)ticus,* from Gr. *arktikes,* "the bear, the pole star," for the bird's range. **Common L.** ME. *commun,* OF. *comun,* L. *communis,* from L. *com,* "with," and L. *munus,* "bound," meaning obligatory services, a widespread obligation. Hence "usual" when applied to this loon. **Pacific L.** another name for the Arctic Loon. **Red-throated L.** for the dark red throat patch in the breeding season. **Yellow-billed L.** for the yellow color of the bill.

MAGNIFICENT FRIGATEBIRD Magnificent, through F. *magnifique,* from L. *magnus,* "great"; L. *facio,* "make"; Frigate, through F. *fregate,* from I. *fregata,* "a frigate."

MAGPIE Also called Magpye, Magotpie, Maggotypie, and Maguerite. All dictionaries agree that *mag* is a pet form of E. *Margaret,* F. *Marguerite,* L. *Margarita* and Gr. *margarites,* in which it means "a pearl." The etymologists do not speak as one concerning *pie.* Skeat says, "ME. *pie,* F. *pie,* L. *pica,* "a magpie." MacLeod goes one step further in stating that the name may have been first imitative of the bird's call. Weekley says, "It has been suggested that it (the bird's name) may have to do with the magpie's habit of making miscellaneous collections." We are warned that the name seems to have no connection with the bird's habit of picking maggots from the backs of sheep. The British, having only one member of this genus, call their bird simply "Magpie." **Black-billed M.** Although this bird is the same species as the one found in Britain, it is so called because the color of the bill is the main difference between it and the one other American magpie, the **Yellow-billed M.** The Black-billed Magpie is sometimes called the American Magpie. The L. *picus,* "woodpecker," possibly comes from the same source. This supposition is reinforced by Sa., *pikas,* "Indian Cuckoo." L. *pipio,* "chirp," is also most likely related, indicating that the ancestral word was imitative of the bird's voice. At any rate, the magpie has long been known for its fairly continuous chattering. It gave rise no doubt to the old legend that it was the only bird that refused to enter the ark, preferring a perch on its roof from which it could jabber about the discomfiture of those caught in the rising flood. Leviner records that Aristotle was impressed by the bird's loquacity, stating that "the pica often times changes its notes, for almost every day it utters different cries." We are certain Pliny was referring to the magpie when he made the following improbable contribution to ornithological lore: Turner translates Pliny, "Not only do they learn, but they delight to talk, and meditating carefully and thoughtfully within themselves hide not their earnestness. They are known to have died when overcome by difficulty in a word, and, should they not hear the same things constantly, to have failed in their memory, and while recalling them to be cheered up in wondrous wise, if meanwhile they have heard the word." One modern philologist has the ornithological effrontery to suggest that our word "pie" for the pastry, a collection of edibles in one dish, is derived from observing the magpies habit of collecting miscellaneous objects. He is in error as the bird does not, but to balance this he informs us that the "pie" in "piebald" when applied to the pattern of a horse's coat comes from the contrasting light and dark of the bird's plumage.

MALLARD ME. *malard* from OF. *malard,* "the mallard." From OF. *male,* "male," which derives from L. *masculinus,* extended from L. *masculus,* "male," and L. *mas,* "a male," plus the intensifying suffix -*ard* from HG. *hart,* an adjective meaning "bold, hardy," akin to the E. *hard.* It generally has a pejorative sense as in drunkard, dullard and sluggard. The suffix seems to fit well the mallard male who exemplifies in his relations with the female a singular concentration on the physical union alone. The female, after she is snatched bald-headed, gets the eggs to hatch, the ducklings to raise, and her drake's name.

MAN-O'-WAR BIRD A name in general use for the Magnificent Frigatebird.

MARSH HEN Used for both the Clapper Rail and the Common Gallinule.

MARTIN F. *Martin,* "Martin," a proper name in French as in English. It originated as a pet name derived from L. *Mars,* the stem of which is *mart.* Add to this the diminutive suffix -*in* and we have Martin or little Mars. Robin is derived in the same manner from Robert. The pet name is found not only in F. *Martin* but also in F. *martinpecheur,* "the king fisher." It appears also in F. *martinet,* "swift." We can conjecture that the nickname Martin had become established as a proper name and in making it into a pet name the second time, another diminutive suffix -*et* was added, giving us the F. *Martinet* "little little

Mars." Making its way into English as a bird name, the word seems to have dropped its connotation of swift in favor of the swallows, as we have in the British dialect of English House Martin and Sand Martin. That this was a gradual evolution is suggested by an old term for the House Martin which appears in Shakespeare's *Merchant of Venice*: "like the martlet builds in the weather on the outside walls." Although the Americans superseded Sand Martin with Bank Swallow, they found a use for the word martin by naming their largest swallow the Purple Martin. The French not only call their swifts martinets to this day, but have commemorated their patron saint, St. Martin of Tours, in their name for the Hen Harrier, Busard Saint Martin. Did the Romans call the swallows and swifts "little Mars" because they appeared at the time of the first month on their calendar, when the dancing priests of Mars, the Salii, took out their sacred shields and spears to initiate the warring season? If no war was contemplated for the winter the weapons were stored away at a time commemorated by another festival. This festival was a very popular one and metamorphosed into Martinmas, November 11th, which is the feast day of Saint Martin. Not only is he the patron saint of France, but of innkeepers, drinking companions and reformed drunkards. Could it be possible that the erratic flight of swifts and swallows, bringing to mind the wavering walk of the dedicated celebrants of Saint Martin, was the inspiration for the nickname of the bird, "little Martin"? **Purple M.** for the male's dark plumage.

MEADOWLARK   AS. *mead,* "a place where grass was cut"; the longer form meadow is due to the addition of a case inflection and refers to the bird's habitat. AS. *lawerce* through ME. *laverock,* to E. *lark,* "a lark." The English colonists probably called our eastern bird a lark because its fine song reminded them of the song of the old world Skylark. Our American bird, however, is in the blackbird and oriole family and is not a true lark. **Eastern M.** for its range in eastern North America. **Western M.** for its more western range.

MERGANSER L. *mergus,* "a diver"; L. *anser,* "a goose"; hence "diving goose." **Common M.** Common is meaningless. **Hooded M.** AS. *hod,* "a hat," allied to E. *hat,* for the bird's crest. **Red-breasted M.** referring to the breast of the male.

MERLIN OE. *marlin, marlion,* "merlin"; in the days of falconry the term for the female bird. OF. *esmerillon.* Merlin is the name approved by the British Ornithologists' Union for the same species of bird for which the American Ornithologists' Union till 1973 approved the name Pigeon Hawk. Both organizations approve the same scientific name. As the American Ornithologists' Union Nomenclature Committee has made some effort to erase dialect differences between the common names of some species, as in giving its stamp of approval to Whimbrel and Dunlin, it is now gratifying that the name Pigeon Hawk has given way to Merlin which is already in general use.

MOCKINGBIRD One of the meanings of mock is to imitate in fun, although the connotation of derision still lingers in the meaning. ME. *mokken* from OF. *mocquer,* where it had both the meanings "to wipe the nose" and "to deride"; from LL. *muccere,* "to wipe the nose." I. *moccare* means both "to wipe the nose" and "to mock." The word is likely onomatopoeic for the sound of a nose being blown like a trumpet. The name is appropriate as the bird imitates the songs of many species.

MOTHER CAREY'S CHICKEN A sailor's name for petrel. Yarrell, who wrote *A History of British Birds* in 1843, stated, "The name was given by Capt. Carteret's

sailors, from some unknown hag of that name." It
has also been suggested that she is a witch of the sea
accompanied by imps in the form of the little black
birds. According to others she is the aunt of Davy
Jones. Weekley conjectures that the term is English
sailor corruption of I. *madre cara,* "dear mother," to
whom the sailors of southern Europe were wont to
breathe a prayer when the gales began to blow.

MUD-HEN Local name for the coot. For its habitat, the
muddy marsh.

MURRE Probably of Celtic dialect for a guillemot or
auk. **Common M.** about as equally common as the
Thick-billed M. **Thick-billed M.** for its heavy bill.

MURRELET Diminutive of murre, a little murre. **Ancient M.** for its gray coloring. **Craveri's M.** for F.
craveri (see Appendix). **Kittlitz's M.** for F. H. Kittlitz
(see Appendix). **Marbled M.** for the black and white
winter plumage, reflecting the scientific name.
Xantus M. for John Xantus (see Appendix).

NIGHTHAWK ME. *night,* "night," for the bird's hunting
insects in the dusk. For hawk, see Hawk. **Common N.**
as its range is over most of North America. **Lesser N.**
for its smaller size.

NIGHTJAR A provincial name in America for the
Whip-poor-will but the common name in Britain for
the European member of the same genus. The song
of the European Nightjar is, according to Peterson,
"a loud rapid churring, rising and falling and sus-
tained for as long as five minutes." Its effect is jarring
and E. *jar* is likely derived from imitation of the
song. **Buff-collared N.** another name for Ridgway's
Whip-poor-will.

NODDY See Tern, Noddy T.

NONPAREIL F. *non pareil,* "not equal." For the Painted
Bunting whose plumage is unequaled in splendor.

NUTCRACKER Another poor name as one of its favorite
foods is the nut of the piñon pine, which it swallows

whole as it does other seeds. **Clark's N.** for Captain William Clark who discovered the bird near Kamiah, Idaho, on August 22, 1805 (see Appendix).

NUTHATCH AS. *hnutu,* "a nut"; *hatch* is from *hack* for the bird's occasional technique of wedging a nut too large for it to swallow whole into a crevice and hacking it into small pieces. **Brown-headed N.** for the brown crown of the male. **Pigmy N.** for its small size. **Red-breasted N.** for its plumage. **White-breasted N.** for its plumage.

OLDSQUAW AS. *eald,* OE. *ald,* "old"; Massachusetts Indian, *Squa,* "woman." Bent states, "If there is any one thing for which the old squaw is justly notorious it is for its voice. It is certainly a noisy and garrulous species at all seasons, for which it has received various appropriate names, such as old squaw, old injun, old wife, noisy duck, hound, etc. . . . The names south-southerly, cockawee, quandy, coal and candle light" as well as many others suggest its notes. With all this Bent says he would prefer the name Long-tailed Duck. We might as well add more names for this bird which few can equal in evoking such a lengthy, humorous and poetic list: long-tailed hareld, swallow-tailed duck, south-southerland, old granny, old molly, old Billy, John Connally, Uncle Huldy, my Aunt Huldy, cowhen, calaw, calloo, scoldenore, scolder, and quandy. And finally, the Crees called the bird Hah-ha-way, which we prefer to Mr. Bent's prosaic Long-tailed Duck which is also the British name.

ORIOLE The American orioles got their name because of their similarity in appearance to the European Golden Oriole. ML. *oriolus,* "golden," from L. *aureolus,* "golden"; L. *aurum,* "gold." The old-world orioles belong to the family Oriolidae, while ours belong to the family Icteridae, which includes the blackbirds and meadowlarks. **Baltimore O.** Mark

Catesby, in his *The Natural History of Carolina,
Florida and the Bahama Islands* published in 1731,
made a plate of the bird which he called the
Baltimore-Bird. He so named the bird because its
colors were the same as those of the Baltimores, the
colonial proprietors of Maryland. It is interesting to
note that Catesby did not call the bird an oriole in
either the common or scientific name he gave it.
Linnaeus used Catesby's plate as the basis of his
description. It is now a subspecies of the Northern
O. **Black-headed O.** a helpful name for the bird
watcher as it is the only oriole with a black head
whose black does not extend down the back below
the neck. **Bullock's O.** for William Bullock (see
Appendix). This is now a subspecies of the Northern
O. **Hooded O.** for the yellow plumage at the top of
the head. **Lichtenstein's O.** for M. H. Lichtenstein
(see Appendix). **Northern O.** a new species name
including both the Baltimore and Bullock's Oriole.
Orchard O. for its preference for orchards. AS. *wort,
"plant"; AS. geard,* "yard." OE. *oregeard,* "orchard."
Scott's O. for Winfield Scott (see Appendix). **Spotted-breasted O.** for its plumage.

OSPREY L. *ossifragus, ossifraga,* "an osprey," from L.
os, "bone," and L. *frangere,* "to break." The bird the
old Romans called ossifragus is not the fish hawk.
The ossifragus mentioned by Pliny was the Lammergeier, a German name, which means literally "lamb
vulture." It received its Latin name from its habit of
dropping bones and even tortoises from a height in
order to fragment their ossified bodily parts. It is
difficult to tell when the word came into English,
when it obtained its present form, and when it came
to mean the particular bird it now does. Latin and
French (a modified Latin) words came into English
in immense numbers from 1300 on. As most literary
Englishmen of the fourteenth and fifteenth century

were adept in both tongues, they may have borrowed from either for any word. Turner in 1544 and Aldrovandus in 1599 use osprey or an approximation of it for the Osprey. Things then become puzzling. The writers of the King James version of the bible in 1610 have: (Leviticus, 11, 13) "And these are they which you shall have in abomination among the fowls; they shall not be eaten, they are an abomination: the eagle, and the ossifrage, and the ospray" ends the list of proscribed fowls. It is explained in the foreword of most current editions of the bible that the center column running down each page contains references, "an aid in clearing up for the reader obscure passages." Here one finds that the ossifrage is "a species of eagle" and the osprey is "the black eagle." The introduction also contains suggestions on where to find "a cure for ignorance," "aid when discontented," and "sustaining faith when facing difficulty." The commentators responsible for the column were no better ornithologists than the writers of the King James version. This seems a bit odd as Shakespeare had not long before written in *Coriolanus*, "As is the osprey to the fish, who takes it by sovereignty of nature." Willughby and others of his time (1676) still confuse it with the Sea Eagle. His name for the osprey was Baldbusardus anglorum. Tristram is quoted by Driver: "the eagle is really the griffon-vulture; the ossifrage, the bearded vulture, the largest and most powerful of the vulture tribe." This latter is the Lammergeier. Driver goes on to say that the Osprey is the Short-toed Eagle. One is inclined to think that this great Hebrew scholar of the turn of the century did a bit of bird watching. Aeschylus, the Greek tragic dramatist, is said to have been killed by a Lammergeier (ossifrage) dropping a turtle on his bald head which it mistook for a stone. This cannot be verified as the Athenian mortuary records along with most of the plays of Aeschylus have been lost.

OUZEL, OUSEL AS. *osle,* "blackbird." Another name for the American Dipper. A name used in the past in Britain for their blackbird but now used only for the Ring Ouzel, a thrush which is a close relative of the European blackbird. The European Ring Ousel, which resembles the blackbird in coloration and size in Europe, was also called the Water Ouzel. This name was also used for the Dipper found in America.

OVENBIRD For the resemblance of the bird's nest on the forest floor to a miniature Dutch oven. AS. *ofn,* "oven."

OWL The statement that *owl* is simply a Cockney shortening of *howl* suggests what happened in the development of the original root of the word and what has occurred repeatedly in several languages. The word is onomatopoeic and derived from the bird's call. Our word is from AS. *ule,* "an owl." This is cognate with L. *ulula,* "a screech owl," found in Pliny. From L. *ululo,* "to cry out in pain." Related also to Gr. *alale,* "an outcry," and Gr. *ololuge,* "an outcry" although this is tied up with *ololugon,* "the croaking of frogs." Sa. *uluka,* "an owl," suggests the antiquity of the word's origin. Cf. E. *owlet, howl, halloo, hallabaloo,* and *hallelujah* which we have borrowed from Hebrew. **Barn O.** for one of its favorite nesting sites. **Barred O.** for its striped throat. **Bog O.** the Short-eared O. **Boreal O.** from its range in the north. **Burrowing O.** for its nesting in burrows. **Elf O.** as it is small and elusive. **Ferruginous O.** for its reddish color. **Flammulated O.** from the scientific name "reddish." **Great Gray O.** for its large size and gray plumage. **Great Horned O.** from the resemblance of the feather tufts to horns. **Hawk O.** The bird appears to be half hawk and half owl. **Hoot O.**

another name for the Barred and Great Horned Owls for their calls. **Long-eared O.** for the feather tufts on its head. **Monkey O., Monkey-faced O.** local name for the Barn Owl. **Pygmy O.** for its smallness. **Saw-whet O.** from its notes' resemblance to the sharpening of a saw. **Screech O.** rather a libel on this bird which has a liquid, wavering whistle for its call. **Short-eared O.** as the ears or feather tufts are almost invisible. **Snowy O.** for its white plumage. **Spotted O.** for the whitish dots on its back. **Whiskered O.** from the thin, hairlike feathers of its "moustache."

OYSTERCATCHER Coues says, "Oyster opener would be a better name, as oysters do not run fast." Other ornithologists also belittled the sprinting ability of the oyster. The word has been traced back to Mark Catesby, 1731, and it is interesting to note the opposite of the usual practice in this case of naming the European bird after its American counterpart, not only in English but also in French, *huitrier,* and German, *austermann.* Although it is too late to edify Dr. Coues, the verb "catch" need not imply that the victim is on the run. Someone may be caught unawares or in an indefensible position. Mark Catesby had probably observed the Oystercatcher feeding upon bivalves at low tide when the shell is partially open, allowing the bird to insert its beak and then cut the adductor muscles. To do this it had to catch the bivalve at the right time. **American O.** a location word given before it was realized there was another species on the west coast of America. **Black O.** from its plumage.

PARAKEET, PAROQUET E. *parakeet* or *paroquet* is most likely from F. *parroquet* or OF. *paraquet,* which may have come from Sp. *periquito* or I. *parocchetto.* Although the relationship is uncertain the meaning in all was "little Peter," a pet name for a little parrot. **Carolina P.** for the range of this now extinct bird.

Monk P. A reflection of the scientific name meaning "monk or solitary" although the bird nests in colonies and flies about in small flocks. Its name is not in the last American Ornithologists' Union *Check-list* (1957) as it was first recorded in 1967 or 1968 in the vicinity of the New York transoceanic airports. This has led to the conjecture that some birds escaped from a South American shipment. It has spread throughout New Jersey and been recorded as far west as Ohio. As its normal range is partially in temperate South America, it may be able to survive over winter in its incipient new range.

PARROT F. *Perrot,* "little parrot," a nickname, diminutive of F. *Pierre,* "Peter." L. *petrus,* Gr. *petros,* "a rock." **Sea P.** the Puffin. **Thick-billed P.** for the heavy bill.

PARTRIDGE **Gray P.** Gray from its coloring. Partridge upset Ingersoll who says, "Partridge is the most abused word in American Bird-talk; abused in form, spelling, pronunciation and significance; it is a distorted descendant of *perdix.*" First of all, the American Ornithologists' Union has paid heed, and, in the *Check-list* of 1957, suggests that those who happen across this introduced species should limit the use of the word to the Gray Partridge. As for the other concerns, let us remember that the word has traveled extensively over a long period of time and has been used by many diverse peoples. The present correct spellings of several words are a crystallized mistake, for example, *brid* is now in the form of *bird,* causing no perturbation to schoolteachers. The Gr. *perdix* moved to L. *perdix* without alteration in spelling. Then it moved as a common Romanic word into all the languages derived from Latin except Rumanian. We can recognize it in Sp. and Por. *perdix,* and I. *pernice.* In Old French we find the word as *perdriz, -triz.* Here we find the second *r,* which the etymologists call intrusive, a polite way of saying that something has appeared unreasonably. In Modern French we have *perdrix,* the second *r* remaining but the final *z* reverting to *x.* The Middle English word appears as *pertriche* and *partrich.* In Yorkshire it came out not only *patrick* but *patrig.* The change from -ch to -dge in the final syllable was the last one making patrich finally partridge. We find this paralleled in knowledge, sausage, and other words.

PAURAQUE This name is derived, according to Bent, "from a fancied resemblance to one of its notes."

PEABODY BIRD The White-throated Sparrow. For its song, "Peabody, Peabody, Peabody."

PEEP A general name for the smaller shorebirds. For their call notes.

PELICAN From F. *pelican,* from L. *pelicanus,* from Gr. *pelikan, pelikas;* "woodpecker" named for its pecking from Gr. *pelekus,* "axe." Gr. *pelekaw* means "I hew with an axe." In ancient times the word applied to birds notable for their bills, in addition to the woodpecker. W. Turner, writing about birds in 1544, used Pelecanus as a synonym for the Shovelard or Spoonbill. However, according to Swann, "The Pelican of Aristophanes is the Woodpecker, or joiner bird, which with its bill hewed out the gates of 'Cloud-Cuckoo Land.'" **Brown P.** AS. *brun,* "brown," as it is largely of this color. **White P.** as it is mostly white.

PETER BIRD Tufted Titmouse. For its song, "Peter, Peter, Peter."

PETREL After mentioning that earlier variants of the word *pitteral* and *pittrel* are obscure, the *Oxford Dictionary of English Etymology* goes on to say that Dampier as early as 1703 ". . . has the spelling *petrel* and derives the name from that of St. Peter in the allusion to his 'walking upon the lake of Genneserath,' (Matt. XIV 30)." It is satisfying to pin down such an early allusion even if it raises another question. Was Dampier recording an allusion already given common acceptance, or did he originate it (and the spelling) himself? At any rate, his explanation of the origin of the name is now given credence, as the petrels when alighting on the water dangle their feet and hesitate to alight, seeming, like St. Peter, to doubt their ability to remain above its surface. William Dampier, who Swann feels quite certain is the Dampier referred to in the dictionary, was an English buccaneer and navigator. He was the pilot on the expedition that rescued Alexander Selkirk (Robinson Crusoe) from his lonely island, which was a minor incident on a voyage that made a profit of $200,000. It is interesting to note that F. *petrel* is derived from English, which is contrary to most derivations. If Dampier is correct, *petrel* is a diminutive of Peter. L. *petrus,* from Gr. *petros,* "a stone." **Ashy P.** OE. *aesce,* "ash," for its uniform dull coloration. **Bermuda P.** for its nesting site. **Black P.** for its dark plumage. **Black-bellied P.** for its dark under plumage. **Black-capped P.** OE. *blac,* "black"; OE. *cap,* "a head covering," possibly from L. *caput,* "head." For the black top of the head. **Cape P.** for the Cape of Good Hope, probably the area of the first specimen. **Fork-tailed P.** AS. *forca,* cf. L. *furca,* "a fork"; AS. *taegl,* "a tail." For the shape of its tail. **Galapagos P.** for the islands where it breeds. **Harcourt's P.** for E. V. Harcourt (see Appendix). **Leach's P.** for William E. Leach (see Appendix). **Least P.** as it is our smallest petrel. **Scaled P.** ME. *scale,* from OF. *escale,* from Old High German *scala* akin to AS. *scalu,* "a shell, a scale." The word can be traced back to an Indo-European root and has derivatives in many languages such as G. *skallein,* "to stir up or to hoe." Our E. *shale, shell, skill* are related. The back of the bird in flight is somewhat scaly in appearance. **White-faced P.** AS. *hwit,* "white"; F. *face,* from L. *facies,* "face." For the coloring of the head. **Wilson's P.** for Alexander Wilson (see Appendix).

PEWEE From the note of the Eastern Wood Pewee. **Eastern Wood P.** from its eastern range and habitat. **Western Wood P.** from its western range and habitat.

PHAINOPEPLA Derived from part of the scientific name of the bird. It seems rather a pity that the American Ornithologists' Union *Check-list* committee decided on this common name rather than either "Shining Fly-snapper" which Coues preferred, or "Silky Fly-snapper" which still has quite a vogue.

PHALAROPE Borrowed from the scientific name. **Grey P.** so called by the British who prefer the name descriptive of the winter plumage rather than the American name, Red P. **Northern P.** from its northern breeding grounds. **Red P.** for the color of the underparts in the breeding plumage. **Red-necked P.** The British prefer this name, taken from the reddish neck of the breeding plumage, rather than the American name, Northern P. **Wilson's P.** for Alexander Wilson (see Appendix).

PHEASANT F. *faisan,* "pheasant"; Gr. *phaisianos,* "pheasant," E. for the river Phasis, where the bird ranged. **Ring-necked P.** for the necklace of white feathers.

PHOEBE In imitation of the bird's call. **Black P.** for its dark plumage. **Eastern P.** for its range. **Say's P.** for Thomas Say (see Appendix).

PIGEON F. *pigeon,* "a pigeon," from OF. *pijon,* "a young bird," from L. *pipio,* "to peep." Imitative as E. *peep, cheep.* **Band-tailed P.** alluding to the bands on the tail. **Passenger P.** "Passenger" as used for this extinct bird has a special meaning, as in the phrase "bird of passage," "migratory." Cf. the special meaning in "passage of arms," implying an event, which the word retained from the original meaning, "tournament." L *passare,* "to pass"; L. *passus,* "a step." **Red-billed P.** for the color of the bill. **White-crowned P.** from the white feathers on the top of its head.

PINTAIL For the long pointed tail of the male.

PIPIT F. *pipit,* "a pipit," from L. *pipio,* "to chirp." **American P.** another name for the Water Pipit. **Sprague's P.** after Isaac Sprague (see Appendix). **Water P.** for a European race which is usually found near water although the American is not.

PLOVER OF. *plovier,* "plover," from L. *pluvarius, pluvialis,* "rainy"; L. *pluvia,* "rain." MacLeod lists several authorities with their explanations of the association of the bird's name with rain: "caught more easily in rainy weather, haunt rainy places, arrive in flocks in the rainy season, have markings on their upper plumage like raindrops, and foretell rain by their restlessness." None of these holds water. The German name *regenpfeifer,* "rain piper," suggests the bird sings in the rain. There seems to be no justification or known valid reason for the name. **American Golden P.** for the color of its breeding plumage. **Barnyard P.** for the Solitary Sandpiper, as it frequents barnyards. **Black-bellied P.** for its breeding plumage although the black on its underparts is not as extensive as in the Golden Plover. **Grey P.** British name for the Black-bellied P. **Mountain P.** from its breeding in mountains. **Piping P.** for its note. **Ringed P.** used at times for the Semipalmated P., but it is the name for a different European species which superficially resembles the American Semipalmated P. **Semipalmated P.** L. *semi,* "half"; L. *palma,* "palm of the hand," for the partially webbed foot. **Snowy P.** for its pale plumage. **Thick-billed P.** a popular name for Wilson's P. **Upland P.** Bent says, "Let us be thankful that this gentle and lovely bird is no longer called Bartramian Sandpiper. It is a sandpiper truly enough, but one that has adopted the haunts and many of the habits of the plovers." In spite of this moving plea, the American Ornithologists' Union's *Thirty-second Supplement* to the *Checklist* feels that "to avoid misleading taxonomic implications, where a better name already has wide acceptance," the name should be changed to Upland Sandpiper. **Wilson's P.** for Alexander Wilson (see Appendix).

POOR JOE A local name for the Great Blue Heron, probably for its lonely habit and unpleasant squawk.

POOR-WILL Suggests the bird's call.

POPINJAY Originally parrot. Cf. Sp. *papagavo,* "parrot." F. *papegoe,* "papingay," had a double meaning which carried over to Middle English, "a target for archers or an overdressed or noisy fop." Possibly the earliest target was a painted parrot on a stick, and then, as the target became any type of gaudily painted bird, the word continued to mean the target. As the popularity of archery declined, the meaning for an obtrusive fool has become the main one.

PRAIRIE CHICKEN See Chicken.

PREACHER BIRD From the Red-eyed Vireo's reiteration of its song, which to some says "First on the one hand . . . and then on the other" and to others, "Here I am, see me, up here."

PTARMIGAN From the Gaelic, *tarmachan,* "mountaineer?" or "White game?" Here, at least, we can pin down a misspelling. The *p* was added to the word by Sibbald in *Scotia Illustra,* 1684. He probably thought the word was of Greek origin, like *ptaer* or *ptarmike,* "yellow." Weekley says, "Earlier spelling *termagant* suggests possibly a nickname based on some folklore belief." **Rock P.** from its habitat. **White-tailed P.** the only ptarmigan with an all-white tail. **Willow P.** from its predilection for the buds of the willow.

PUFFIN E. *puff,* and *-in,* the diminutive suffix; literally "little puff" from the downy young or the puffed-up appearance of the mature bird. **Common P.** "Atlantic" more fitting. **Horned P.** for the small stiff plume over the eye. **Tufted P.** for the tuft back of the eye during the breeding season.

PYRRHULOXIA A reflection of the scientific name. (See Pyrrhuloxia.)

QUAIL OF. *quaille,* "quail." Cognate with quack, imitative of the call of the European species. A fairly popular name for the Bobwhite. **California Q.** a locality designation. **Gambel's Q.** for William Gambel (see Appendix). **Harlequin Q.** from its feather pattern (see Duck, Harlequin D.). **Mountain Q.** for its habitat. **Scaled Q.** from the appearance of the feathering.

RAIL Probably a combination of French and Teutonic sources: F. *rale,* "a rail." OF *raale,* to make a scraping noise; L. *raelare,* "to scrape." **Black R.** for its color. **Clapper R.** E. *clap,* "a noise made by striking the hands together," from the call of the bird. **King R.** a compliment to its appearance. **Virginia R.** Its range does not justify its name. **Yellow R.** for its yellow plumage.

RAIN BIRD Another name for the American cuckoos. From an old superstition that its call foretold the coming of rain. A local name in England for the Green Woodpecker.

RAVEN AS. *hraefn,* "a raven." Imitative of the bird's cry. **Common R.** common only in the far north and west. **White-necked R.** for the scarcely visible ring of white neck feathers.

RAZORBILL From the sharp-edged bill. Also, mainly in the past, used for the Puffin and Guillemot.

REDBIRD Local name for the Cardinal.

REDBREAST Old name for Robin, especially in Britain.

REDHAMMER The Red-shafted Flicker. For the pinkish

red underwing and tail, and the tattoo it beats with its bill.

REDHEAD From the color of the head.

REDPOLL OE. *red,* for the color of the spot on its head. ME. *pol,* "head," as in taking a poll, i.e., counting heads. **Common R.** only in comparison with the Hoary Redpoll. **Hoary R.** AS. *har,* "hoar" or "white." For the whitish bird.

REDSTART The American bird was so called for its resemblance to the European Redstart. AS. *read,* "red"; AS. *steort,* "tail." **American R.** as distinguished from the European. **Painted R.** in the same genus as the one above but, alas, no red in its "start."

REED-BIRD A local name for the Bobolink, particularly in the Middle Atlantic states where it congregates in the reedy marshes during the fall migration.

RICE-BIRD A local name for the Bobolink, particularly in the past on the southeast coast where it frequented the rice fields. This was Audubon's name for the bird.

ROADRUNNER From its habit of running on the ground.

ROBERT O'LINCOLN A name for the Bobolink suggested by the common name Bobolink, in turn suggested by the bird's song.

ROBIN Wherever the English have settled they have tended to bestow the name Robin on any bird with a noticeable amount of red or russet in the plumage. If the russet is on the breast, the name is practically inevitable. The early settlers in America, who had more pressing concerns than the niceties of ornithological nomenclature, named the Robin because of its resemblance to the English bird with the orange-red face and breast. Gradually the name is becoming limited to this one species. In the past the Bluebird was also called Robin. The Towhee, alias Chewink, labored under the name of Ground Robin. Then, too, the Robin Snipe might be either the Knot or the Dowitcher. Calling the Baltimore Oriole the Golden Robin seems to be going a little too far. But things began to get out of control when the Cedar Waxwing was labeled the Canadian Robin, to say nothing of christening the Redbreasted Merganser the Sea Robin. Robin, a diminutive nickname of Robert, is of French origin. Both forms of the name were in common use near the beginning of the Middle English period. According to Weekley the name was originally HG. *Ruodperht* (G. Ruprecht), from HG. *hrode, ruod,* "fame," plus *berht,* "bright." The English have the sole responsibility for attaching the name Robin to the bird. It was first Redbreast, then the pet name Robin was added. Finally Redbreast was dropped. The process did not go as far with Jackdaw and Magpie. The *Dictionary of Word Origins* tells us "The use of the bird's name, robin in 'round robin' a petition signed in a circular manner to avoid giving prominence to any one signature," had its origin on the brig *Catherine* at Gibralter in 1612. The crew was discontented but well aware that the captain had the right to enforce discipline by hanging to the yardarm whoever he decided was the chief dissenter. The first name signed to a petition was likely to be taken as sufficient evidence of leadership and justify the extreme penalty. To avoid this fate for any one individual the crew decided to append their names in the form of a circle. Thus all signatures were on an equal basis and the captain could scarcely hang the whole crew. The story goes that a statuette of a Robin on a circular base was close at hand. This was used to trace a circle which formed a guide for writing the signatures around it. This device to protect individual petitioners henceforth became known as a "round robin." Newton writing in 1894 says of the name in England, "Robin, a well-known nickname of the 'REDBREAST,' which in common use has almost supplanted the stock on which it was grafted." **American R.** This is now the name sanctioned by the American Ornithologists' Union as there are other birds in the world named Robin.

RUBYTHROAT The Ruby-throated Hummingbird.

RUFF, REEVE Reeve most likely preceded ruff as the name for the bird. AS. *gerifa*, "one in authority," from which is derived *reeve*, the chief officer of a town or district" and our modern word "sheriff." The bird was perhaps so named for the pugnacious-appearing display of the males at the onset of the breeding season. It is debatable whether the bird was named for the starched linen neckwear popular in Elizabethan times or the neckwear named for the bird. At any rate, "ruff" is generally used for the male bird and "reeve" for the female. Ruff is short for ruffle, which we still use to describe the raising of the feathers when it assumes a threatening posture. The ruff in the Elizabethan costume was open in front and widest and longest behind, while the bird's ruff is most evident in front and hardly noticeable behind the head.

SANDERLING AS. *sand*, "sand," from the habitat; *-er*, AS. and Germanic suffix, "one who has to do with," *-ling*, AS. diminutive suffix, often applied to animals, "little"; so literally the whole word means "the little one of the sand." Then, probably, from Ic. *sanderla*, a name for a shorebird.

SANDPIPER AS. *sand*, "sand"; AS. *pipe*, from LL. *pipa*, from L. *pipare*, "to chirp." We find this imitative word in I., Ic., Sp., Sw., *pipa*, G. *pfeife*, D. *pibe*, and in F. *pipe*. All are imitative of the cry of a young bird. E. suffix, *-er*, "one who." Thus we have "one who chirps on the sand." **Baird's S.** for Spencer F. Baird (see Appendix). **Bartramian S.** for William Bartram (see Appendix). Name for the Upland Plover used mainly by those whose scientific conscience rebels at calling a sandpiper a plover. **Buff-breasted S.** for the color of its breast. **Curlew S.** for its curlew-like bill. **Least S.** It is. **Pectoral S.** L. *pectus,* "breast"; not from the distinct shield of dark breast feathers but from the inflationary sac under this which gives resonance to the male's amatory outpourings. **Purple S.** for the purplish tone of its back. **Red-backed S.** popular name for the Dunlin. **Rock S.** for its habitat. **Semipalmated S.** for its partially webbed feet. **Sharp-tailed S.** for its pointed tail. **Solitary S.** generally alone, never in large flocks. **Spoon-bill S.** for the shape of its bill. **Spotted S.** for the spotted underparts in the breeding plumage. **Stilt S.** for its comparatively long legs. **Upland S.** As this bird is taxonomically a sandpiper, the American Ornithologists' Union now prefers to call it that rather than Upland Plover. **Western S.** more common in western North America than eastern. **White-rumped S.** for the obvious field mark.

SAPSUCKER   From the habit of drilling holes in the bark of trees and eating the sap and insects attracted thereto. **Yellow-bellied S.** for its yellowish underparts. **Williamson's S.** for Robert S. Williamson (see Appendix).

SAWBILL   For all the mergansers whose bills are serrated.

SAW-FILER   A local name for Saw-whet Owl.

SCAUP   A Scottish variation of *scalp,* which meant not only the hairless top of a bald head but also a ledge which at times might be partially exposed above the surface of the water. *The Oxford Dictionary of English Etymology* states that *scaup* comes from *scaup bank* which provides a bed for shellfish on which the birds feed. MacLeod states that *scaup* originally meant a shell and that it is cognate with *scallop* and *scalp.* Possibly the old word for a shelf in the sea and a shellfish, being the same, is close enough in relation to the bird's habits that both played a part in giving in the name of scaup. The **Greater S.** is about an inch longer than the **Lesser S.**

SCOTER Probably a variation of coot, which is used by hunters for the scoters. In support of this MacLeod points out that *macreuse* in the north of France means a scoter, and in the south, a coot. It might also be connected with *"scot,"* a local name for the Guillemot and Razorbill. **Black S.** for its dark plumage. This is a much needed change from **Common S. Surf S.** from diving for shellfish in the surf. **Velvet S.** name for a European species sometimes mistakingly given to the Common S. **White-winged S.** for its white speculum.

SEA PIGEON Local name for the Black Guillemot for its resemblance to the domestic pigeon.

SEEDEATER OE. *saed,* "seed"; OE. *aet,* "eat." **White-collared S.** for the white band about the neck.

SEWICK The Least Flycatcher. For its song.

SHAG An accepted name for one of the cormorant family in Britain and used loosely in America for the Double-crested Cormorant. For the crest of feathers on the head which give it a shaggy appearance.

SHEARWATER E. *shear,* "to cut close with a large pair of scissors"; E. *water,* "the element which makes up the sea." For the bird's manner of flight in skimming the water. **Audubon's S.** for John J. Audubon (see Appendix). **Black-tailed S.** for the dark shade on the underside of the tail. **Cory's S.** for Charles B. Cory (see Appendix). **Flesh-footed S.** for the color of its feet. Formerly called **Pale-footed S. Greater S.** for its large size. **Little S.** for its smallness. **Manx S.** for the Isle of Mann where it formerly bred in great numbers but has not done so since 1800. **New Zealand S.** for the New Zealand islets where it breeds. **Pinkfooted S.** for its flesh-colored feet. **Short-**

tailed **S.** as this is the name used in its breeding region. Formerly called **Slender-billed S. Sooty S.** for its dark-brown color.

SHELDRAKE, SHELD DUCK A colloquial name for the merganser. *Sheld, shell,* English dialect words for "dappled, variegated," applied to birds and to animals which are particolored.

SHITE POTE An attempt to render more delicate by a change in spelling a name for the bird derived from its habit of ejecting effluent when making a startled departure. In America applied indiscriminately to the Black-crowned Night Heron, the Green Heron and the Bittern.

SHORE LARK Local name for the Horned Lark. Where it is found in winter.

SHOVELER From the shape of the large bill. AS. *scoff,* "shove."

SHRIKE Turner first used the name for the bird in English in 1544, and states that he only saw it twice in England although more frequently in Germany. Possibly from AS. *scric,* "a shrieker," or OE. *scric,* "a thrush." It is evidently related to "shriek" as is S. *shrika,* "a jay." Turner seems to have been unaware that the name was probably in use for the Mistle Thrush. **Loggerhead S.** "loggerhead" is applied to animals with large heads and is similar to blockhead in derivation. Log is akin to Nor. *laag,* "a fallen tree," and Ic. *lag,* "a log." The bird's head is larger in proportion to its body than most birds' heads are. **Northern S.** for its more northern range. The English call the bird the Great Grey Shrike.

SICKLE BILL A local name for the Long-billed Curlew.

SISKIN Closely related to the European Siskin. It gets its name from the Old World bird. Authorities differ as to its exact derivation in English as it may have been adopted from a number of sources of common origin; D. *sisgen* or *sidsken,* "a chirper"; S. *siska,* "a chirper"; Ic. *zieske, ziseke,* "a siskin"; Middle Dutch, *siseken.* Slavic forms of the word appear in Czech, *ciz,* and Russian, *chizh,* "siskin or small bird." **Pine S.** for its partiality for breeding in conifers.

SKIMMER Black S. For the color of the upper parts and the bird's method of procuring food by immersing its lower bill in the water while skimming over its surface. Pennant bestowed the name "The Black Skimmer" on the bird in 1773, evidently preferring this to Catesby's "cutwater."

SKUA A Faroese name for the bird.

SKYLARK Whence come "the profuse strains of unpremeditated art." The European bird introduced on Vancouver Island, British Columbia.

SNAKE BIRD, SNAKE KILLER Local names for the Anhinga and the Roadrunner.

SNIPE AS. *snite,* "snipe," from Ic. *snipa,* "snipe," as a snipper, akin to modern *snip* and *snap.* **Common S.** more common in western Europe than the other two species of snipe found there, the Great Snipe and the Jack Snipe. **Red-breasted S.** is the accepted British name for the Dowitcher. We also have grass snipe for the Pectoral Sandpiper, robin snipe for the Knot, rock snipe for the Purple Sandpiper and sea snipe for the Phalaropes. **Wilson's S.** was an old name for the Common Snipe. **Telltale S.** for the Yellow Leg's readiness to sound its alarm notes.

SNOW BIRD For the Junco in its winter range.

SNOWFLAKE Another name for the Snow Bunting.

SOLITAIRE For its elusive habits. F. *solitaire,* "alone." **Townsend's S.** after J. K. Townsend who found the first specimen near the Columbia River (see Appendix).

SORA One of the few native American Indian bird names that has endured.

SPARROW AS. *spearwa,* "sparrow," literally "flutterer," applied to any small bird. The word has an Indo-

European base, *sper,* "flutter, quiver," and hence figuratively "to struggle, kick or jerk." Thus we have L. *parra,* "a bird of ill omen," and L. *spernere,* "to spurn"; Gr. *sporgiles,* "a sparrow," and Gr. *spairein,* "to struggle." E. *spavin* means lameness in a horse which has a bird-like hopping motion due to a swelling of a joint. Spur originally meant to spur a horse as a rider would seem to flutter his legs, and from there on to the word spurn, i.e., to kick against or reject. Newton points out, "Perhaps the earliest instance of nicknaming birds is to be found in Landland's Piers' 'The Plowman,'" written soon after 1400, where the sparrow is called 'Philip.'"
Bachman's S. named by Audubon for his friend John Bachman (see Appendix). **Baird's S.** for Spencer F. Baird (see Appendix). **Black-chinned S.** for its black throat. **Black-throated S.** for the black throat of the male. **Botteri's S.** for M. Botteri (see Appendix). **Brewer's S.** for Thomas M. Brewer (see Appendix). **Cape Sable S.** for its breeding range on the coast of southern Florida. This is now a subspecies. **Cassin's S.** for John Cassin (see Appendix). **Chipping S.** for its song of short quick notes. **Clay-colored S.,** as clay means fine grained earth and may be of various colors, the term is meaningless. **Dusky Seaside S.** for its dark plumage. This is now a subspecies. **English S.** a popular name for the House S. **European Tree S.,** introduced from Europe but as yet confined to the area about St. Louis, Missouri. **Field S.** from its habitat. **Fox S.** for its reddish, fox-like color. **Golden-crowned S.** for its golden pate. **Grasshopper S.** from its song which resembles that of the insect. **Harris' S.** for Edward Harris (see Appendix). **Henslow's S.** for John S. Henslow (see Appendix). **House S.,** AS. *hus,* "house"; from the bird's fondness for association with man's dwellings. **Ipswich S.** for Ipswich, Massachusetts, from where the first specimen came. It is

now a subspecies. **Lark S., AS.** *lawerc,* "lark," ME.
Laverock, "a lark." Probably because of its musical
notes. **Le Conte's S.** for Dr. John Le Conte (see
Appendix). The name is a reflection of one of the
previous trivial scientific names for this bird.
Changes in scientific nomenclature particularly in
such a large and complex family as the Fringillidae
became necessary as new species were discovered
and knowledge of them and their relation to each
other accumulated. The first description was made
by the English ornithologist John Latham in 1790
from a specimen from the interior of Georgia. He
named it *Fringilla caudacuta* (L. "little finch with the
sharp tail"). This placed it in the European genus
Fringilla in company with the Chaffinch and the
Brambling. As there was at that time no American
genera, the bird was placed in one of the six genera
of the European family Fringillidae. It was a lost
species until Audubon rediscovered it in South
Dakota in 1843. Thinking it a new species, he named
it *Emberiza leconteii* placing it in the European genus
with the bunting rather than the finches. This was
possibly a slight improvement as there was not as yet
any American classification. By 1872, the date of the
publication of the first edition of Coues *Key to North
American Birds,* the British had added six genera and
the Americans twenty-four genera to the family
Fringillidae. Breaking away from the British nomenclature in this edition and in the three subsequent
editions of his book, the bird was called *Coturniculus
leconteii.* It then came to light that Gray in 1849 had
called the genus *Ammodromus* and Le Conte's Sparrow joined the genus accompanying Henslow's Sparrow. So, conforming to the law of priority the name
Ammodromus leconteii appeared in the first (1886)
and second (1895) editions of the American Ornithologists' Union *Check-list.* Coues, who was chair-

man of the committee responsible for the *Check-list*, changed the name in latter editions of his *Key to North American Birds.* Previous to the publication of the third (1910) edition of the *Check-list,* it was felt that a group of which LeConte's Sparrow was one should be reclassified. While casting about for a new name for the proposed new genus a bibliographical check proved rewarding as it was discovered that C. J. Maynard in 1895 had proposed the name *Passerherbulus* for the group. The Nomenclature Committee adopted this and the name appears in the third (1910) edition of the *Check-list* as *Passerherbulus lecontei,* the only casualty being the loss of the final *i.* Another difficulty arose. It was found that the bird that had been lost for over fifty years had a name that had been lost for over a hundred years. *Passerherbulus* could remain, but *lecontei,* according to the sacred law of priority, had to be dropped for the original *caudacuta,* with a change of gender to *caudacutus.* But there was already a *Passerherbulus caudacutus,* the Sharp-tailed Sparrow. Much to the satisfaction of the nomenclature committee, we can be sure, it was found that this bird really belonged in the genus *Ammospiza,* where it was placed, leaving LeConte's Sparrow in undisputed possession of the name *Passerherbulus caudacutus* in the fourth (1931) and fifth (1957) editions of the *Check-list.* This state of nomenclatural quiescence lasted for forty-two years until shattered in the *Thirty-second Supplement* to the *Check-list (Auk;* vol. 90, no. 3). It is decided that, after all, LeConte's Sparrow belongs to the genus *Ammospiza.* As there is already an *A. caudacuta* and it would not do to have two species so named, leconteii is revived, giving us *A. leconteii.* The common name which had remained only as a reflection of the scientific one now regains its former significance. The common name, which is not sub-

ject to the decisions of learned taxonomists, remains
as a memento of the bird who not only was lost, but
when found had proven to be very elusive. A cynic is
supposed to have said that taxonomy is a branch of
science concerned mainly with recording errors.
Lincoln's S. for Thomas Lincoln (see Appendix).
Olive S. for the dull, olive-colored plumage. **Pine-
woods S.** a popular name for Bachman's S. **Rufous-
crowned S.** for its reddish crown. **Rufous-winged S.**
for the reddish wings. **Sage S.** for its habitat.
Savannah S. for Savannah, Georgia, where Alexander Wilson obtained his specimen, thus giving this
bird the widest range between its scientific, *sandwichensis,* and common names. **Seaside S.** for its habitat
in the coastal marshes. **Sharp-tailed S.** It has. **Song
S.** for its habit of continuously singing its pleasant
song. **Swamp S.** from its predilection for wetlands.
Marsh sparrow would do just as well. **Tree S.** for its
breeding habitat. **Vesper S.** from its habit of singing
at dusk. **White-crowned S.** for the distinctive white
crown. **White-throated S.** for its white throat.

SPOONBILL Referring to the wide, flat shape of the end
of the bill. Formerly in England a name for the
Shoveler. AS. *spon,* "a thin piece of wood." **Roseate
S.** for the salmon shade of the plumage.

SPRIG A local name for the Pintail.

STAKE DRIVER A local name for the Bittern. Suggested
by its call.

STARLING AS. *stear, stearn,* and *sterlving,* "a starling,"
with the diminutive suffix *-ling.* In the west and north
of England and in Ireland *stare* is still a term for the
bird. In German the name of the bird is star and in
Swedish stare. *Sterling* is possibly from the four birds
on the silver coins of Edward the Confessor. It is
thought by some that the name may mean "little
star" suggested by the silhouette of the bird in
flight.

STILT ME. *stilte,* "stilt," refers to the disproportionally long legs in which it is only outdone by the flamingo. **Black-necked S.** refers to the black on the back of the neck in contrast to the European bird, the **Black-winged S.** whose black is confined to the wings and back.

STORK OE. *storc,* "stork," supposed to refer to the bird's rigid habit. E. *stark* and *starch* are related. **Wood S.** as it nests in woods. This name is now preferred to Wood Ibis.

SUGARBIRD A local name for the Bananaquit.

SUMMER REDBIRD For the Summer Tanager which is only a summer resident compared to the Cardinal, also called a red bird, which is non-migratory.

SURFBIRD From its addiction to the rocky shoreline in winter.

SWALLOW AS. *swalewe,* "swallow." **Bank S.** for its nesting sites. In Britain called the Sand Martin. **Barn S.** for its nesting sites. In Britain it is just plain Swallow. **Cave S.** for its nesting sites. **Cliff s.** for its nesting sites. **Rough-winged S.** from the recurved hooklets on the outer web of the first primary feather. **Tree S.** for its nesting in holes in trees. **Violet-green S.** from the color of its upper back.

SWAN AS. *swan,* "swan." It was formerly often spelled swanne. The male is termed cob and the female, pen. G. *schwan* may go back with English in origin to an association with the musical note of such a species as the Whooper. The Indo-European roots *swon, swen* are seen in Sa. *svanas,* "noise." L. *sonere,* "to sound," probably has the same derivation. **Mute S.** Mute is a misnomer as the bird is not silent though not as vocal as the two other swans known to the English, the Whooper and Bewick's. Until about 1800 it was commonly called the Tame Swan. **Trumpeter S.** from its trumpet-like call. **Whistling S.** so named from its call, although it has a nasal quality.

SWIFT Aptly named as it is among the fastest flyers. **Black S.** for its dark plumage. **Chimney S.** from its roosts and nesting sites. **Vaux's S.** for William S. Vaux (see Appendix). **White-throated S.** for its white throat.

TANAGER From *tangara,* a kind of bird in Tupi, a South American Indian language. **Hepatic T.** L. *hepaticus,* "liver-colored," i.e., rusty red; this term was taken from the former scientific term which referred to the coppery color of the male's plumage. **Scarlet T.** from the bright crimson color of the body plumage of the male. **Summer T.** Catesby christened the bird Summer Red Bird possibly to differentiate it from the Cardinal, which he called the Red Bird, an all-year-round resident. **Western T.** for its range in western North America.

TATTLER For its rapid tinkling notes. **Wandering T.** for its wide ranging, particularly over vast distances of water. Also used for the Yellow Legs and other sandpipers whose alarm notes alert other birds to the hunter's dismay.

TEACHER BIRD The Ovenbird which is said to call "Teacher, Teacher, Teacher."

TEAL Did not appear in English until the thirteenth or fourteenth century, although the authorities differ on this. All agree that the term is not Anglo-Saxon but that it is cognate with Du. *teling,* "a teal." **American Green-winged T.** This was formerly the Green-winged T. but is now classified as a subspecies of it. **Baikal T.** refers to its range around Lake Baikal, Siberia. **Blue-winged T.** for the bright blue speculum. **Cinnamon T.** for the cinnamon red of its head and underparts. **Common T.** common in Eurasia but casual in North America. **Eurasian Green-winged T.,** the former Common T., is now also classified as a subspecies of the Green-winged T. **European T.** formerly used in America for the Eurasian Green-

winged T. **Green-winged T.** for the green speculum.
This is now the specific name which includes both
the American and the Eurasian Green-winged Teals
which have been reclassified as subspecies.

TEETER BIRD   For the Spotted and to a lesser extent the
Solitary Sandpiper. For their rocking habit.

TERN   Norse *taerne,* S. *tarna,* "tern." Most likely first
applied to the Sandwich Tern, other terns being
called sea swallows. **Aleutian T.** for its breeding
range. **Arctic T.** for its breeding grounds. **Black T.**
alluding to the dark breeding plumage. **Black Noddy
T.** for its plumage and resemblance to the Noddy T.
Bridled T. for the pattern of the head plumage.
Cabot's T. for Dr. Samuel Cabot (see Appendix). At
the time Cabot originally described this tern, which
he collected on the coast of Yucatan in 1847, the
practice of recognizing and naming subspecies was
not yet established. It did not become accepted until
the end of the century. So this term received both a
scientific and common name. The common name
Cabot's Tern, honoring the describer, came into
wide use in this country. When it became clear that
this bird was a subspecies of the Old World Sandwich Tern, the American Ornithologists' Union
sanctioned this name in accordance with the conven-
tion of dropping subspecific common names. **Caspian T.** for the Caspian Sea, the site of the first
specimen. **Common T.** widespread in North America
and Europe. **Elegant T.** from the scientific term,
elegans. **Forster's T.** for John R. Forster (see Appendix). **Gull-billed T.** from the shape of its bill. **Least T.**
for its small size. **Noddy T.** E. *noddy,* "simpleton," an
appropriate name given to the bird by sailors because it did not take alarm at their approach.
Roseate T. for the faint tinge of pink color on its
breast in breeding plumage. **Royal T.** for its impressive size and appearance. **Sandwich T.** for Sandwich,

Kent, England, the site of the first specimen. **Sooty T.** for its dark plumage. **Trudeau's T.** as there is only one record for this bird, its authenticity has been repeatedly questioned. De Schauensee in *Species of Birds of South America and Their Distribution* (1966) says, "The type supposedly was taken on the coast of New Jersey, U.S.A., but the accuracy of the locality has been questioned." The American Ornithologists' Union *Check-list* lists the record as valid although it credits Audubon with taking the specimen instead of Trudeau. Audubon says in his *Ornithological Biography* (1839), "This beautiful tern, which has not hitherto been described, was procured at Egg Harbor, in New Jersey, by my much esteemed and talented friend, J. Trudeau, Esq., of Louisiana, to whom I have great pleasure in dedicating it. Nothing is known of its range, or even the particular habits in which it may differ from other species. The individual obtained was in the company of a few others of the same kind. I have received from Mr. Trudeau an intimation of the occurrence of several individuals on Long Island." It seems that Trudeau sent the specimen to London where Audubon made the drawing in 1838. Unfortunately, there is no record of the date when Trudeau procured the bird; but most fortunately, the type of specimen, which Audubon used for his description and painting of the bird, formerly at Vassar College, is now in the collection of the American Museum of Natural History, no. 156650. The label on it was not made by either Trudeau or Audubon. There is no question about the validity of the species. The only doubt is about the site of the record, which to be valid would mean that Trudeau was mistaken as to where he procured the specimen he sent Audubon. It seems highly improbable that he obtained the bird in South America and then deliberately misled Audubon. The A.O.U.

Check-list says type specimen was taken by Audubon at Great Egg Harbor. This is an error. **Wilson's T.** an old name for the Common T.

THRASHER From E. *thrusher* from *thrush;* q.v., not connected with *thrash,* "to beat." **Bendire's T.** for Charles E. Bendire (see Appendix). **Brown T.** for its coloring. **California T.** for its range. **Crissal T.** for the rusty color of the under-tail coverts, the crissum; the only thrasher so marked. **Curve-billed T.** for the bill's shape. **LeConte's T.** for John L. LeConte (see Appendix). **Long-billed T.** reflection of the appropriately descriptive scientific term, *longirostre,* "long bill." **Sage T.** from its type of habitat.

THRUSH ME. *thrusch,* AS. *thryce,* "a thrush"; possibly allied to G. *trizo,* "to twitter." **Gray-cheeked T.** for the gray feathering behind the eye. **Hermit T.** from its solitary habits especially in the winter. **Olive-backed T.** a popular name for Swainson's T., for the very dull greenish tinge of the plumage of the back. **Swainson's T.** for William Swainson (see Appendix). **Varied T.** from the diversified plumage. **Wilson's T.** local name for the Veery. **Wood T.** from its habitat.

THUNDER PUMPER The American Bittern. For its impressive vocalizing.

TIERCEL A falconer's term for the male peregrine or male goshawk considered to be a third smaller than the female.

TIMBER DOODLE More prosaically known as the Woodcock.

TIP-UP For the Spotted and Solitary Sandpipers' see-saw habit.

TITLARK A popular name for the Water Pipit.

TITMOUSE Ic. *tittr,* anything small; AS. *mase,* a name used for small birds, e.g., AS. *fraecmase, colemase, spicmase,* all names of small birds. True plural should be titmouses, but due to confusion with mouse, it is titmice. **Black-crested T.** for the black tuft of feath-

ers. L. *crista,* "a comb or tuft on a bird's head."
Bridled T. from the bridle-like pattern on the face.
AS. *bridel,* "a bridle." **Plain T.** It has a crest, too, but
not much color. **Tufted T.** E. *tuft* from F. *touffe,* "a
lock of hair." For the crest of feathers.

TOMTIT, TIT Occasionally used for the Tufted Titmouse.

TOWHEE Imitative, for the bird's call note, as is
chewink which the American Ornithologists' Union
Check-list ignores in the interest of conformity.
Abert's T. for Major James W. Abert (see Appendix).
Brown T. for the color of its plumage. **Green-tailed T.**
a reflection of the scientific term, which ignores the
fact that the dark green of the plumage is not
confined to the tail. **Rufous-sided T.** for the plumage.

TROGON Gr. *trogon,* "a gnawer." For the tooth-like
edge of the bill. **Coppery-tailed T.** for the color of the
male's tail.

TROPICBIRD From E. *tropic,* the name of the lines
bounding the Tropics where the sun appears to turn.
Gr. *tropikos,* "relating to a turn." For the range of
the birds. **Red-billed T.** AS. *bile,* "bill." For the bill's
red color, which the following also has. **White-tailed
T.** for the white tail, which the Red-billed T. also has.

TURKEY Our wild turkey derives its name from the
domestic turkey which is a descendent of turkeys
brought alive from Mexico to Spain in 1630. *The
Oxford Dictionary* says the name was first applied to
the African bird (Guinea fowl) because it was
brought from Guinea through Africa by the Portuguese, and later applied to the American bird.
However, it is more generally agreed that the name
turkey became attached to the bird from a widespread misconception of the country of its origin,
Turkey. Ignorance as to the bird's place of origin is
not confined to its reflection in English, as we find G.
calecutischer hahn, literally "a cock of Calicut"; F.

coc d'Inde, literally "a cock of India"; and the I. *gallo d'India,* "cock of India." One wonders whether or not some of the early settlers in America were a bit puzzled when they found the bird ahead of them.

TURNSTONE From its penchant for turning over stones, shells and small bits in search of food. The name, according to Newton, appears to be first used by Willughby in 1676. **Black T.** for its dark appearance. **Ruddy T.** for its reddish color.

VEERY Probably imitative of the bird's song.

VERDIN Alexander Wetmore says it is "the French word for yellow head."

VIREO L. *viridos,* "green." As some of the vireos have a greenish tinge in their plumage. William Turner in *A Short and Succinct History of the Principle Birds Noticed by Pliny and Aristotle* (1544), as translated by A. H. Evans (1905), says, "These are the words of Aristotle:—'The Vireo, which is entirely green, is singled out as easy to be caught, and clever for the business of life; but it flies badly and its color is unpleasing.' So far for Aristotle." In the Latin from which the above is translated the word Vireo is present as it is in Evans' translation. The bird referred to is probably the Greenfinch, common in Europe. Despite this record of the name vireo for a bird in English in 1544, it never appears to have been accepted, not appearing in Swann who lists 5,000 names of British birds. In America the name has fared much better, being widely accepted. It probably is a reflection of the scientific name vireo, first used by Vieillot in 1807. **Bell's V.** for J. G. Bell (see Appendix). **Black-capped V.** almost a complete reflection of the scientific name, describing the dark plumage of the head. **Black-whiskered V.** Its whisker marks are rather thin and modest but they are there. **Gray V.** for the gray plumage. **Hutton's V.** for William Hutton (see Appendix). **Philadelphia V.** for the site of the type specimen. **Red-eyed V.** for the red eye of the mature bird. **Solitary V.** a reflection of the scientific name possibly both because of its preference during the breeding season for more secluded woodland areas than other vireos and also because it migrates earlier in the spring and later in the fall than the others. Perhaps poets will keep alive the name "blue-headed" which scientists in their striving for simplicity in nomenclature frown upon. **Warbling V.** Bent says, "Wherever we turn in the literature of the warbling vireo we find that the author, after commenting on the bird's inconspic-uousness, speaks enthusiastically of its song, pointing out the differences from the songs of the other vireos, the length of the song period, and the charm of the smoothly flowing warble." So the bird is named for its most attractive feature. **White-eyed V.** for its white eyes. **Yellow-green V.** a reflection of the scientific name which refers to the coloration. **Yellow-throated V.** for its yellow throat.

VULTURE   L. *vultur,* "a vulture"; in old Latin it was *vulturus,* literally, "tearer," from *vuellere,* "to pluck or tear." **Black V.** for its black plumage. **Turkey V.** from its resemblance in appearance only to the bird which is honored at Thanksgiving.

WAGTAIL   For the pumping of the tail. **Yellow W.** for its yellow underparts. **White W.** for the whitish plum-age.

WAKE UP   Another name for the Flicker. For its loud and early calling.

WANDERING TATTLER   From its extensive range and its notes which supposedly give away the presence of the fowler to other birds.

WARBLER   The word which means to sing with trills and quavers was first used for a genus (*Sylvia*) of birds by Pennant in 1773, although the birds are not all good singers. The word has become attached to the American Parulidae family which are not scientifically akin to the European warblers and have now been given the distinguishing name of wood warblers. **Arctic W.** for its northern breeding range. **Audubon's W.** for John J. Audubon (see Appendix). This has been dropped as a species but may be used for the subspecies. **Bachman's W.** for John Bachman (see Appendix). **Bay-breasted W.** for its chestnut sides and throat. **Black-and-white W.** for its plumage. **Blackburnian W.** Bent cites Bagg and Eliot as follows: "Some time in the later eighteenth century, a specimen (apparently female) was sent from New York to England, and there described and named for a Mrs. Blackburn [see Appendix] who collected stuffed birds and was a patron of ornithology." However, an earlier description came to light and took over the scientific name, although the popular name has remained. **Blackpoll W.** for its black cap. **Black-throated Blue W.** for its plumage. **Black-throated Gray W.** for the dark throat. **Black-throated Green W.** for the black throat and blue-black of the male's plumage. **Blue-winged W.** from its plumage. **Canada W.** refers to the breeding range although it is not limited to Canada. **Cape May W.** Named by Alexander Wilson for a specimen taken by his friend, George Ord, in Cape May County, New Jersey, in 1811. **Cerulean W.** for the sky blue plumage. **Chestnut-sided W.** from its appearance. **Colima W.** for the site where it was first collected, Sierra Nevada de Colima, by W. B. Richardson in 1889. **Connecticut W.** named by Wilson for the state where he first found it. **Golden-cheeked W.** for the facial patches. **Golden-winged W.** for its bright yellow epaulets. **Grace's W.** for Grace D. Coues (see Appendix under Grace). **Hermit W.** possibly because it was thought to be rare when first found. **Hooded W.** for the ring of black feathers about the head suggesting a hood. **Kentucky W.** named by Wilson for the state where he found it abundant. **Kirtland's W.** for Jared P. Kirtland (see Appendix). **Lucy's W.** for Lucy Baird (see Appendix under Lucy). **MacGillivray's W.** Both the scientific and common names were given by Audubon to honor his collaborator and friend, William MacGillivray (see Appendix). The original specimens collected by J. K. Townsend were given to Audubon for publication in his *Birds of America.* It seems that Audubon first confused the bird with the Mourning Warbler and then published it as MacGillivray's by which name it was known scientifically for years. As it has been shown that Townsend's description was published two months previous to Audubon's, the name of MacGillivray has been replaced by *tolmiei* in the scientific term although not in the popular name. Possibly, Townsend was somewhat mollified to find that Audubon had named a bird Townsend's Solitaire as he had named Audubon's Warbler. **Magnolia W.** So called by Wilson who shot the first specimen in a magnolia tree. **Mourning W.** so named by Wilson for whom the markings on the breast suggested the black clothes of grief for the dead. Bent and Forbush lament the name "for it seems as happy and active as most of the birds." Our only comment is, "Good grief." **Myrtle W.** from its fondness for the berries of the wax myrtle (*Myrica cerifers*). This has been dropped as a species but the name may be used for the subspecies. **Nashville W.** named by Alexander Wilson, who discovered it near Nashville, Tennessee. **Necklace W.** for the Canada W.; for the ring of black spots on the throat. **Olive W.** from its coloration. **Olive-backed W.** for its plumage. As the species was enlarged the name is changed to **Tropical Parula W. Orange-crowned W.** for the orange feathers in the crown. **Palm W.** as first describer probably found the bird in palm trees in Hispaniola. **Parula W.** from the scientific name meaning little titmouse. This is changed to **Northern Parula W. Pine W.** Both Wilson and Audubon called this bird the Pine Creeping Warbler, which has given way to pine. It comes from the bird's habitat. **Prairie W.** The name is misleading as the bird is not found on prairies but in cut-over areas and in fairly open woods. **Prothonotary W.** a reflection of the scientific name, *Protonotaria.* **Red-faced W.** from the color of its face. **Swainson's W.** for William Swainson (see Appendix). **Tennessee W.** named by Alexander Wilson who discovered it on the banks of the Cumberland River in the state. **Townsend's W.** for John K. Townsend (see Appendix). **Virginia's W.** for Mrs. W. Anderson (see Appendix under Anderson, Virginia). **Wilson's W.** for Alexander Wilson (see Appendix). **Worm-eating W.,** a translation of the scientific name. **Yellow W.** for its coloration. **Yellow-rumped W.,** a former local name for Myrtle W., but now to be used to include both it and the former Audubon's W. **Yellow-throated W.** for the yellow plumage of its throat.

WATER BELCHER   The American Bittern whose call has given him many colorful common names.

WATEROUZEL   See Ouzel.

WATERTHRUSH   Although not really a thrush, Forbush says it is well named as it is "disguised as a thrush" and is generally associated with water along the margins of streams and ponds. **Louisiana W.** The name implies it breeds to the south of the northern. While this is true, it breeds in the eastern United States except in the deep south. **Northern W.** from its northern breeding range.

WATERTURKEY   Another name for the Anhinga, as the bird looks somewhat like a small, thin turkey.

WAVY   Kortright tells us in *The Ducks, Geese and Swans of North America* that in the Canadian West it (the lesser snowgoose) goes by the name of "wavy," a corruption of the Indian word "wa wa."

WAXWING For the bright red coloring of the bare shafts of the tips of some of the secondary wing feathers which resembles the color of sealing wax. **Bohemian W.** Newton says it was "apparently first so-called by Stephens in 1817, having been before known as the 'Silk tail.' " The British, having only one species, called this bird the Waxwing. The reason for calling this species Bohemian is obscure. It cannot be a place name as Bohemia is outside both the breeding and winter range in Europe. **Cedar W.** for the bird's fondness for the berries of the evergreen commonly called cedar.

WHEATEAR MacLeod says, "Two derivations have been given for this name. According to Ray's translation of Willughby the name was given 'because (in) the time of wheat harvest they (the birds) wax very fat.' Others, however, say that 'wheat' is derived from 'white,' and ear from a vulgar name for 'rump,' and certainly the bird's white rump is a very distinctive feature, which is reflected in the alternative name of 'whitetail.' "

WHIMBREL Whim is said to sound like the bird's call; *-rel* is a diminutive suffix. Peter Matthiessen in *Shore Birds of North America* says, "In North England, curlews and whimbels were called 'Gabriel's Hounds'; the name whimbrel comes from 'whimpernel' which, in the *Durham Household Book* of 1530, refers to a habit attributed to it of sound, like whimperings."

WHIP-POOR-WILL Suggests the bird's call. **Ridgway's W.** for Robert Ridgway (see Appendix).

WHISKEY JACK, WHISKEYJAY A popular name for the Gray Jay altered from Whiskey John from the American Indian (Algonquin) Whiskatjan.

WIGEON From F. *vigeon,* "a whistling duck." Skeat

suggests that it possibly comes from L. *vipio,* "a small crane." This was Pliny's name for a small crane. As Pliny's birds were not accurately described, this apparent change of meaning for the bird from a small crane to a duck is not implausible. **American W.** the species that is common in North America but casual in Europe. The common names for this and the following species seem sensible and are in contrast to the naming of the two teals which have comparable distributions. **European W.** the species that is common in Europe but casual in North America.

WILLET Imitative of the bird's call.

WOODCOCK AS. *wudu-coc,* "woodcock." From its habitat. (For cock, see Chicken.) **American W.** as distinctive from the European as it is a different species from the **European W.,** which is much larger.

WOODPECKER E. *wood* from AS. *wudu,* "wood." As wood means either timber or a growth of trees, the name applied to the bird may refer either to its habit of pecking wood or to its habitat in woods. E. *peck* from either AS. *pican,* "to peck," or from L. *picus,* "a woodpecker"; both have a common Indogermanic source, *spi-g.* Suffix *-er,* "one who." Thus a woodpecker is one who pecks wood or pecks in the woods. **Acorn W.** from its favorite food, more apt than the scientific name. **American Three-toed W.** an old name for the Northern Three-toed W. **Ant W.** the Flicker, for its un-woodpeckerlike habit of procuring ants on the ground. **Arctic Three-toed W.** a local name for the Black-backed Three-toed W. **Arizona W.** from its range. **Black-backed Three-toed W.** rather full but apt. **Downy W.** for its shaggy and hairy appearance, the name is a translation of the scientific one. **Gila W.** Gila, a river in Arizona in the vicinity of which the bird is found. **Golden-fronted W.** AS. *gold,* "gold," L. *frons,* "forehead." For the yellow forehead, as in the scientific name. **Golden-winged W.** a local name for the Flicker. **Hairy W.** for its rather hairy and shaggy appearance. It reflects the meaning of its scientific name. **Ivory-billed W.** for its large ivory-colored bill. **Ladder-backed W.** for its transverse stripes on the back, although several are so marked. **Lewis' W.** for Meriwether Lewis (see Appendix). **Northern Three-toed W.** for its range. **Nuttall's W.** for Thomas Nuttall (see Appendix). **Pileated W.** from the scientific name meaning capped. **Red-bellied W.** alluding to a very slight pink on the belly. **Red-cockaded W.** cockade, "a knot of ribbon on a hat." From its resemblance to a cock's comb, because of red patches on the side of the head. **Red-headed W.** for its head plumage. **White-headed W.** for its outstanding white head.

WREN AS. *wraenna*, "wren." **Bewick's W.** for Thomas Bewick (see Appendix). **Brown-throated W.** for its buffy throat. **Cactus W.** for its nesting sites. **Canyon W.** for its habitat in deep gorges. **Carolina W.** a loose term for its range. **House W.** AS. *hus*, "house"; as it stays about dwellings. **Long-billed Marsh W.** for its bill and habitat. **Rock W.** as it is commonly found among the rocks. **Short-billed Marsh W.** comparing its bill with its codweller in the marshes. **Winter W.** for its winter range in mideastern and southern United States.

WRENTIT "A little bird like a wren." (See Titmouse).

YELLOWHAMMER Another name for the Flicker. For its yellow underwing and habit of drumming on dead limbs.

YELLOWLEGS From the color of the legs. **Greater Y.** the larger one. **Lesser Y.** the smaller one.

YELLOWTHROAT From its bright yellow throat. As we have a Yellow-throated Warbler it is well to omit the word warbler from this bird's name as has happily been sanctioned by popular usage.

The earth obey'd and straight
Op'ning her fertile womb teem'd at a birth
Innumerous living creatures, perfect forms,
Limb'd and full grown . . .
The grassy clods now calv'd; now half appear'd
The tawny lion, pawing to get free
His hinder parts, then springs as broken from bonds,
And rampant shakes his brindled mane;

John Milton, *Paradise Lost*, VII

I can entertain no doubt that the view that each
species has been independently created is erroneous. I
am fully convinced that species are not immutable; but
that those belonging to what are called the same genera
are lineal descendents of some other and generally
extinct species, in the same manner as the acknowl-
edged varieties of any one species are the descendents
of that species.

Charles Darwin, *The Origin of Species*, Introduction

Scientific Names

For out of olde feldes, as men seith,
Cometh al this newe corn from yeer to yere;
And out of olde bokes, in good feith,
Cometh al this newe science that men lere.
  Chaucer, *The Parlement of Foules*, The Proem

Construction of the Name

The scientific name of a bird has two parts: first, a
group or generic name, and second, a trivial or individual name. Somewhat the same scheme is used for the
identification of individual persons. John Jones is a
complete name made up of a personal name, John, and
a family name, Jones. The second word in the scientific
name is sometimes called the specific term. This may
cause confusion if it is understood that this word alone
names the bird scientifically. Both words in the scientific designation must be used to give a bird its correct
scientific name, i.e., its name as a species. A third term
may be added to the group and individual term to
denote subspecific status. This is a refinement added to
the original system of Linnaeus.

The generic term, the first one given, is a noun and is
capitalized. It means that any bird having this name in
common with another one has some characteristics
which both share. Thus *Passerina cyanea* (Indigo Bunting) and *Passerina amoena* (Lazuli Bunting) have

enough features in common to be placed in the same group, and the generic name shows this relationship.

The specific term, the second one given, is usually an adjective modifying the first term although it may be a noun in apposition or in the genitive form. This second term indicates that this kind of bird has distinctive characteristics which it does not share with any other kind.

At the time of Linnaeus' invention of binomial nomenclature, Latin was the language of the learned. We still preserve the remnants of this means of communication in the Latin inflections used in scientific terms and generally call them Latin. Many of the words have Greek or Latin origins. Some come from other languages, while some commemorate a person or a geographic location. It is the privilege of the original describer to give the bird its scientific name. While Alexander Wilson often used place names, John Audubon was inclined to honor his friends and associates.

The name of the original describer using the binomial system follows the name of the bird. If this name is in parenthesis it means that the original name has been changed. For example, the American Ornithologists' Union *Check-list* has *Troglodytes troglodytes* (Linnaeus). This means that the name has been changed from the name given by Linnaeus, *Motacella troglodytes*. As the practice of taxonomists is to make as few changes as possible, only the generic name was changed, letting the specific name stand, and means that the bird is no longer retained in the genus where the original describer placed it.

The fact that most birds have had their names changed is not in any way an implication that the original describers were at fault, but rather that so much has been learned since their time that revisions in nomenclature are a necessary means for the incorporation of new knowledge into the system. In "Recent Advances in Systematics," *Bio Science*, December 1968, Edward O. Wilson points out, ". . . according to insulin structure, we find that the pig is closer to whales than it is to the cow, horse and sheep." This gives a hint of the continuing new implications for revisions of nomenclature that are coming from contemporary research. One of the chief virtues of the binomial system is that it is a resilient tool adaptable to the continuous growth of knowledge. It is pleasant to contemplate that this scientific system invented by Linnaeus a century before Darwin has so readily lent itself to the progress of science.

Origin and Development

The binomial system of nomenclature was first used for plants by Linnaeus in *Species Planatarium* in 1753. Five years later, in the tenth edition of his *Systema Naturae*, birds were first so classified. Before Linnaeus the scientific community identified plants and animals by means of descriptive phrases and clauses in Latin. While binomial terms were used occasionally, they were not developed into a comprehensive system which showed the relationship of one species to another. Linnaeus' system did this, and also replaced an unwieldy superfluity of words with a concise two-word term.

The acceptance of a single worldwide term for each species makes it possible for scientists, regardless of the language they use, to know the identity of any bird with which they are concerned. This is not to say, however, that there is complete and universal agreement. There are still some minor areas of confusion. For example, the latest *Check-list of the Birds of Great Britain and Ireland* prepared by the List Subcommittee of the British Ornithologists' Union in 1952 has as the second bird on its list:

Colymbus immer Brunnich   Great Northern Diver
                                   Common Loon

The latest *Check-list of North American Birds* prepared by a committee of the American Ornithologists' Union in 1957 has as the first bird on its list:

Gavia immer (Brunnich): Common Loon.

This means that, as indicated by the parenthesis, the name given by Brunnich has been changed by the committee on this side of the Atlantic but not on the other. Going back a little further into the question we find that this is not altogether the case. The British explain in a footnote how they handled the problem. It seems that the original designation of the genus made by Linnaeus in 1758 was *Columbus*. Although this spelling had page priority it would "make the spelling of the family name identical with that of the Pigeons (Columbidae)." So the British decided on the family name of Colymbidae for the Loons and Columbidae for the pigeons. The American group seems to have thought that there would be still less possibility of confusion if the whole word was changed rather than one letter. Neither publication notes that its choice of words results in a difference in the scientific name for this or any other species.

Linnaeus' great contribution to biological nomenclature in classifying plants and animals as well as naming them became in a comparatively short time almost universally accepted. The value of his system lay not only in its contribution to systematizing the knowledge of his day, but also in its providing both for a revision of that knowledge and for the inclusion of new knowledge in the future. The development of a universally accepted set of rules as a guide for scientists of diverse nationalities for solving difficulties of nomenclature has been one of the major concerns of various international scientific congresses. A botanical congress concerned with botanical nomenclature met in Paris in 1867. In 1889, also in Paris, the International Zoological Congress first met. As a result of the deliberations of these bodies, a set of regulations was formulated in the hope that its acceptance would further the continuation of a common understanding and interpretation of systematics, which the binomial system had made possible in the first place. One can readily imagine how confusing the results would be without the formulation of precise and comprehensive rules. In practice, too much would depend on the personal and individual interpretation of every authority naming a new organism or changing the species status of an old one.

The Law of Priority

One of the most important contributions to the regulation of nomenclature was the formulation of the law of priority. Its basic provision is that each distinct living thing retain inviolate its original and unique binomial name as long as it is scientifically valid. If new data and interpretation should require the change of a species from one genus to another, the generic name would be changed but the specific name would remain. Cf., *Colymbus immer* became *Gavia immer*.

The name given to a new species by its original describer stands if the publication in which it first appeared is considered adequate. And it stands in its initial form despite mistakes in the name of the color, place of geographic origin, misspelling, grammar or other error. It is practically inviolate. It must be remembered that the words given to name a species assume a new and special function and become technical terms. That some of them are etymologically incorrect has no bearing on their usefulness as technical scientific labels.

Categories

Taxonomy, according to Ernst Mayr, is "the theory and practice of classifying organisms. It may be thought of as the name for the rules of the game of classification. Linnaeus invented the first good set of rules. These rules worked well for putting the pieces (the species) into appropriate pigeonholes in accordance with the knowledge and concepts of the mid-eighteenth century. Linnaeus used only four categories: class, order, genus and species. He thought every species was created in a distinct form which clearly differentiated it from all others and that this form had been retained from the moment of creation and would continue unchanged into eternity. In justice to him we must say that in his later writings, as his increasing collection made evident variations in species, he had become aware that his original system was not comprehensive enough to include all the new data that were accumulating.

The system invented by Linnaeus rapidly gained wide acceptance. Organisms already known had their names changed into binomial ones, and those newly discovered were henceforth named in conformity with the Linnaean scheme. The ever-increasing number of species made the relationships among them progressively obscure. Larger and more comprehensive collections made it evident that there was much variation among specimens often of so minute a nature that it became increasingly difficult to justify species status for many specimens. In addition to the problem of insufficient and appropriate categories of the original system, there was difficulty because it viewed living things as unchanging over eons of time. This static species concept became increasingly inadequate and a handicap to correct classification.

A century after Linnaeus, Darwin, who tells us quite vividly how he pondered upon the variety among the finches of Galapagos, and Wallace, noting the variations among the mammals, birds and insects of the Malay Archipelago, realized at about the same time in the middle of the last century the inadequacy and falseness of the static concept as a basis for understanding living things. Mayr, in his *Systematics and the Origin of Species*, points out " 'good species' were found to be connected by intermediates or in which one species had slightly different attributes in different parts of its range. This showed clearly that a static species concept was no longer tenable and that it had to be replaced by a dynamic one. This change was hastened by the confusion caused by the species splitters." It is interesting to note that until the ruling of the United States Supreme Court in 1969, it was illegal in some sections of the United States for biology teachers to explain the relationships of living things by means of the dynamic (evolutionary) concept.

Subspecies—A Lower Category

Mayr points out that even before the publication of *The Origin of Species* by Darwin in 1859, Schlegel "was apparently the first author (from 1844 on) to use trinomials consistently (even though hesitatingly) for geographic subdivisions of species." This custom gradually became more widely accepted during the latter half of the nineteenth century and is now the common practice. A subspecies is considered to be a group of individuals with characteristics sufficiently distinctive to differentiate it from other groups (especially on a geographic basis) while at the same time having so much in common as to place it in the same species. The validity of a subspecies is the decision of the taxonomist and depends on the number of individuals with distinctive and like characteristics in a geographic area. This decision is difficult as a subspecies in nature is not always a clear-cut unit, and the dividing line between races frequently has to be arbitrary.

The Song Sparrow, *Melospiza melodia,* in the American Ornithologists' Union *Check-list* is subdivided into thirty-one subspecies or races. These subspecies are not given a common name in the *Check-list* as it would only be of limited local value. They are all given a trinomial scientific name, the first two parts of which they have in common. The first word of the trinomial shows that all are in the same genus and the second that all are in the same species.

Although we are not including either the common or scientific subspecific names in this study, we are making one exception because it has such a good story behind it. It is *Troglodytes aedon parkmanii,* originally named as a species *Troglodytes parkmanii* by Audubon, before subspecies were used in classification in 1835, for his friend and probable benefactor Dr. George Parkman, a prominent and wealthy member of one of Boston's most eminent families. His nephew was Francis Parkman, the historian. The generous doctor gave to Harvard University not only the ground on which to build its medical school, but also a chair of anatomy which the university named for him in appreciation. This chair was filled by Dr. Oliver Wendell Holmes whose lecture room was above the office of Dr. John White Webster, professor of chemistry and mineralogy. This gentleman, who had been helped financially by Dr. Parkman, found the erstwhile helpfulness of his benefactor turn to a nagging and annoying insistence for repayment after his dishonest manipulations came to light. He secretly sold a cabinet of minerals which were part of the security for his loan from Dr. Parkman. Dr. Parkman was last seen entering the building in which was the office of his debtor. Some of his anatomical remains were found in a bricked-in vault below this office. Rufus Choate, whose advice to plead guilty in the hope of avoiding a first-degree conviction was ignored, refused to handle the case. After what was left of Parkman's false teeth were shown to fit the mold of his dentist, a first-degree conviction was a foregone conclusion. A belated confession failed to save Webster from the gallows. The Webster-Parkman tragedy which was long considered America's most celebrated murder case is fading while the name of an obscure little bird still carries with undiminished permanence the name of Parkman whom it was meant to honor. So much for *Troglodytes aedon parkmannii.*

The Higher Categories

As the development of scientific ornithology necessitated the reorganization of the taxonomy of some species into subspecies, it also necessitated the reorganization of categories above the species level. The genera of Linnaeus were much more inclusive than those of today. In fact, his genera, which often included species that were based on rather minute morphological differences, became so numerous that their value for classification in showing relationships became questionable. To have value a genus should bring together both those species that are most alike in form and structure (morphologically) and also those that presumably have a common ancestry (phylogenetically).

One means of clarifying the taxonomic muddle was the addition of a new category above that of the genus, the family. This new pigeonhole was quite akin in its inclusiveness to the original one of the genus as it was first used by Linnaeus. It is now in universal use. All genera in the same family have characteristics in common of a grosser kind than those in the genera to which they belong. Moving in the same direction, all members of the same family have characteristics of a finer distinction than that of the next higher category which is the order. Taxonomists have further refined classification by establishing sub- and super-stages for various categories. In the following table we can see how the Greater Scaup fits into the general taxonomic scheme of things.

Organization of Categories

Beginning with the highest category we shall move down to the smallest unit to which *Aythya marila,* the Greater Scaup, belongs.

Category	Division in Category
KINGDOM	ANIMAL The Greater Scaup is one of over a million species of animals and not a vegetable or a mineral.
PHYLUM	CHORDATA The bird belongs in this phylum of a little over one hundred thousand species that have spinal chords.
SUBPHYLUM	VERTEBRATA Birds are subdivided into this classification of animals that have a backbone protecting the spinal chord. There are seven vertebrate classes.
CLASS	AVES Here we find the nine thousand species of heavier-than-air machines which fly through the air, with the exception of a few such as the Ostrich and the Kiwi. Adaptation to flight has evolved in them special

characteristics such as feathers, wings, and light-weight bones.

ORDER   **ANSERIFORMES** The ordinal names of birds end in *iformes*. Alexander Wetmore in his *Revised Classification of Birds* lists twenty-seven orders of living birds and seven extinct orders.

SUBORDER   **ANSERS** This contains the ducks, geese, and swans, eliminating the screamers.

FAMILY   **ANATIDAE** Family names end in *idae*. Although it is the only family in its suborder, it is divided into several subfamilies; one each for the swans, geese, tree ducks, surface feeding, ducks, diving ducks, ruddy and masked ducks, and mergansers. Just why there could not be several families instead of subfamilies illustrates the difficulties faced by taxonomists in deciding where to place birds. In this case it seems that they felt that the differences among the groups were too small to justify family status, but still sufficient to place them in a lower category as a subfamily.

SUBFAMILY   **AYTHYINAE** The diving ducks are placed here.

GENUS   **AYTHYA** Boie This is the first category followed by the name of a person. It signifies that he was the one whose definition of the genus was accepted as valid. The American Ornithologists' Union *Check-list* numbers eight species in this genus, which is quite a drop from the one million in the first category.

SPECIES   **AYTHYA MARILA** (Linnaeus) This is the Greater Scaup. It is generally written *Aythya marila,* the first word being a noun and the second an adjective. The parentheses around the name of Linnaeus indicates that he was the first to describe the bird in the bino-mial system but the name he origi-nally gave it has been changed, in this case because it has been shifted to another genus.

SUBSPECIES   **AYTHYA MARILA NEARCTICA** Stejneger As there is a difference between the American and the European Greater Scaup which is too minor to justify placing each in a separate species but still worthy of note, a third word is added signifying that it is a sub-species. Stejneger's name without pa-rentheses indicates that his original description of the subspecies still stands for the American race.

Authority for Nomenclature

The American Ornithologists' Union is the recog-nized authority responsible for the nomenclature of American birds. The work is delegated to a committee of experts who not only check on the material to be published but submit the sections to collaborators throughout the United States and Canada who have specialized knowledge about a family or an area for their correction or comment. "The consideration of newly described forms, records of forms new to the *Check-list* area, revision of names and status, and the deletion of species included in the fourth edition on the basis of inadequate data or false identification have required much study." This quotation is from the preface to the fifth edition of the *Check-list of North American Birds* published in 1957. Previous editions were published in 1886, 1895, 1910, and 1931. Changes in status or other revisions of the *Check-list* are published in *The Auk*, the journal of the American Ornithologists' Union from time to time between *Check-lists* and serve to keep nomenclature up to date. The latest *Check-list* covers 1686 species and subspecies found in North America north of Mexico, with inclusion of Greenland, Bermuda and Baja California. The birds are listed in systematic order according to their categories and subcategories.

The British Ornithologists' Union performs a comparable service for the nomenclature of the birds of Great Britain and Ireland. The fourth and most recent edition of their *Check-list of the Birds of Great Britain and Ireland* appeared in 1952. It is uncluttered by the designation of super- and sub-classifications of categories. It contains, as the American list does not, a "Short Explanation of Scientific Terms Used in This Checklist." This is a very helpful way of informing users of the *Check-list* of the terms used in the taxonomic game. Another helpful inclusion is the American name for a bird when that name differs from the British one.

When the name of the original describer of a species or subspecies is not enclosed in parentheses it means that the name given by him has remained unaltered. When the name of the person is enclosed in parentheses it means that the name of the bird is not the same as the original. The change that is most commonly made is in part of the name due to reclassification of the bird into another genus. For example, Borlausen first described the genus *Acanthis* and as the name of this genus is still valid there is no parenthesis around his name. Linnaeus

originally named the Redpoll *Fringilla flammea,* but
with the refinement of nomenclature this was changed
to *Acanthis flammea.* Thus the parentheses around
Linnaeus' name signifies that the name he originally
gave the bird has been altered.

List of Scientific Names

ACANTHIS Borlausen Gr. *acanthis,* "a bird fond of
thistles, the linnet." **A. flammea** (Linnaeus): COM-
MON REDPOLL—REDPOLL; L. *flammea,*
"flame-colored," for its plumage. **A. hornemanni**
(Holboell): HOARY REDPOLL—ARCTIC RED-
POLL; for J. W. Hornemann (see Appendix).

ACCIPITER Brisson L. *accipiter,* "hawk," from L. *ad,*
"after"; L. *capito,* "take." **A. cooperii** (Bonaparte):
COOPER'S HAWK for William Cooper (see Ap-
pendix). **A. gentilis** (Linnaeus): GOSHAWK; LL.
gentilis, "noble." L. *gentilis* meant belonging to the
same clan, from L. *gens* "tribe or clan." From this
the descendants of the word have come to mean
those qualities which at one time were considered the
special attributes of the well born. They were qualities to be admired and by medieval times could be
readily applied to a bird which was courageous,
domesticated and much admired; the Goshawk. The
L. *gens* from which we inherit, gentle, gentile, genus
was derived from an Indo-European root which was
also the progenitor of E. *king* and E. *kin.* The word
gentilis was a term used by falconers who divided
their birds into two classes. The members of the first
class were the long- and pointed-winged falcons.
They were called "noble" for their spectacular
plunging after prey. In the second class were the
rounder- and shorter-winged hawks. As their catching of prey was less entertaining they were called
"ignoble." An exception was made for the Goshawk

which in spite of its physical affinity to the round-winged hawks was a thrilling hunter and by courtesy was admitted into the "noble" class of falcons. Albertus Magnus described it as "the most noble kind of all falcons." The word *gentilis* was often applied only to the female. In naming the bird *Falco gentilis* Linnaeus implies that it was one of the "noble" hawks traditionally reserved for the pleasure of the nobility in the sport of falconry. This does not seem to be the case. Grossman and Hamlet say, "by the Twelfth Century even the citizens of London— the merchant, the baker and the candlestick maker kept sparrowhawks (accipiters) and goshawks, 'the short-winged hawks.' Gyrfalcons and Peregrines, 'the long-winged hawks,' were . . . reserved . . . for . . . the nobility." The Eurasion Sparrowhawk and the Goshawk, "the birds of the yeoman and the priest. And last of all, at the bottom of the social ladder, reserved for knaves, servants and children, was the pliable, brave little Old World Kestrel." Linnaeus' *Falco gentilis* was, according to Swann, an immature Goshawk based on a description Albin published in 1738. Linnaeus also had a *Falco alumbarius,* which was most likely the description of a bird in mature plumage. Brisson in 1760 removed the accipiters from the falcons, thus giving them a new generic name. As his name is not in parentheses we see that his generic designation is still valid while Linnaeus' name, in parentheses, indicates a change was made, substituting *Accipiter* for *Falco.* **A. striatus** (Vieillot): SHARP-SHINNED HAWK; L. *striatus,* "striped," for the streaks on the underside.

ACTITIS Illiger   Gr. *aktites,* "a dweller on the sea coast." **A. macularia** (Linnaeus): SPOTTED SANDPIPER; L. *macula,* "spot," for the spots on the underparts in the breeding season.

ADAMASTER Bonaparte   The name of a mysterious and

hideous phantom said to have appeared to Vasco da Gama on his voyage to the East Indies. **A. cinereus** (Gmelin): BLACK-TAILED SHEARWATER; L. *cinereus,* "ash-colored."

AECHMOPHORUS ML. term coined by Coues. Gr. *aichme,* "spear"; Gr. *phoreus,* "bearer"; for the spear-like bill. **A. occidentalis** (Lawrence): WESTERN GREBE; L. *occidentalis,* "western," for its range in western North America.

AEGOLIUS Kaup Gr. *aigolios,* "a kind of owl," mentioned by Aristotle. Remotely from the resemblance of its notes to the bleating of a goat. Gr. *aigos,* "a goat." **A. acadicus** (Gmelin): SAW-WHET OWL; L. *acadicus,* "of Acadia," for Nova Scotia where first specimen was found. **A. funereus** (Linnaeus): BOREAL OWL; L. *funereus,* "mournful," as its call has been likened to the "slow tolling of a soft but high-pitched bell."; cf. E. *funereal.*

AERONAUTES Hartert Gr. *aer,* "air"; Gr. *nautes,* "a sailor." **A. saxatalis** (Woodhouse): WHITE-THROATED SWIFT; L. *saxatilis,* "rock-dweller," from its habitat.

AETHIA Merrem Gr. *aithya,* "a sea bird." **A. cristatella** (Pallas): CRESTED AUKLET; L. *cristatellus,* diminutive of *cristatus,* "crested." **A. pusilla** (Pallas): LEAST AUKLET; L. *pusillus,* "very small," apt term as it is the least in size being 5¼ inches in length. **A. pygmaea** (Gmelin): WHISKERED AUKLET; L. *pygmaea,* "dwarfish," from Gr. *pygmaioi,* "mythical dwarfs whose height was the length of a *pygme,*" i.e., from the elbow to the knuckles of the closed fist (13 to 14 inches). Gr. *pygme* also meant fist as did L. *pugnus,* the base of E. *pugnacious* and *pugilist.* Close to the length of the *pygme* was the L. *cubitus,* "cubit," the length from the elbow to the end of the middle finger (18 to 22 inches). Happily for the translators of the King James version of the Bible, the length of the cubit and the length of the Hebrew *ammah* is the same. They were thus saved arithmetical calculation when they could write, "Goliath of Gath whose height was six cubits and a span."

The Pygmies, according to Homer, were forced in bloody battles to defend their fields of grain in their homeland near the sources of the Nile every winter when the migrating cranes threatened to devastate their fields.

AGELAIUS Vieillot   Gr. *agelaios,* "flocking." **A. phoeniceus** (Linnaeus): RED-WINGED BLACKBIRD; Gr. *phoinikeos,* L. *phoeniceus,* "red," the color introduced into Greece by the Phoenicians. This is the Tyrian (Tyre, the Phoenician city) dye used in robes of state. It was violet-purple and was obtained from shellfish. **A. tricolor** (Audubon): TRI-COLORED BLACKBIRD; L. *tricolor,* "three-colored," red, white, and black in the plumage.

AIMOPHILA Swainson   Gr. *aima, "blood"*; Gr. *phila,* "fond of." Swanson is credited with naming this genus in 1837, its lone species being *A. aestivalis.* The four other species of the same genus were first described later. It would appear that Swanson made a separate genus for one species and then gave the genus a singularly inappropriate name. "What's so blood-loving about a sparrow?" **A. aestivalis** (Lichtenstein): BACHMAN'S SPARROW; L. *aestivalis,* "summery," L. *aestas,* "summer." **A. botterii** (Sclater): BOTTERI'S SPARROW for M. Botteri (see Appendix). **A. carpalis** (Coues): RUFOUS-WINGED SPARROW; L. *carpalis,* "having to do with the wrist," L. *carpus,* "wrist." As the wing is rufous, this might be stretched to mean the bend of the wing suggested a wrist. **A. cassinii** (Woodhouse): CASSIN'S SPARROW for John Cassin (see Appen-

dix). **A. ruficeps** (Cassin): RUFOUS-CROWNED
SPARROW; L. *ruficeps*, "red-headed," for the red
crown.

AIS Boie Gr. *aix*, "a kind of waterfowl." **A. sponsa**
(Linnaeus): WOODDUCK; L. *sponsa*, "betrothed,"
i.e., dressed for a wedding, from the bird's attractive
appearance.

AJAJA Reichenbach Ajaja is a South American native
name for the spoonbill. **A. ajaja** (Linnaeus): ROSE-
ATE SPOONBILL.

ALAUDA Linnaeus L. *alauda*, "lark," possibly from
Celtic *al*, "high"; *aud*, "song." **A. arvensis** Linnaeus:
SKYLARK; L. *arvensis*, "of the cultivated field,"
alluding to its habitat.

ALCA Linnaeus S. and Ic. *alka*, "auk." **A. torda** Linnaeus: RAZORBILL; *torda*, name of the bird in the
Gottland province of Sweden.

ALECTORIS Kaup Gr. *alektor*, "a cock." **A. chukar**
(Meisner): CHUKAR, a range name for one of its
geographical races.

ALLE Link S. *alle*, "the dovekie." **A. alle** (Linnaeus):
DOVEKIE–LITTLE AUK.

AMAZILLA Lesson *Amazilia*, a barbarism, which is a
lexicographer's term for a word of no known derivation or meaning. **A. verticalis** (Deppe): VIOLET-
CROWNED HUMMINGBIRD; L. *verticalis*, "pertaining to the top of the head," as the bird has a
conspicuous crown. **A. yucatanenis** (Cabot): BUFF-
BELLIED HUMMINGBIRD; ML. *yucatanensis*,
"of Yucatan," locality of original specimen.

AMMODRAMUS Swainson Gr. *ammos*, "sand"; Gr.
dramein, "to run," not particularly apt. **A. bairdii**
(Audubon): BAIRD'S SPARROW for Spencer F.
Baird (see Appendix). **A. henslowii** (Audubon):
HENSLOW'S SPARROW for John S. Henslow (see
Appendix). **A. savannarum** (Gmelin): GRASSHOP-

PER SPARROW; L. *savannarum,* "of the meadows," as the bird frequents a grassy habitat.

AMMOSPIZA Oberholser   Gr. *amme,* "sand"; Gr. *spiza,* "a finch." **A. caudacuta** (Gmelin): SHARP-TAILED SPARROW; L. *cauda,* "tail"; L. *acuta,* "sharp," descriptive of the tail. **A. leconteii** (Audubon): LE CONTE'S SPARROW for Dr. John Le Conte (see Appendix). **A. maritima** (Wilson): SEASIDE SPARROW; L. *maritima,* "seaside," for the bird's habitat. **A. mirabillis** (Howell): CAPE SABLE SPARROW; L. *mirabilis,* "marvelous." Here the poet got ahead of the scientist as the bird is a very pretty little sand finch. Now a subspecies of A. maritima. **A. nigrescens** (Ridgway): DUSKY SEASIDE SPARROW; L. *nigrescens,* "dusky," for the dark plumage. Also now a subspecies of **A. maritima.**

AMPHISPIZA Coues   Gr. *amphi,* "on both sides"; Gr. *spiza,* "a finch"; "alluding to the close relation of the genus to those about it" according to Coues. **A. belli** (Cassin): SAGE SPARROW; for John G. Bell (see   Appendix). **A. bilineata** (Cassin): BLACK–THROATED SPARROW; L. *bilineata,* "two-lined," alluding to the stripes on the head.

ANAS Linnaeus   L. *anas,* "a duck." **A. acuta** Linnaeus: PINTAIL; L. *acutus,* "sharp," in reference to the tail. **A. americana** (Gmelin): AMERICAN WIGEON; ML. *americana,* "American," for its range. **A. crecca carolinensis** Gmelin: AMERICAN GREEN-WINGED TEAL; ML. *carolinensis,* "of Carolina." This is now considered a subspecies of **A. crecca** (see below). It was originally described as being from Carolina to Hudson's Bay. This was shortened to the first geographical area. **A. clypeata** (Linnaeus): SHOVELER; L. *clypeata,* "furnished with a shield." Possibly for the reddish patches on the sides of the male. **A. crecca** Linnaeus: GREEN-WINGED

TEAL. The Gr. *krex* means a long-legged bird, which does not fit. Macleod suggests it is a coined word that "probably represents the bird's incessant calling; cf. the onomatopoeic Gr. *kreko*, 'cause a string to sound by striking it.'" **A. cyanoptera** Vieillot: CINNAMON TEAL; Gr. *chyaneous*, "dark blue"; Gr. *pteron*, "wing"; referring to the blue patch on the wing which is easily observed in flight. **A. diazi** Ridgway: MEXICAN DUCK; for Augustin Diaz (see Appendix). **A. discors** (Linnaeus): BLUE-WINGED TEAL; L. *discors*, "discordant," according to most authorities in reference to the bird's harsh call. The difficulty with this is that the call of the bird is not harsh. Bent, in *Life Histories of American Wildfowl*, pt. II, p. 118, says "About the vocal powers of this teal there is very little to be said. Dawson (1903) has covered the ground very well in the following words, 'In addition to the whistling of the wings, the teals have a soft whistling note, only remotely related to the typical anatidine quack, and it is uttered either in apprehension or encouragement.'" While the male peeps, the female has a soft quack. Contrary to Macleod, Jorday and Eaton suggest that the derivation may be *disc* from Gr. *discos*, "a disc," and L. *os, oris*, "pertaining to the mouth." Thus *discors* may mean "disc about the mouth" and refers to the well-known field mark of the bird, the oral disc. **A. formosa** Georgi: BAIKAL TEAL; ML. *formosa*, Latinized form referring to the island of Formosa, one of the places in its winter range. **A. fulvigula** Ridgway: MOTTLED DUCK; L. *fulvus*, "reddish-yellow"; L. *gula*, "the throat." **A. penelope** (Linnaeus): EUROPEAN WIGEON–WIGEON. Coues, Eaton and others suggest that *penelope* is a mistake for *penelops*, a kind of goose mentioned by Aristotle and Pliny. But Linnaeus may not have erred too much in using the name of a goose for a wigeon. Conrad Gessner (1516–1565), the German-Swiss naturalist, cites an old legend that Penelope was thrown into the sea by her parents (no reason given) and rescued by sea birds (species not cited) whose name she was given. At any rate Penelope survived to win renown as the virtuous and patient model of Greek propriety who waited twenty years for her husband, Ulysses, to return from the Trojan War, and who used weaving as a device to forestall her suitors. As Gr. *penelope* means "weaver," we may surmise that our bird was named for a skill, a woman, or a sea bird that just possibly may have been a wigeon. **A. platyrhynchos** Linnaeus: MALLARD; Gr. *platus,* "broad"; Gr. *rhynchos,* "bill." **A. rubripes** Brewster: BLACK DUCK; L. *ruber,* "red"; L. *pes,* "foot." **A. strepera** Linnaeus: GADWALL; L. *streperus,* "noisy."

ANHINGA Brisson   A South American native (Tupi) name for the Water Turkey. **A. anhinga** (Linnaeus): ANHINGA.

ANOUS Stephens   Gr. *anous,* "stupid," referring to the bird's failure to take alarm. **A. stolidus** (Linnaeus): NODDY TERN; L. *stolidus,* "stupid," so the stupid, stupid bird also gets it over again in (see) Noddy. **A. tenuirostris** (Temminck): BLACK NODDY TERN; L. *tenuis,* "thin"; L. *nostrum,* "bill."

ANSER Brisson   L. *anser,* "goose." **A. albifrons** (Scopoli): WHITE-FRONTED GOOSE; L. *albus,* "white"; L. *frons,* "forehead," for the white forehead of the adult.

ANTHUS Bechstein   Gr. *anthos,* "a kind of bird." It received its name from a youth who changed into a bird after being killed by his father's horses. **A. spinoletta** (Linnaeus): WATER PIPIT; ML. *spinoletta,* a mistake for I. *spipoletta,* "water pipit." **A. spragueii** (Audubon): SPRAGUE'S PIPIT for Isaac Sprague (see Appendix).

APHELOCOMA Cabinis Gr. *aphelos,* "smooth"; Gr. *koms,* "hair"; as there is no crest. **A. coerulescens** (Bosc): SCRUB JAY; L. *caeruleus,* "dark blue," for the plumage. **A. ultramarina** (Bonaparte): MEXICAN JAY; L. *ultra,* "beyond"; L. *marina,* "marine"; deeper blue in color than the sea.

APHRIZA Audubon Gr. *aphros,* "sea foam"; Gr. *zoa,* "to live." **A. virgata** (Gmelin): SURFBIRD; L. *virgatus,* "striped."

AQUILA Brisson L. *aquila,* "eagle," perhaps related to L. *aquilus,* "dark brown," hence a dun-colored bird; *aquilus* is from *aqua,* "water." E. *aquiline,* "like an eagle," used in describing a human nose hooked like an eagle's beak. **A. chrysaetos** (Linnaeus): GOLDEN EAGLE; Gr. *aetos,* "eagle"; Gr. *chrysos,* "golden." The bird was called *chrysaetos* by Aelian, a Roman who wrote in Greek in the third century A.D.

ARAMUS Vieillot Unknown origin. **A. guarauna** (Linnaeus): LIMPKIN; Guarauna is the name of a tribe inhabiting the delta of the Orinoco in Venezuela, hence, a locality name for the bird that does likewise.

ARCHILOCHUS Reishenback Gr. *arch,* a prefix meaning "chief"; Gr. *lochos,* "a body of people," here meaning "first among the birds." Naming the hummingbirds has caused the systematists difficulty. Unique to the New World, their first describers had no background for their scientific classification. Hindsight shows us that the problem was further compounded by the fact that most hummingbirds have their range in the western part of the country. As new species were discovered one by one the relationship of each to the as yet unknown ones was impossible to determine. The consequence of this was that the original names had to be changed when fuller knowledge of the hummingbird made a more valid classification possible. Alexander Wilson knew only the Rubythroat and Audubon included only four in his *Birds of America*. Baird in 1858 named seven. Coues could name only ten in 1872, although he was able to list eighteen in 1890. The A.O.U. *Check-list* of 1957 names eighteen, all but one having its original name revised. Since then two more species of hummingbirds have been recorded in the United States. **A. alexandri** (Bourcier and Mulsant): BLACK-CHINNED HUMMINGBIRD for Dr. Alexandre (see Appendix). **A. colubris** (Linnaeus): RUBY-THROATED HUMMINGBIRD; L. *colubris,* "a serpent," so inappropriate that a misspelling by Linnaeus is more likely. The word is from F. *colibre,* "hummingbird."

ARDEA Linnaeus   L. *ardea,* "heron." **A. herodias** (Linnaeus): GREAT BLUE HERON; Gr. *herodios,* "a heron." **A. herodias occidentalis** (Audubon): GREAT WHITE HERON; L. *occidentalis,* "western." This makes it conspecific with the Great Blue Heron.

ARENARIA Brisson   L. *arenaria,* "having to do with sand," from L. *arena,* "sand." **A. interpres** (Linnaeus): RUDDY TURNSTONE–TURNSTONE; L. *interpres,* "interpreter, go-between" or, in this case, "tell-tale," for its notes of alarm that warn other birds. Coues says that the name was given in error by Linnaeus who misunderstood the native name "tolk" used for the Redshank on the island of Gottland in the early 1700s. The "tolk" does alarm other birds more than the Turnstone. **A. melanocephala** (Vigors): BLACK TURNSTONE; Gr. *melas,* "black"; Gr. *cephalos,* "head"; for its dark head.

ARREMONOPS Ridgway   Gr. *arremon,* "silent," a name of a South American genus, and Gr. *opsis,* "appearance," for the resemblance to the southern genus. **A. rufivirgata** (Lawrence): OLIVE SPARROW; L. *rufus,* "reddish"; L. *virgata,* "striped"; for the inconspicuous reddish stripes on the head. It is more easily identified in the field by its notes which sound like a ping-pong ball bouncing on a hard surface.

ASIO Brisson   L. *asio,* "a kind of horned owl." **A. flammeus** (Pontoppidan): SHORT-EARED OWL; L. *flammeus,* "flame-colored," for its tawny plumage. **A. otus** (Linnaeus): LONG-EARED OWL; Gr. *otos,* "an eared owl."

ASYNDESMUS Coues   Gr. *a,* "without"; Gr. *syn,* "together": Gr. *desmos,* "a band." Coues, who made this name, says it alludes "to loosened texture of feathers in certain parts." **A. lewis** (Gray): LEWIS' WOODPECKER for Meriwether Lewis (see Appendix).

AURIPARUS Baird   L. *aurum,* "gold," for the yellow head. L. *parus,* "a titmouse." **A. flaviceps** (Sundevall): VERDIN; L. *flaviceps,* "yellow head."

AYTHYA Boie   This one really aroused Coues' dander. He said, "I am willing to follow the A.O.U. in adopting the genus, but not in violating plain rules for the transliteration from the Greek to the Latin, which give us neither AYTHYA BOIE, nor *Aithya* KAUP, nor *Aithyia* Bp., nor anything but Æthyia." Gr. *aythya,* "a kind of waterbird," in Homer's *Odyssey* and Aristotle's *Natural History.* **A. affinis** (Eyton): LESSER SCAUP; L. *affinis,* "related," i.e., to the species above. **A. americana** (Eyton): RED-HEAD; L. *americana,* "American." **A. collaris** (Donovan): RING-NECKED DUCK; L. *collaris,* "collared," referring to the ringed neck. **A. marila** (Linnaeus): GREATER SCAUP; probably Gr. *marile,* "charcoal." **A. valisineria** (Wilson): CANVAS-BACK; *valisineria* should be spelled *vallisneria* as it is spelled by Coues and Eaton. It refers to one of the main foods of the bird, *Vallisneria americana,* the wild or water celery. The plant was named in honor of an eminent Italian physician and naturalist,

Antonio Vallisneri or Vallisnieri (1661–1730). While it is debatable as to whether the botanists or the ornithologists are the worse spellers, the ornithologists go way ahead on this one. Wilson in discussing the bird's food says, "The plant is said to be a species of valisineria." He thus admits his inability to be more definite.

BARTRAMIA Lesson   In honor of William Bartram (see Appendix). **B. longicauda** (Bechstein): UPLAND SANDPIPER; L. *longus,* "long"; L. *caudus,* "tail."

BOMBYCILLA Vieillot   A coined word from L. or Gr. *bombyx,* "silk"; ML. *cilla,* which through error was taken to mean "tail." *Cilla* is the last part of L. *motacilla,* "wagtail." This word according to Macleod is most likely derived from L. *motax, motacis,* "mover," and L. *illa,* the feminine diminutive suffix. Thus the word means "little mover." Varro, the Roman scholar, explained the word which he used, "The bird owes its name to the fact that it is always moving its tail (*caudam*); and this clearly gave rise to the idea that *mota,* the first part of the word, meant 'moving'; *cilla,* the second part of the name, meant 'tail.' " It is obvious, however, that if there had been such a word as *cilla,* Varro would have said in his explanation of *motacilla* that the bird moves its *cilla* and not its *cauda.* **B. cedrorum** (Vieillot): CEDAR WAXWING; L. *cedrorum,* "of the cedars," from the bird's partiality to this tree. **B. garrulus** (Linnaeus): BOHEMIAN WAXWING–WAXWING; L. *garrula,* "chattering," as its crest makes it resemble the European Jay known as *garrulous,* which is quite noisy. Cf. E. *garrulous.*

BONASA Stephens   L. *bonasum,* Gr. *bonasos,* "the aurochs, a wild ox," the drumming of the bird being likened to the bellowing of a bull. It is suggested that consideration be given to L. *bonus,* "good," plus L.

assum, "a roast." **B. umbellus** (Linnaeus): RUFFED
GROUSE; L. *umbellus,* "a sunshade," alluding to
the neck tufts.

BOTAURUS Stephens ML. *botaurus,* "a bittern," from
either ME. *boter* or F. *butor* probably derived from
L. *butio,* "a bittern." Both the French and English
names may be imitative of the bird's call. MacLeod
says, "Possibly *Botaurus* was also intended to suggest
a derivation from two old L. words *bos,* 'ox,' and
taurus, 'bull'; in allusion to the bittern's old L. name
taurus, which according to Pliny (X, 57) had its
origin in the bird's imitating a bull's bellowing." At
any rate, in this case we have the correct tie-up of the
bird's name with its vocalizing. **B. lentiginosus**
(Rackett): AMERICAN BITTERN; L. *lentiginosus,*
"freckled," from L. *lent,* "a lentil," referring to the
freckled or lentil-shaped spotting of the bird's upper
parts.

BRACHYRAMPHUS Brandt Gr. *brachus,* "short"; Gr.
ramphos, "beak," from Gr. *ramphis,* "a hook"; not
too appropriate as it implies "hooked." **B. brevirostris** (Vigors): KITTLITZ'S MURRELET; L. *brevis,*
"short"; L. *rostrum,* "beak." As all the murrelets and
their relatives have small bills, the name does not
imply special distinction for this bird. E. *rostrum,* "a
platform used by speakers," comes from L. *rostra,*
"beaks." The Romans used the word rostrum for the
pointed bronze ram on the prow of a war galley as its
shape resembled the beak of a bird. In classical times
before the use of gunpowder, the most effective ship
in naval combat was the war galley. Propelled by
banks of oars, it had great speed and maneuverabil-
ity compared to cargo ships, which relied mainly on
sail. On the prow of the war galley was a heavy
pointed ram mounted slightly above water level.
This ram easily penetrated the side of a wooden ship.
The Romans in 338 B.C. sent the consul Maenius to

remove the menace to their trading ships by the pirates at Antium, now Anzio. He was victorious and brought back as mementos the rostra, "beaks," of six of the destroyed pirate galleys. These were hung on the platform used by speakers in the forum, which was from that time on called the *rostra.* **B. marmoratus** (Gmelin): MARBLED MURRELET; L. *marmoratus,* "marbled," from its underparts in breeding plumage.

BRANTA Scopoli ML. *branta,* coined from English *brant* from AS. *bernan, brennan,* "to burn," with reference to the charred or burnt appearance of the bird's plumage, particularly around the neck. Also possibly a corruption of Gr. *brentha,* "an unknown water bird." **B. bernicla** (Linnaeus): BRANT– BRENT GOOSE; Nor. *bernicla,* "barnacle"; the Latinized form of ME. *bernekka* was first Latinized as *bernaca* by Giraldus Cambrensis who originally "put forth the tale" about 1175 that the bird hatched from the shellfish of the name *bernaca,* "barnacle." Although repeating the tale, Turner, writing in 1544, remarks "that no one has seen the Bernicle's nest or egg as evidence of this spontaneous generation" as Swann points out. Disregarding this doubt, Gerard, in his *Herbal* of 1597, states, "As it groweth greater, it openeth the shell by degrees till at length it is all come forth and hangeth only by the bill; in short space after, it cometh to full maturity and falleth into the sea, where it gathereth feathers." The *Oxford Dictionary* says, "All the evidence shows that the name was originally applied to the bird which had the marvelous origin, not to the shell which produced it." This leaves the derivation of the name of the bird unresolved; but no matter which came first, the chicken or the egg, in the legend, barnacles are whitish and the bird does have a burnt coloration. **B. canadensis** (Linnaeus): CANADA GOOSE; M. *ca-*

nadensis, "Canadian," referring to the bird's main summer range. **B. leucopsis** (Bechstein): BARNA-CLE GOOSE; Gr. *leukos,* "white"; Gr. *ophis,* "face." **B. nigricans** (Lawrence): BLACK BRANT; L. *nigricans,* "black."

BUBO Dumerill L. *bubo,* "the great horned owl," cognate with Gr. *buas,* "the great horned owl" from Gr. *buzo,* "to hoot," **B. virginianus** (Gmelin): GREAT HORNED OWL; ML. *virginianus,* "Virginian." Considering the extent of its range, *americanus* would be more appropriate.

BUBULCUS Bonaparte L. *bubulus,* "concerning cattle" —Ardeola, British Ornithologists' Union *Check-list.* L. *cus,* "suffix denoting belonging to." **B. ibis** (Linnaeus): CATTLE EGRET; L. *ibis* from Gr. *ibis* who borrowed the word from the ancient Egyptians' *ibis.* The Egyptians also called the bird *hab.* Both the glossy and sacred ibis have been identified from mummies. The sacred ibis was sacred to Thoth, one of the greatest gods in the Egyptian pantheon, who was the patron of learning. The birds are frequently portrayed in Egyptian hieroglyphics. Just why Linnaeus named this straight-billed egret an ibis is puzzling.

BUCEPHALA Baird Gr. *bous,* "ox or bull," plus Gr. *kephale,* "head"; for the shape of the head and not for the famous horse of Alexander. **B. albeola** (Linnaeus): BUFFLEHEAD; L. *albus,* "white"; L. *-olus,* diminutive suffix; "little white head," which is appropriate as the predominant color is white. **B. clangula** (Linnaeus): COMMON GOLDENEYE– GOLDENEYE; L. *clangula,* diminutive of *clangor,* "noise," referring to the little noise of the whirring wings. **B. islandica** (Gmelin): BARROW'S GOLDENEYE; ML. *islandica,* "of Iceland," one of the bird's breeding localities.

BUTEO Lacepede L. *buteo,* "a hawk," probably akin to E. *buzzard.* **B. albonotatus** (Kaup): ZONE-TAILED

HAWK; L. *albus,* "white"; L. *notatus,* "marked." **B. albicaudatus** Vieillot: WHITE-TAILED HAWK; L. *albus,* "white"; L. *caudatus,* "tailed." **B. brachyurus** (Vieillot): SHORT-TAILED HAWK; Gr. *brachys,* "short"; Gr. *·ours,* "tail." **B. jamaicensis** (Gmelin): RED-TAILED HAWK; ML. *jamaicensis,* "of Jamaica," site of original specimen. **B. jamaicensis harlani** (Audubon): HARLAN'S HAWK for Dr. R. Harlan (see Appendix). **B. lagopus** (Pontoppidan): ROUGH-LEGGED HAWK; Gr. *lagos,* "a hare"; Gr. *pous,* "foot"; probably in reference to the feathered shanks. **B. lineatus** (Gmelin): RED-SHOULDERED HAWK; L. *lineatus,* "striped," most likely for the black and white stripes on the wings seen from above. **B. nitidus** (Latham): GRAY-HAWK; L. *nitidus,* "bright, shining." While lighter in color than most buteos, the common name more aptly portrays its color. **B. platypterus** (Vieillot): BROAD-WINGED HAWK; Gr. *platys,* "broad"; Gr. *pteron,* "wing." **B. regalis** (Gray): FERRUGINOUS HAWK; L. *regalis,* "royal." **B. swainsoni** Bonaparte: SWAINSON'S HAWK for William Swainson (see Appendix).

BUTEOGALLUS Lesson   L. *buteo,* "a hawk"; L. *gallus,* "a domestic cock"; roughly "a chicken hawk." **B. anthracinus** (Deppe): BLACK HAWK; L. *anthracinus,* "coal black," from Gr. *anthrax,* "coal."

BUTORIDES Blyth   Butorides is etymologically uncertain. It is a coined Modern Latin word, probably allied to L. *butio,* "bittern," and Gr. *eidos,* "resembling." **B. virescens** (Linnaeus): GREEN HERON; L. *virescens,* "growing or becoming green." Possibly it is loosing its green, of which the bird has very little.

CALAMOSPIZA Bonaparte   Gr. *calamos,* L. *calamus,* "a reed"; Gr. *spiza,* "a finch." **C. melanocorys** Stejneger: LARK BUNTING; Gr. *melanos,* "black," for the predominant color of the male's plumage. Gr. *corys,* "a lark," possibly for its singing on the wing like the European Skylark.

CALCARIUS Bechstein L. *calcar,* "a heel," in reference to the enlarged hind claw of the genus. **C. lapponicus** (Linnaeus): LAPLAND LONGSPUR–LAPLAND BUNTING; L. *lapponicus,* "of Lapponia," Lapland. Breeds in the Arctic and sub-Arctic regions of the Northern Hemisphere. Possibly Linnaeus saw it on his trip to Lapland. At any rate, it was the site of the type specimen. **C. mccownii** (Lawrence): MCCOWN'S LONGSPUR for J. P. McCown (see Appendix). **C. ornatus** (Townsend): CHESTNUT-COLLARED LONGSPUR; L. *ornatus,* "adorned," for its striking plumage. **C. pictus** (Swainson): SMITH'S LONGSPUR; L *pictus,* "painted," for the gay summer plumage of the male.

CALIDRIS Merrem Gr. *calidris,* "a gray speckled sandpiper." The genera Crocethia, Eurentes, and Erolia are now merged in Calidris (1973). **C. acuminata** (Horsfield): SHARP-TAILED SANDPIPER; L. *acuminata,* "sharp-pointed," for the pointed tail. **C. alba** (Pallas): SANDERLING; L. *alba,* "white," for the light colored winter plumage. **C. alpina** (Linnaeus): DUNLIN; L. *alpina,* "alpine," for its breeding in an alpine-like climate which may be on the Arctic tundra as well as in the mountains. **C. bairdii** (Coues): BAIRD'S SANDPIPER for Spencer F. Baird (see Appendix). **C. canutus** (Linnaeus): KNOT; ML. *canutus,* "King Canute," said to be named for Canute because (1) the birds and the king both came from Denmark, (2) the species when broiled was his favorite food, (3) the birds frequent the scene of his famous rebuke. The story is that Canute, bored by the outrageous flattery of his courtiers, commanded the tide to stay its advance. Its disregard of his edict suggested that the courtiers, too, be realistic. Swann gives Camden (1607) responsibility for originating the tale. Coues says, "Named for King Canute by Linnaeus, who accepted the dubious tradition that connected this bird with a story of the Danish king Knut, Cnut, Canut, etc. The name appears in the poems of Michael Drayton (1563–1631) and Knotts are named in MSS. of the sixteenth century. Sir T. Browne has Gnatts or Knots, c. 1672. Other forms are Gnat, Knat, Knet, etc." More likely Linnaeus thought the tale interesting and gave it no more credence than the mythological stories which inspired his naming of some birds. **C. ferruginea** (Pontoppidan): CURLEW SANDPIPER; L. *ferruginea,* "rusty red," for the color of the underparts. **C. fuscicollis** (Vieillot): WHITE-RUMPED SANDPIPER; L. *fuscus,* "dusky"; L. *collum,* "neck." As the bird does not have a dark neck, the name is misleading. **C. maritima** (Brunnich): PURPLE SANDPIPER; L. *maritima,* "belonging to the sea." It is partial to the rocky sea coasts. **C. melanotos** (Vieillot): PECTORAL SANDPIPER; Gr. *melas,* "black"; Gr. *notos,* "the back." As the bird does not have a black back, it looks like more carelessness on the part of Vieillot. **C. minutilla** (Vieillot): LEAST SANDPIPER–AMERICAN STINT; L. *minutilla,* "very small," apt name for the smallest sandpiper. **C. ptilocnemis** (Coues): ROCK SANDPIPER; Gr. *ptilon,* "feather"; Gr. *cnemis,* "a greave," the shin armor of a Greek foot soldier comparable to the shin guard of an American baseball catcher. The term refers to the feathering on the leg from the knee to the heel. **C. pusillus** (Linnaeus): SEMIPALMATED SANDPIPER; L. *pusillos,* "very small."

CALLIPEPLA Wagler Gr. *kallos,* "a beauty"; Gr. *peplos,* "a robe"; hence "beautifully dressed." **C. squamata** (Vigors): SCALED QUAIL; L. *squamatus,* "scaled," as the plumage suggests.

CALOTHORAX Gray   Gr. *calos,* "beautiful"; Gr. *thorax,* "chest"; not too accurate as it is the throat and not the chest that has color. **C. lucifer** (Swainson): LUCIFER HUMMINGBIRD; L. *lucifer,* "light bearer," like a small torch sailing in the air.

CALYPTE Gould   Gr. *Calypte,* "a proper name of unknown significance." **C. anna** (Lesson): ANNA'S HUMMINGBIRD for Anna, Duchess of Rivoli (see Appendix). **C. costae** (Bourcier): COSTA'S HUMMINGBIRD for Marquis de Costa (see Appendix).

CAMPEPHILUS Gray   Gr. *campa,* "a caterpillar"; Gr. *philos,* "loving." **C. principalis** (Linnaeus): IVORY-BILLED WOODPECKER; L. *principalis,* "principal," hence principal caterpillar lover or grub lover.

CAMPTORHYNCUS Bonaparte   Gr. *camptos,* "bent"; Gr. *rhynchos,* "beak"; **C. labradorius** (Gmelin): LABRADOR DUCK; LL. *labradonum,* "of Labrador," for the bird's range.

CAMPTOSTOMA Sclater   Gr. *kamptos,* "bent"; Gr. *stoma,* "mouth"; referring to the fact that the bill is compressed and not depressed as is usual in the other members of the Tyrannidae. **C. imberbe** Sclater: BEARDLESS FLYCATCHER; L. *imberbis,* "beardless," as it does not have the hairlike feathers at the base of the bill common to the other flycatchers.

CAMPYLORHYNCHUS Spix   Gr. *campylos,* "curved"; Gr. *rhynchos,* "beak." **C. brunneicapillus** (Lafresnaye): CACTUS WREN; L. *brunneus,* "brown"; L. *capillus,* "hair"; for its brownish plumage.

CANACHITES Stejneger   Gr. *kanacheo,* "to make a noise, to crow." **C. canadensis** (Linnaeus): SPRUCE GROUSE; ML. *canadensis,* "Canadian," found mostly in Canada.

CAPELLA L. *caper,* "goat"; L. *-ella,* a feminine diminutive; "little female goat," from the resemblance of the sound made particularly in the breeding season by the male bird to the bleating of a goat. MacLeod points out that a Scotch name is "heather-bleater." **C. gallinago** (Linnaeus): COMMON SNIPE; gallinago, coined from L. *gallina,* "a hen." The use of "go" as a suffix is more puzzling than the reason for making the goat a female in the first suffix, giving us the little goatlike hen or vice versa.

CAPRIMULGUS Linnaeus L. *caprimulgus,* "goat milker." The Romans got the traditional superstition though not the name from the Greeks, Gr. *aigothelas,* "goat milker," from Gr. *aix,* (genitive, *aigos*), "goat"; Gr. *thelazo,* "to suckle." Aristotle evidently accepted the belief of the shepherds when he stated, "Flying to the udders of she-goats, it sucks them, and thus gets its name." **C. carolinensis** Gmelin: CHUCK-WILL'S WIDOW; ML. *carolinensis,* "of Carolina"; L. *Carolus,* "Charles"; from the area where Catesby obtained the bird, named from the colony of the English king. **C. ridgwayi** (Nelson): RIDGWAY'S WHIP-POOR-WILL, for Robert Ridgway (see Appendix). **C. vociferus** Wilson: WHIP-POOR-WILL; L. *vociferus,* "noisy" literally "voice-carrying."

CARACARA Merrem Probably a South American native name for the bird, derived from its call, a low rattle. **C. cheriway** (Jacquin): CARACARA. Coues says that cheriway is probably a South American native name.

CARDELLINA Bonaparte Possibly from L. *carduelis,* "some kind of finch." **C. rubifrons** (Giraud): RED-FACED WARBLER; L. *ruber,* "red"; L. *frons,* "forehead"; not only the forehead but the whole face and neck are red.

CARDINALIS Bonaparte L. *cardinalis,* "important," from L. *cardo,* "the hinge of a door," which came to mean figuratively "important," something upon which an object or an idea hinged or depended. A cardinal is an important church official upon whose decisions matters of administration and policy depend. His robe and hat are red. Hence the name of the bird whose plumage is the same color. **C. cardinalis** (Linnaeus): CARDINAL.

CARDUELIS Brisson L. *carduelis,* "goldfinch"; L. *carduus,* "thistle," the bird's favorite food. **C. carduelis** (Linnaeus): EUROPEAN GOLDFINCH–GOLDFINCH.

CARPODACUS Kaup Gr. *carpos,* "fruit"; Gr. *dacos,* "biting." A questionable name for a genus of seed-eating birds. **C. cassinii** Baird: CASSIN'S FINCH for John Cassin (see Appendix). **C. mexicanus** Muller: HOUSE FINCH; ML. *mexicanus,* "of Mexico." To Muller, who first described the bird in 1776, Mexico, the site of his specimens, meant "Valley of Mexico." He could not have known that the term did not signify the major portion of the bird's range, which is to the north. **C. purpureus** (Gmelin): PURPLE FINCH; L. *purpureus,* "crimson" or other reddish color, from Gr. *porphura,* "a shellfish," from which the Tyrean purple dye was obtained (see *Agelaius phoeniceus*). To the Romans the word meant either the color or the cloth dyed with it. So in the classical sense the color is correct for the plumage of the male bird. Now the E. *purple,* which originated in the Latin, means a color obtained from mixing red and blue (OE. *purpur*) and means a color less reddish.

CASMERODIUS Gloger Gr. *chasma,* "open mouth"; Gr. *herodios,* "a heron." As there is nothing open-mouthed about the egret, the name seems nonsensical. **C. albus** (Linneus): GREAT EGRET; L. *albus,* "white."

CASSIDIX Lesson L. *cassidis,* "helmet." The application of this term to the bird is obscure. **C. major** (Vieillot): BOAT-TAILED GRACKLE; L. *major,* "larger." This new species contains the more eastern and northern subspecies. Major was the subspecific name for the eastern race. It was the term used by Vieillot when he first described the bird as a species in 1819.

C. mexicanus (Gmelin): GREAT-TAILED GRACKLE; ML. *mexicanus*, "of Mexico," where the bird is common.

CATHARACTA Brunnich Gr. *kathartes*, "a purifier"; Gr. *akta*, "the sea shore"; from its scavenging for food at sea rather than along the shore. **C. skua** Brunnich: SKUA–GREAT SKUA; Faroese name for the bird.

CATHARTES Illiger Gr. *kathartes*, "a purifier." **C. aura** (Linnaeus): TURKEY VULTURE. Jordan says *aura* is a South American name for the bird.

CATHARUS Gr. *catharos*, "pure." Just how this applies to the genus is obscure. **C. fuscescens** (Stephens): VEERY; L. *fuscus*, "dark"; L. *-escens*, a qualifying suffix, "slightly." **C. guttata** (Pallas): HERMIT THRUSH; L. *gutta*, "a drop," hence a drop-like spot, for the spotted breast. **C. minimus** (Lafresnaye): GRAY-CHEEKED THRUSH; L. *minimus*, "least"; seems inapplicable as this bird is if anything slightly larger than its closest relatives. **C. ustulata** (Nuttall): SWAINSON'S THRUSH; L. *ustulata*, "singed," for its brownish color.

CATHERPES Baird Gr. *catherpes*, "a creeper." **C. mexicanus** (Swainson): CANYON WREN; ML. *mexicanus*, "Mexican," as the type specimen was obtained in Mexico.

CATOPTROPHORUS Bonaparte Gr. *katoptron*, "mirror"; Gr. *phero*, "to bear"; mirror bearing alluding to the white patches in the wings. **C. semipalmatus** (Gmelin): WILLET; *Semipalmatus* for the partially webbed feet (see *Charadrius semipalmatus*).

CENTROCERCUS Swainson Gr. *kentron*, "a point"; Gr. *kerkos*, "tail." **C. urophasianus** (Bonaparte): SAGE GROUSE; Gr. *oura*, "tail"; Gr. *phasianos*, "pheasant"; so we have the pointed-tailed pheasant tail.

CENTURUS Swainson Gr. *kentron*, "a prickle"; Gr. *oura*, "tail"; for the stiff feathers in the tail. **C. aurifrons** (Wagler): GOLDEN-FRONTED WOOD-PECKER; L. *aurus*, "gold"; L. *frons*, "forehead"; for its bright yellow forehead. **C. carolinus** (Linnaeus): RED-BELLIED WOODPECKER; ML. *carolinus*, "of Carolina." **C. uropygialis** Baird: GILA WOOD-PECKER; Gr. *ouropygion*, "the rump," which, being banded, is a field mark for this species.

CEPPHUS Pallas Gr. *kepphos*, "a kind of sea bird." **C. columba** Pallas: PIGEON GUILLEMOT; L. *columba*, "a pigeon," from the size and shape of the bird. **C. grylle** (Linnaeus): BLACK GUILLEMOT; S. *grylle*, the name for the bird in Gothland, an island in the Baltic.

CERORHINCA Bonaparte Gr. *keros*, "a horn"; *rhyncos*, "beak"; which is rhinoceros backwards. **C. monocerata** (Pallas): RHINCEROS AUKLET; Gr. *monos*, "single"; *keros*, "horn"; this gives us the single-horned horned beak.

CERTHIA Linnaeus L. *certhius*, "a creeper." **C. familiaris** Linnaeus: BROWN CREEPER–TREE CREEPER. L. *familiaris*, "domestic, homelike," hence friendly.

CHAETURA Stephens Gr. *chaite*, "a bristle"; Gr. *oura*, "tail." **C. pelagica** (Linnaeus): CHIMNEY SWIFT; Gr. *pelagios*, "marine." In commenting on the use of *pelagica* for this land bird, Coues says, "In 1758 Linnaeus named it *Hirundo Pelagica*, but in 1766 he changed the specific term to *pelasgia*. The *Pelasgi* were anciently a nomadic tribe, and the implication of the term in ornithology is supposed to be the bird's migration, without any reference to the sea." Coues goes on to say that L. *pelasgius* from a Greek form means Grecian or Hellenic and that *Pelasgia*, the noun, is the name of a district of Thessaly. Coues used *pelasgica* for a time, but finally went back to *pelagica,* the term used by the American Ornithologists' Union. Possibly Linnaeus made a slip in spelling and tried to retrieve it. Coues in reverting to the original spelling evidently realized the futility of his brief endeavor. This was fortunate as his interpretation of *pelasgic* is questionable. L. *pelasgia* meant the Peloponnesus after *Pelasgos,* the mythical progenitor of the natives living there. A name once given to a species has the primary function of identifying that animal regardless of initial error or subsequent refinement of meaning. **C. vauxi** (Townsend): VAUX'S SWIFT for William S. Vaux (see Appendix).

CHAMAEA Gamber Gr. *chamai,* "on the ground." **C. fasciata** (Gambel): WRENTIT; L. *fasciata,* "striped," from L. *fascis,* "a bundle of faggots." Seems to refer to both bird's fondness for staying close in the underbrush and the striped underparts.

CHARADRIUS Linnaeus Gr. *charadrios,* L. *charadrius,* "a plover," from Gr. *charadra,* "a gully," from the nesting site. **C. alexandrinus** Linnaeus: SNOWY PLOVER; named for Alexandria, since the first specimen came from that city in Egypt. **C. melodus** Ord: PIPING PLOVER; L. *melodus,* "a melody," from the notes of the bird. **C. montanus** (Townsend): MOUNTAIN PLOVER; L. *montanus,* "of the mountains," although it is found mostly in the high plains. **C. semipalmatus** Bonaparte: SEMIPALMATED PLOVER; L. *semi,* "half"; L. *palma,* "palm of the hand"; literally half-webbed referring to the feet. **C. vociferus** Linnaeus: KILLDEER–KILLDEER PLOVER; L. *vociferus,* "vociferous," from its loud call. **C. wilsonia** Ord: WILSON'S PLOVER for Alexander Wilson (see Appendix).

CHEN Boie Gr. *chen,* "goose." **C. caerulescens** (Linnaeus): SNOW GOOSE; L. *caerulescens,* "bluish." As **C. hyperborea** is now considered the white morph of a polymorphic species whose dark morph has been known as **C. caerulescens,** the name for both becomes **C. caerulescens** as this term has priority being used for the blue morph by Linnaeus in 1758, while **C. hyperborea** was not used for the white morph till 1769. **C. rossii (Cassin): ROSS' GOOSE for Bernard R. Ross (see Appendix).**

CHILIDONIAS Rafinesque Should be spelled cheldonias. Gr. *chelidon,* "a swallow," ML. *-ias,* suffix, "denoting or characteristic of." **C. niger** (Linnaeus): BLACK TERN; L. *niger,* "black," from the breeding plumage.

CHLOROCERYLE Kaup Gr. *chloros,* "greenish"; Gr. *kerylos,* "kingfisher." **C. americana** (Gmelin): GREEN KINGFISHER; ML. *americana,* "American."

CHLORURA Sclater Gr. *chloros,* "green"; Gr. *oura,* "tail." Not only the tail but the wings and back are a dark green, while the Greek word means light green. **C. chlorura** (Audubon): GREEN-TAILED TOWHEE; a bit repetitious.

CHONDESTES Swainson Gr. *chondros,* "a grain, grit, a lump of salt"; Gr. *odestes,* "an eater." Swainson certainly abbreviated this one. He probably meant seed eater. **C. grammacus** (Say): LARK SPARROW; Gr. *grammicus,* "marked with a line, streaked," from Gr. *gramme,* "a line, writing," to indicate the line on the head. We agree with Coues that the term is "badly selected and badly spelled."

CHORDEILES Swainson Gr. *choros,* most likely "a circular dance" hence "a moving about"; Gr. *deile,* "evening"; alluding to the bird's spectacular flight and call when hawking for insects at that time of day. **C. acutipennis** (Hermann): LESSER NIGHTHAWK; L. *acutus,* "sharp"; L. *penna,* "a feather"; alluding to the sharp pointed wings. **C. minor** (Forster): COMMON NIGHTHAWK; L. *minor,* "smaller." When described in 1771, it was so called as it was then smaller than the only other bird in the same family known at that time, the Nightjar of Europe.

CINCLUS Borkhausen   Gr. *kinklos,* "a bird," mentioned by Aristotle; possibly the Water Ousel or Wagtail. **C. mexicanus** Swainson: DIPPER; ML. *mexicanus,* "Mexican," from the range of a subspecies.

CIRCUS Lacepede   L. *circus,* from Gr. *kirkos,* "a kind of hawk"; from its circling in the air; mentioned by Aristotle who most likely did not mean a harrier which infrequently circles. **C. cyaneus** (Linnaeus): MARSH HAWK; Gr. *kyaneous,* "dark blue" referring to the blue of the male's back.

CISTOTHORUS Cabanis   Gr. *cistos,* "a shrub"; Gr. *thouros,* "leaping" or "running through." **C. platensis** (Latham): SHORT-BILLED MARSH WREN; Gr. *plates,* "flat, broad," probably compared with the bill of the long-billed marsh wren.

CLANGULA Leach   ML. *clangula,* "noise," from Gr. *klange,* "a noise or sound." **C. hyemalis** (Linnaeus): oldsquaw–LONG-TAILED DUCK; L. *hiemalis,* "wintry." Older ornithologists were for a time confused by the different plumages which they thought belonged to two species, naming one *hyemalis* and the other *glacialis.*

COCCYZUS Vieillot   Gr. *kokkux,* "a cuckoo." **C. americanus** (Linnaeus): YELLOW-BILLED CUCKOO; ML. *americanus,* "American," as is the other in the same genus. **C. erythropthalmus** (Wilson): BLACK-BILLED CUCKOO; Gr. *erythros,* "red"; Gr. *ophthalmos,* "eye"; which it is not, as the red is confined to the eyelids. **C. minor** (Gmelin): MANGROVE CUCKOO; L. *minor,* "smaller" although it is about the same size as the other cuckoos.

COEREBA Viellot   Brazilian name of a small bird. **C. bahamensis** (Reichenbach): BAHAMA HONEY-CREEPER; ML. *bahamensis,* "of the Bahamas,"

COLAPTES

from the bird's range where the birds found in Florida originated; becomes **C. flaveola bahamensis** (Linnaeus): BANANAQUIT, as this is now the approved name; L. *flavus*, "yellow," for the plumage.

COLAPTES Vigors Gr. *kolapto*, "to peck with the bill, chisel." **C. auratus** (Linnaeus): COMMON FLICKER; L. *auratus*, "golden." This is the name for the enlarged species and includes the former **C. auratus, C. cafer**, and **C. chrysoides. C. auratus cafer** (Gmelin): RED-SHAFTED FLICKER. Following is Coues' reaction to the term *cafer:* "With every disposition to follow the dogma and ritual of the A.O.U., I cannot bring myself to call this bird *C. cafer*, for no better reason than because *Picus cafer* Gm. 1788 was mistaken for a bird of the Cape of Good Hope! Say what we please in our canons, there *is* something in a name after all, and 'the letter of the law killeth' when wrenched from its spirit, in defiance of science and common sense. Individually I cannot incur the penalty of deliberately using for a North American bird a name only applicable to one from South Africa. The fact that *Cafer* is a sort of Latin for Caffraria or Caffrarian makes its use in this connection as bad as 'Hottentot Woodpecker' or Zulu Flicker would be; and how would such a combination sound in plain English?" The original specimen described by Gmelin in 1778 came from the Bay of Good Hope, Nootka Sound, Vancouver Island, British Columbia. So Gmelin confused the Bay and the Cape of Good Hope. Coues chose the name *C. mexicanus* in his writings, but the A.O.U. *Check-list* Committee in deference to the law of priority retained *cafer*. **C. auratus chrysoides** (Malherbe): GILDED FLICKER. Formerly a species.

COLINUS Goldfus Sp. *colin*, from "zolin," meaning a partridge, in Nahuatl, a Central American Indian

tongue. **C. virginianus** (Linnaeus): BOBWHITE;
ML. *virginianus,* "of Virginia."

COLUMBA Linnaeus L. *columba,* "a dove, pigeon." **C.
fasciata** Say: BAND-TAILED PIGEON; L. *fascia,*
"a band"; ML. *-ata,* "a suffix signifying an adjective"; for the striking band of the tail. **C. flavirostris**
Wagler: RED-BILLED PIGEON; L. *flavis,* "yel-
low"; L. *rostrum,* "bill." Not a very good name as the
bill is red with only a yellow tip. **C. leucocephala**
Linnaeus: WHITE-CROWNED PIGEON; Gr. *leu-
cos,* "white"; Gr. *cephala,* "head." **C. livia** Gmelin:
ROCK DOVE; L. *lividus,* "to be bluish," for the
bird's bluish-gray color.

COLUMBINA Boie L. *columba,* "a dove, pigeon." **C.
passerina** (Linnaeus): GROUND DOVE; L. *passerina,* "sparrow-like." We have now the end product of
the changes in nomenclature which gives us "sparrow-like, domestic hen-like pigeon." It may be an
improvement in scientific accuracy even if the bird
does not look like either a hen or a sparrow. Gone
into limbo is Catesby's *Turtur minimus guttatus,* "the
little spotted dove" and Baird's *Chamaepelia passerina,* "sparrow-like ground dove."

CONTOPUS Cabinis Gr. *kontos,* "short"; Gr. *pous,*
"foot"; as its feet are very small. **C. pertinax** Cabanis
and Heine: COUES' FLYCATCHER; L. *pertinax,*
"closer to," meaning (closely) allied to the Olive-
sided Flycatcher which, at the time *pertinax* was first
described, was in the same genus, but is now in a
different one. Thus the term is meaningless. **C.
sordidulus** Sclater: WESTERN WOOD PEWEE; L.
sordius, "dirty, foul," L. *ulus,* diminutive suffix;
hence "the dirty little one." Possibly so called out of
exasperation of the systematist who had to distinguish it from *C. virens.* **C. virens** (Linnaeus): EAST-
ERN WOOD PEWEE; L. *virens,* "greenish."

CONUROPSIS Salvadori   Gr. *conos,* "a pine cone"; Gr. *oura,* "tail"; Gr. *-opsis,* "appearance of"; hence, with a tail shaped like a cone. **C. carolinensis** (Linnaeus): CAROLINA PARAKEET; ML. *carolinensis,* "of Carolina," suggesting a southern range.

CORAGYPS Geoffroy   Gr. *korax,* "raven"; Gr. *gyps,* "vulture"; the griffon-vulture of Homer. **C. atratus** (Bechstein): BLACK VULTURE; L. *atratus,* "clothed in black as for mourning."

CORVUS Linnaeus   L. *corvus,* "a crow." **C. brachyrhynchos** Brehm: COMMON CROW; Gr. *brachys,* "short"; Gr. *rhynchos,* "beak"; which it is compared to a raven's. **C. caurinus** Baird: NORTHWESTERN CROW; L. *caurinus,* "northwestern," from L. *caurus,* "the northwest wind." **C. corax** Linnaeus: COMMON RAVEN; Gr. *korax,* "raven," imitative of the call, cognate with Gr. *krazo,* "to croak." **C. cryptoleucus** Couch: WHITE-NECKED RAVEN; Gr. *cryptos,* "hidden," which is very apt as the Gr. *leucos,* "white," of the neck is rarely seen in the field. **C. ossifragus** Wilson: FISH CROW; L. *ossifragus,* "bone breaker," puzzling as a name for the bird (see Osprey).

COTURNICOPS Gray   L. *coturnix,* "quail"; Gr. *opsis,* "appearance"; thus looking like a quail. **C. novaboracensis** (Gmelin): YELLOW RAIL; ML. *Noveboracum,* "New York"; L. *-ensis,* a suffix meaning "belonging to"; a poor place name as the bird is rare in New York. L. *novus,* "new"; L. *Eboracum,* the Roman name for "York," England.

CREX Bechstein   Gr. *krex,* the name used by Aristotle for a long-legged bird and by Herodotus for a bird the size of an ibis; name imitates call. **C. crex** (Linnaeus): CORN CRAKE; a better imitation of its call when both words are used.

CROTOPHAGA Linnaeus   Gr. *kroton,* "a bug"; Gr. *phagos,* "eating." **C. ani** (Linnaeus): SMOOTH-BILLED

ANI; Brazilian *ani,* "ani." **C. sulcirostris** (Swainson): GROOVE-BILLED ANI; L. *sulcus,* "furrow"; L. *rostrum,* "bill."

CYANOCITTA Strickland Gr. *cyanos,* "blue"; Gr. *kitta,* "a jay." **C. cristata** (Linnaeus): BLUE JAY; L. *cristata,* "crested." **C. stelleri** (Gmelin): STELLER'S JAY after George Wilhelm Steller (see Appendix).

CYANOCORAX Boie Gr. *cyanos,* "blue"; Gr. *corax,* "a croaker, the raven." **C. yncas** (Boddaert): GREEN JAY; *yncas,* same as Inca, the name of the chief of the aboriginal natives of Peru, not of Mexico. As the bird ranges in Mexico and not in Peru, the name is misleading. Same confusion seems to have occurred in naming *S. inca,* the Inca dove.

CYCLORRHYNCHUS Kaup Gr. *kyklos,* "circle"; Gr. *rhynchos,* "beak." **C. psittacula** (Pallas): PARAKEET AUKLET; L. *psittaculus,* "a little parrot."

CYGNUS Bechstein L. *cygnus,* "swan," from Gr. *kyknos,* "swan." **C. olor** (Gmelin): MUTE SWAN; L. *olor,* "swan." *Olor* was used by Pliny and according to MacLeod "appears to be of Celtic origin."

CYNANTHUS Swanson Gr. *kyon,* kynos, "a dog"; Gr. *anthos,* "flower"; possibly for the bird "hounding" flowers as it feeds on their nectar. **C. latirostris** (Swainson): BROAD-BILLED HUMMINGBIRD; L. *latus,* "wide"; L. *rostrum,* "beak."

CYPSELOIDES Streubel Gr. *kypselos,* L. *cypselus,* "the European Swift"; Gr. *eidos,* "resembling." **C. niger** (Gmelin): BLACK SWIFT; L. *niger,* "black," from the dark plumage.

CYRTONYX Gould Gr. *kyrtos,* "curved"; Gr. *onyx,* "claw." **C. montezumae** (Vigors): HARLEQUIN QUAIL; after Montezuma, the Aztec emperor of Mexico at the time of the Spanish conquest. The name is a Nahuati word meaning "angry chief." A gastric disturbance which affects some visitors to Mexico is known as Montezuma's revenge.

DAPTION Stephens Gr. *dapte,* "devour"; L. *-ion,* suffix meaning "having to do with." The name may be explained by this quote from Murphy's *Oceanic Birds of South America,* "Cape Pigeons are eager devourers of garbage and it would not be unnatural if bands of the birds sometimes pursued vessels a considerable distance." **D. capense** (Linnaeus): CAPE PETREL; ML. *capensis,* "of the Cape," referring to the Cape of Good Hope in the area of which the type specimen was obtained.

DENDRAGAPUS Elliott Gr. *dendron,* "a tree"; Gr. *agape,* "love"; tree-loving. **D. obscurus** (Say): BLUE GROUSE; L. *obscurus,* "dark," from its coloration.

DENDROCOPOS Kock Gr. *dendron,* "a tree"; Gr. *kopis,* "a dagger." **D. albolarvatus** (Cassin): WHITE-HEADED WOODPECKER; L. *albus,* "white"; L. *larvatus,* "masked." **D. arizonae** (Hargitt): ARIZONA WOODPECKER; ML. *arizonae,* "of Arizona," its residence. **D. borealis** (Vieillot): RED-COCKADED WOODPECKER; L. *borealis,* "northern," Gr. *boreas,* "the north wind." Boreas, the North Wind, fell in love with Orithyea but her father, Erechtheus, and the people of Athens wanted nothing to do with another northerner after Tereus' villainry became known. Orithyea, herself, was not entranced but rather repelled by the rough ways of her suitor. Not to be thwarted by the proprieties of permission of relatives or reluctance on the part of the object of his devotion, Boreas, in a great gust of wind, swooped down and carried her off. No subsequent accounts suggest it was an unhappy marriage. Vieillot evidently fumbled the naming of this bird, which has its range in the southeastern United States. The A.O.U. *Check-list,* in citing his description, has noted (*dans le nord des Etats-Unis*—Southern States). We take this to mean that Vieillot was confused. Even if he thought the bird came from the

northern United States, he overdid it a bit. Northern
Canada would be a better justification for the name.
D. nuttallii (Gambel): NUTTALL'S WOOD-
PECKER for Thomas Nuttall (see Appendix). **D.
pubescens** (Linnaeus): DOWNY WOODPECKER;
L. *pubescena,* "downy," i.e., with the hairs of puberty
and not quite so virily unkempt as *villosus.* **D. scalaris**
(Wagler): LADDER-BACKED WOODPECKER;
L. *scalaris,* "ladder-like"; L. *scals,* "a flight of stairs";
alluding to the plumage of the back. **D. villosus**
(Linnaeus): HAIRY WOODPECKER; L. *villosus,*
"hairy," from its rather shaggy appearance especially
about the head.

DENDROCYGNA Swainson Gr. *dendron,* "a tree"; Gr.
kyknos, L. *cygnus,* "swan." **D. autumnalis** (Linnaeus):
BLACK-BELLIED TREE DUCK; L. *autumnalis,*
"autumnal." The reason for the name is unknown.
D. bicolor (Vieillot): FULVUS TREE DUCK; L. *bi,*
"two"; L. *color,* "color."

DENDROICA Gray Gr. *dendron,* "a tree"; Gr. *oicos,*
"inhabit"; tree-dweller. **D. coronata auduboni** (Townsend): AUDUBON'S WARBLER in honor of J. J.
Audubon (see Appendix). Changed to subspecies,
1973. **D. caerulescens** (Gmelin): BLACK-
THROATED BLUE WARBLER; L. *caerulescens,*
"becoming blue." **D. castanea** (Wilson): BAY-
BREASTED WARBLER; L. *castanea,* "a chestnut,"
for the color of the breast. **D. cerulea** (Wilson):
CERULEAN WARBLER; L. *ceruleus,* "sky blue."
D. chrysoparia Sclater and Salvin: GOLDEN-
CHEEKED WARBLER; Gr. *chrysos,* "golden"; Gr.
pareia, "cheek." **D. coronata** (Linnaeus): YELLOW-
RUMPED WARBLER; L. *coronata,* "crowned," for
the yellow crown. Myrtle Warbler is still available
for the subspecies. **D. discolor** (Vieillot): PRAIRIE
WARBLER; L. *discolor,* "of different colors." **D.
dominica** (Linnaeus): YELLOW-THROATED

WARBLER; ML. *dominica,* "St. Domingo," now Hispaniola where this bird was first found. **D. fusca** (Muller): BLACKBURNIAN WARBLER; L. *fuscus,* "dark." **D. graciae** Baird: GRACE'S WARBLER to honor Grace D. Coues, sister of Elliott Coues (see Appendix, under Grace). **D. kirtlandii** (BAIRD): KIRTLAND'S WARBLER for Dr. J. P. Kirtland (see Appendix). **D. magnolia** (Wilson): MAGNOLIA WARBLER; E. *magnolia,* so named by Wilson, who shot a specimen in a magnolia tree. **D. nigrescens** (Townsend): BLACK-THROATED GRAY WARBLER; L. *nigrescens,* "becoming black." **D. occidentalis** (Townsend): HERMIT WARBLER; L. *occidentalis,* "western," from the bird's range. **D. palmarum** (Gmelin): PALM WARBLER; L. *palmarum,* "of the palms," from its frequenting the palm trees of Hispaniola, whence it was first known. **D. pensylvanica** (Linnaeus): CHESTNUT-SIDED WARBLER; *pen,* a misspelling for Pennsylvania as the first specimen came from Philadelphia, Pennsylvania. L. *sylva,* "woods"; L. *pensylvanic,* "Penn's Woods," from the site of probably the original specimen near Philadelphia, Pennsylvania. **D. petechia** (Linnaeus): YELLOW WARBLER; ML. *petechia,* I. *pettechia,* "purplish spot"; Gr. *pittakia,* "patch." E. *petechiae* is a medical term for reddish or purplish spots that appear as a rash on the skin. Evidently the russet-red streaks on the breast of the male suggested a rash to the original describer. **D. pinus** (Wilson): PINE WARBLER; L. *pinus,* "a pine tree," from its habitat. **D. striata** (Forster): BLACKPOLL WARBLER; L. *striata,* "striped." **D. tigrina** (Gmelin): CAPE MAY WARBLER; L. *tigrina,* "striped like a tiger," with the black stripes on its yellow breast. **D. townsendi** (Townsend): TOWNSEND'S WARBLER for J. K.

Townsend (see Appendix). D. virens (Gmelin): BLACKTHROATED GREEN WARBLER; L. *virens,* "growing green."

DICHROMANASSA Ridgway   Gr. *di,* "two"; Gr. *chroma,* "colored"; Gr. *anassa,* "a lady, a queen." **D. rufescens** (Gmelin): REDDISH EGRET; L. *rufescens,* "reddish."

DIOMEDEA Linnaeus   Diomedes, king of Aetolia and later of Argos, was a Greek hero of the Trojan War, second only to Achilles in renown. He disappeared and possibly was buried on one of the islands in the Adriatic called after him, the Diomedae. Here, according to Ovid, his companions were changed into birds. William Bebe in "Galapagos, World's End" has this to say about the name, " 'Instead of the cross, the albatross about my neck was hung.' Intellectually, man's relation with the albatross has been less spectacular but of equal interest. Linnaeus, one hundred and sixty-eight years ago, first played taxonomic Adam to the albatross, calling it *Diomedea exulans.* Its godfather was probably, therefore, the famous hero of the seige of Troy, but the Grecian etymology provides a much more poetic and appropriate derivation, and it is pleasant to think of the albatross, whether winging over foam crests or at home on its little isle, as being over Diomedea or God-counseled. In its specific appellation Linnaeus was also happy, for to the ordinary observer the wandering albatross is truly exulans 'homeless,' banished apparently from all connection with solid land." **D. albatrus** (Pallas): SHORT-TAILED ALBATROSS (see Albatross). **D. cauta** (Gould): WHITE-CAPPED ALBATROSS; L. *cautus,* "beware," possibly in deference to the sailor's superstition concerning the dire consequences for harming the bird. **D. chlororhynchos** (Gmelin): YELLOW-

NOSED ALBATROSS; Gr. *chloros,* "greenish yellow"; Gr. *rhynchos,* "beak." **D. immutabilis** (Rothschild): LAYSAN ALBATROSS; L. *immutabilis,* "never changing." **D. melanophris** Temminck: BLACK-BROWED ALBATROSS; Gr. *melan,* "black"; Gr. *ophris,* "eyebrow." **D. nigripes** (Audubon): BLACK-FOOTED ALBATROSS; L. *niger,* "black"; L. *pes,* "foot."

DOLICHONYX Swainson   Gr. *dolichos,* "long"; Gr. *onux,* "claw"; for the very large claws. **D. oryzivorus** (Linnaeus): BOBLINK; Gr. and L. *oryza,* "rice"; L. *voro,* "devour"; from the bird's fondness for the grain.

DRYOCOPUS Boie   Gr. *drys,* "a tree"; Gr. *kopis,* "a cleaver or dagger." **D. pileatus** (Linnaeus): PILEATED WOODPECKER; L. *pileatus,* "capped"; L. *pileum,* "a cap"; for the bird's conspicuous red and black crest.

DUMETELLA S.D.W.   The only systematist not identified by name in the A.O.U. *Check-list.* L. *dumus,* "a thorn bush"; L. *-ella,* diminutive suffix giving us "little one of the thorn bush." **D. carolinensis** (Linnaeus): CATBIRD; ML. *carolinensis,* "of Carolina," for the region called Carolina by Marc Catesby.

ECTOPISTES Swainson   Gr. *ectopistes,* "a wanderer," which Coues says is very appropriate. **E. migratorius** (Linnaeus): PASSENGER PIGEON; L. *migratorius,* "migratory."

EGRETTA Forster   F. *aigrette,* "egret." **E. thula** (Molina): SNOWY EGRET. Thula is a Chilean name for the bird used by Molina (1740–1839), a Chilean naturalist, who first described the species in 1782.

ELANOIDES Vieillot   Gr. *elanos,* "a kite," plus Gr. *oideos,* a suffix meaning "resembling." Thus we have "like a kite" for the meaning of the genus. **E. forficatus** (Linnaeus): SWALLOW-TAILED KITE; L. *forficatus,* "deeply forked."

ELANUS Savigny   L. *elanus,* "a kite." **E. leucurus** (Vieillot): WHITE-TAILED KITE; Gr. *leukouros,* "white tailed."

EMPIDONAX Cabanis Gr. *empis,* genitive, *empidos,* "a gnat"; Gr. *anax,* "king"; the genitive is used so we understand the term as "king of the gnats." **E. alnorum** Brewster: ALDER FLYCATCHER; L. *alnorum,* "of the alders" for the bird's habitat. This is a new species made by dividing **E. trailii. E. difficilis** Baird: WESTERN FLYCATCHER; L. *difficilis,* "difficult, undoable," to which Coues says "very appropriate"; because of its close resemblance to *E. flaviventris.* The notes and range are more helpful in identifying it than its plumage. **E. flaviventris** (Baird and Baird): YELLOW-BELLIED FLYCATCHER; L. *flavus,* "yellow"; L. *ventrus,* "the belly." **E. fulvifrons** (Giraud): BUFF-BREASTED FLY-CATCHER; L. *fulvus,* "tawny"; L. *frons,* "forehead," to be interpreted here as the English meaning of front. For the buffy underparts. **E. hammondii** (Xantus): HAMMOND'S FLYCATCHER; for William A. Hammond (see Appendix). **E. minimus** (Baird and Baird): LEAST FLYCATCHER; L. *minimus,* "least." **E. oberholseri** Phillips: DUSKY FLYCATCHER; for Dr. Harry C. Oberholser (see Appendix). **E. traillii** (Audubon): WILLOW FLY-CATCHER; for Thomas S. Traill (see Appendix). When circumstances prevent species identification (by hearing the song in spring), Traill's Flycatcher "remains available for the complex." **E. virescens** (Vieillot): ACADIAN FLYCATCHER; L. *virescens,* "growing green." Possibly the color suggested to Vieillot that of some fruit ripening into greenness but still having a long way to go. **E. wrightii** Baird: GRAY FLYCATCHER; for Charles Wright (see Appendix).

ENDOMYCHURA Oberholser Gr. *ende,* "wanting, in need of"; Gr. *mychos,* "hidden"; Gr. *oura,* "tail." As the tails of the birds in this family are small. **E. craveri**

(Salvadori): CRAVERI'S MURRELET for Frederico Craveri (see Appendix). **E. hypoleuca** (Xantus): XANTUS' MURRELET; Gr. *hypo-,* "below"; Gr. *leukon,* "white"; for the white underparts.

EREMOPHILA Brehm   Gr. *eremos,* "lonely"; Gr. *phileo,* "love"; hence loving solitude, although they gather in flocks in winter. **E. alpestris** (Linnaeus): HORNED LARK; ML. *alpestris,* "alpine." Holarctic in distribution from mountains to deserts, although breeding in mountains is not limited to such a habitat.

EUDOCIMUS Wagler   Gr. *eudokimos,* "famous, in good standing." Wagler quite correctly removed these birds from the genus *Scolopax,* where they had been placed in company with the European Woodcock, and put them into a new genus, *Eudomicus,* which is in an entirely different scientific order. It seems he could not resist naming the genus after his accomplishment in placing the bird in a scientific classification in good standing. **E. albus** (Linnaeus): WHITE IBIS; L. *albus,* "white." **E. ruber** (Linnaeus): SCARLET IBIS; L. *ruber,* "red."

EUDROMIAS Brehm   Gr. *eu,* "good"; Gr. *dromos,* "running"; from its habit of making short quick runs in search of food. **E. morinellus** (Linnaeus): DOTTEREL; ML. *morinellus,* "little fool," a coined word made by adding a Latin diminutive suffix to the Gr. *moros,* "stupid," cf. E. *moron.* Swann quotes Ray as saying "it is a very foolish bird, and is taken in the night time, by the light of a candle, by imitating the gestures of the fowler, for if he stretches out an arm, the bird also stretches out a wing, if he a foot the bird likewise a foot, in brief, whatever the fowler does, the bird does the same, and so being intent upon the man's gestures it is deceived, and covered with the net spread for it." A grain of salt is also useful.

EUGENES Gould Gr. *eugenes,* "well born," and by implication, attractive in appearance. **E. fulgens** (Swainson): RIVOLI'S HUMMINGBIRD; L. *fulgens,* "glittering."

EUPHAGUS Cassin Gr. *eu,* "good"; Gr. *phago,* "to eat"; literally "good to eat." This should not lead to confusion with "the four and twenty blackbirds" of nursery-rhyme renown which belong to the genus *Turdus* of the Old World. **E. carolinus** (Muller): RUSTY BLACKBIRD; referring to the Carolinas where the first specimens were found; L. *Carolus,* after Charles II of England. **E. cyanocephalus** (Wagler): BREWER'S BLACKBIRD; Gr. *cyanos,* L. *cyanus,* "blue"; Gr. *cephale,* "head"; as the plumage of the head is dark blue in contrast with the greenish cast of the body.

EURYNORHYNCHUS Nilson Gr. *euryno,* "to make wide"; Gr. *rhynchos,* "a beak"; refers to the broad beak. **E. pygmeum** (Linnaeus): SPOON-BILL SANDPIPER; Gr. *pygm-ios,* "drawfish," from Gr. *pygme,* "first"; cf. Tomthumb, literally the little wide-beak.

FALCO Linnaeus LL. *falco,* "falcon," from L. *falx,* "sickle," after the shape of the talons and the beak. **F. columbarius** Linnaeus: MERLIN; L. *columbarius,* "a pigeon keeper," but in ML. "pidgeon," an adjective, from L. *columba,* "a dove," plus *-arius* "pertaining to." Referring to the bird's reputation as an occasional pigeon snatcher. **F. femoralis** Temminck: APLOMADO FALCON; ML. *femoralis,* "pertaining to the thighs," refers to the bright coloring of the upper legs. **F. mexicanus** Schlegel: PRAIRIE FALCON; ML. *mexicanus,* "Mexican." **F. peregrinus** Tunstall: PEREGRINE FALCON; L. *per,* a prefix meaning "through," and L. *ager, agri,* "field," plus L. *-inus,* a suffix meaning "pertaining to the nature of"; on the base of these the Romans evolved the L.

peregrinus, "foreign, wandering." Albertus Magnus (c. 1206–1280) gives two reasons for the bird's name: "(1) that it constantly moves from one place to another; (2) that its nest can never be discovered." J. Ray writing in 1713 says it . . . "took its name either from passing from one country to another, or because it is not known where it builds." The medieval falconers, Ingersoll says, "so named 'the bird' because the young were not taken like 'eyas' from the nest, but caught in their passage from the breeding place." **F. rusticolus** Linnaeus: GYRFAL-CON; *rusticolus* is Linnaean Latin. It should be *rusticulus,* a diminutive of *rusticus,* "a rustic," according to MacLeod. Probably for the bird's habitat in the remote tundra. **F. sparverius** Linnaeus: AMERICAN KESTREL; L. *sparverius,* "pertaining to a sparrow," a rather unfortunate term as it implies that the bird preys preeminently on sparrows. **F. tinnunculus** Linnaeus: KESTREL; L. *tinnunculus,* "most likely the Kestrel," from L. *tinnulus,* "ringing," as the bird's notes suggest a ringing bell.

FLORIDA Baird   Named for the state. **F. caerulea** (Linnaeus): LITTLE BLUE HERON; L. *caeruleus,* "dark-colored, dark blue."

FRATERCULA Brisson   ML. *fraterculus,* "friar," diminutive of L. *frater,* "brother"; hence "little brother." MacLeod suggests, ". . . perhaps with reference to the bird's habit, when rising from the sea, of clasping its feet as though in prayer." **F. arctica** (Linnaeus): COMMON PUFFIN–PUFFIN; L. *arctucus;* "arctic," from Gr. *arktikos,* "of the bear," "northern," from the constellations in the northern sky which the Greeks called the Greater and Lesser Bear, but which we know as the Big and Little Dipper. **F. corniculata** (Naumann): HORNED PUFFIN; L. *cornu,* "horn"; L. *cula,* diminutive suffix for the horn-like beak.

FREGATA Lacapede   Now we have the Italian word for frigate spelled correctly by the French naturalist, Conte de Lacepede. **F. magnificens** (Mathews): MAGNIFICENT FRIGATEBIRD; L. *magnus,* "great," L. *facio,* "make."

FREGETTA Bonaparte   I. *fregata,* "a frigate." This looks like two mistakes in spelling in one word, which we would like to lay at the feet of Charles Lucien Jules Laurent Bonaparte, Prince of Canine and Musignano. The family was Corsican and seemed to have trouble with the spelling of classical Italian as in the name Bonaparte for Buonaparte (see Appendix). **F. tropica** (Gould): BLACK-BELLIED PETREL; Gr. *tropikos,* "tropical," for its range near the equator in the Atlantic Ocean.

FULICA Linnaeus   L. *fulica,* "a coot," perhaps from L. *fuligo,* "soot," from the bird's color. **F. americana** (Gmelin): AMERICAN COOT; ML. *americana,* "of America," to differentiate it from the European species.

FULMARUS Stephens   See Fulmar, the common name, of which this is the Latinized form. **F. glacialis** (Linnaeus): FULMAR–FULMAR PETREL; L. *glacialis,* "frozen, full of ice," descriptive of the habitat.

GALLINULA Brisson   L. *gallinula,* "hen." **G. chloropus** (Linnaeus): COMMON GALLINULE; Gr. *chloros,* "green"; Gr. *pus,* "foot."

GAVIA Forster   L. *gavia,* "gull." Turner identifies the bird as the "se cob or see-gell," which could mean any gull without reference to a particular species, in the same way we use the term today. Some modern dictionaries give the meaning of *gavia* as "sea-mew." As obsolete *mew* meant gull we come up with the same translation. The choice of the generic term *Gavia* for the loons was made by Forster in 1789 and has held sway in American ornithological nomenclature. Just why he chose the Latin word for gull for the loons eludes us. The genus was originally named *Colymbus* by Linnaeus in 1758, a term still in vogue, at least in the latest B.O.U. *Check-list*. It is from Gr. *kolymbis*, "a diving bird." *Colymbus* was formerly used as a generic term for some species of grebes, but has now been superseded. As ornithologists could not reach agreement for a better name, the problem was referred to the International Commission on Zoological Nomenclature in 1956. As the decisions of this body are purely advisory we'll have to wait for future editions of *Check-lists* to see if they are accepted. **G. adamsii** (Gray): YELLOW-BILLED LOON–WHITE-BILLED DIVER; in honor of Edward Adams (see Appendix). **G. arctica** (Linnaeus): ARCTIC LOON–BLACK-THROATED DIVER; Gr. *arktikos*, "northern," from Gr. *arktos*, "bear"; the name given to the constellations in the northern sky and hence meaning northern. **Gavia immer** (Brunnich): COMMON LOON–GREAT NORTHERN DIVER; E. *immer*, "diver," was a common name for the bird, possibly from L. *immersus*, "to plunge into." Related to S. *immer* and *emmer* and Ic. *himbrimi*, "the common loon." **G. stellata** (Pontoppidan): RED-THROATED LOON–RED-THROATED DIVER; L. *stellata*, "starred," referring to the spotty appearance of the back of the bird in winter.

GELOCHELIDON Brehm   Gr. *gelos*, "laughter"; Gr. *chelidon*, "a swallow"; literally "laughing swallow." The explanation as to why Alfred Edmund Brehm, when he felt it incumbent upon himself to change the name of the genus from *Hydrochelidon*, substituted *gelos* for *hydro* seems to be that he thought the bird had a call resembling human laughter, which the European subspecies possibly does. The American form, however, is given to short nasal honkings which suggest derisive disapproval generally heard at such nonliterary pursuits as baseball games where it is termed in the parlance of the diamond "the raspberry" or "the bronx cheer." While it is certain that Herr Brehm, the German zoologist and author of "Das Leben der Vogel," never attended a ball game it is not certain that he ever heard the bird call. **G. nilotica** (Gmelin): GULL-BILLED TERN; L. *nilotica,* "of the Nile," whence came the type specimen.

GEOCOCCYX Wagler Gr. *ge,* "the earth, land"; Gr. *kokkux,* "cuckoo"; literally "land cuckoo." **G. californianus** (Lesson): ROADRUNNER; ML. *californianus* "of California," although found throughout southwestern United States and Mexico.

GEOTHLYPIS Cabanis Gr. *ge,* "the earth"; Gr. *thlypis,* "a kind of finch." **G. trichas** (Linnaeus): YELLOW THROAT; Gr. *trichas,* "a thrush." We have to rate Linnaeus low on this one. **G. poliocephala** Baird: GROUND CHAT; Gr. *polios,* "gray"; Gr. *cephale,* "head"; for the gray head of the male.

GLAUCIDIUM Boie Gr. *glaukidion,* diminutive of "glaring" in reference to the eyes, hence Gr. *glaux,* "an owl," sacred to Athene. **G. brasilianum** (Gmelin): FERRUGINOUS OWL; ML. *brasilianum,* "Brazilian," one of the areas where the bird is found. **G. gnoma** Wagler: PYGMY OWL; L. *gnoma,* "a spirit or sprite"; cf. Gr. *gnome,* "intelligence," tied up with the idea of the owl being wise. This association of the owl with wisdom has come down from classical times. Athene, the goddess of wisdom, was prayerfully referred to as "glaucopis Athene" which may be translated as "gleaming eyed" or "owl-eyed Athene."

GRUS Pallas L. *grus,* "crane." The Latin word is derived from an Indo-European root, *g(w)er,* "to cry out." The ancestral word, perhaps imitative,

spawned in its long history. Gr. *geranos,* "a crane";
Gr. *gerus,* "speech"; L. *garrulus,* "chattering," and
via AS. our crane, crow, croon, and care. **G. americana** (Linnaeus): WHOOPING CRANE; ML. *americana,* "of America." **G. canadensis** (Linnaeus):
SANDHILL CRANE; ML. *canadensis,* "of Canada."

GUIRACA Swainson Coues says, "A Mexican or South
American name of some bird." **G. caerulea** (Linnaeus): BLUE GROSBEAK; L. *caerulea,* "blue."

GYMNOGYPS Lesson Gr. *gymnos,* "naked," in reference
to the naked head; Gr. *gyps,* "vulture." **G. californianus** (Shaw): CALIFORNIA CONDOR; ML. *californianus,* "of California," area where remaining
birds are found.

GYMNORHINUS Wied Gr. *gymnos,* "naked"; Gr. *rhinos,*
"nose"; as the nostrils are large and more exposed
than those of most birds. **G. cyanocephalus** Wied:
PINON JAY; Gr. *cyanos,* "blue"; Gr. *cephale,*
"head"; for the plumage.

HAEMATOPUS Linnaeus Gr. *haima,* genitive *haimatos,*
"blood," referring to the color; Gr. *pous,* "foot";
hence blood-red foot. **H. bachmani** Audubon:
BLACK OYSTERCATCHER; named by Audubon
after his friend, the Reverend John Bachman (see
Appendix). **H. palliatus** Temminck: AMERICAN
OYSTERCATCHER; L. *palliatus,* "wearing a
cloak," from the dark feathering of the back.

HALIAEETUS Savigny Gr. *haliaetos,* "the osprey," literally sea eagle from Gr. *hals, halos,* "the sea"; Gr.
aetos, "eagle." The Greeks wrote the word with an
accent mark over the *e.*" This signified that the letter
had a sound of its own and was not part of a
diphthong. Coues, in translating the word, put a
dieresis over the *e* in the Greek word signifying the
same. Savigny, when he separated this genus from
the falcons, evidently transliterated the *e* in the

Greek word into a diphthong *ae*, an error. The old
A.O.U. *Check-lists* followed this. As diphthongs became passé, the fifth edition of the A.O.U. *Check-
List* transliterates the *ae* diphthong into the letters *a*
and *e*. Thus orthography has reinforced a spelling
error which the law of priority perpetuates. **H. leuco-
cephalus** (Linnaeus): BALD EAGLE; Gr. *leukos,*
"white"; Gr. *kephalos,* "head"; for the white plumage of the head.

HALOCYPTENA Coues Gr. *hals,* "the sea"; Gr. *okus,*
"swift"; Gr. *ptenos,* "winged." **H. microssoma** Coues:
LEAST PETREL: Gr. *mikros,* "small"; Gr. *soma,*
"body"; appropriate for the smallest petrel.

HELMITHEROS Rafinesque A misspelling of Gr. *helmin-
thos,* "a bug"; Gr. *theran,* "to hunt"; hence a
bug-hunter. **H. vermivorus** (Gmelin): WORM-EAT-
ING WARBLER; L. *vermis,* "a worm"; L. *voro,*
"eat."

HESPERIPHONA Bonaparte Gr. *hesperis, hesperios,* two
related meanings: (1) of place, "western," where the
sun goes down; (2) of time, "evening," at sunset. As
a plural noun we have *Hesperides,* "the Daughters of
the Night" who dwelt on the western edge of the
world. Gr. *phone,* "voice or sound." This can be
interpreted as either the song of the west or the song
of the evening. **H. vespertina** (Cooper): EVENING
GROSBEAK; L. *vespertina,* derived from the Greek
and having the same double meaning, "evening" or
"western."

HETEROSCELUS Baird Gr. *heteros,* "different"; Gr.
skelis, "a leg"; i.e., different in the leg from all other
sandpipers in regard to the covering with small
scales. **H. incanus** (Gmelin): WANDERING TAT-
TLER; L. *incanus,* "gray," coloring of upper parts.

HIMANTOPUS Brisson Gr. *himantopous,* "a kind of
water bird"; Gr. *himantos,* "strap"; Gr. *pous,* "foot";
for the resemblance of the leg to a thong. **H.**

mexicanus (Muller): BLACK-NECKED STILT; ML. *mexicanus,* "of Mexico," originally described from a Mexican bird.

HIRUNDO Linnaeus   L. *hirundo,* "a swallow." **H. rustica** Linnaeus: BARN SWALLOW–SWALLOW; L. *rustica,* "rustic," as compared with the House Martin which is more urban where both birds occur in Europe.

HISTRIONICUS Lesson   L. *histrionicus,* "histrionic," from L. *histrio,* "a stage player," referring to its plumage as though dressed up to play a part. The common name suggests the same thing. **H. histrionicus** (Linnaeus): HARLEQUIN DUCK, just some more of the same.

HYDRANASSA Baird   Gr. *hydor,* "water"; Gr. *anassa,* "queen." **H. tricolor** (Muller): LOUISIANA HERON; L. *tri,* "three"; L. *color,* "hue."

HYDROPROGNE Kaup   Gr. *hydor,* "water"; Gr. *Prokne,* who was changed into a swallow, was the daughter of Pandion, hence "water swallow." **H. caspia** (Pallas): CASPIAN TERN; ML. *caspia,* "Caspian Sea," site of the first specimen.

HYLOCHARIS Vieillot   Gr. *hyle,* "a wood"; Gr. *charis,* "beauty." **H. leucotis** (Vieillot): WHITE-EARED HUMMINGBIRD; Gr. *leukos,* "white"; Gr. *ous, otos,* "ear."

HYLOCICHLA Baird   Gr. *hyle,* "forest"; Gr. *cichla,* "a thrush." **H. mustelina** (Gmelin): WOOD THRUSH; L. *mustelina,* "weasel-like," i.e., tawny in color; L. *mustela,* "a weasel."

ICTERIA Vieillot   Gr. *ikteros,* "the jaundice," hence yellow. **I. virens** (Linnaeus): YELLOW-BREASTED CHAT; L. *virens,* "green."

ICTERUS Brisson   Gr. *ikteros,* "jaundice," hence yellowish, and also a greenish-yellow bird, the oriole, which was supposed to cure the disease when it was seen. **I. culcullatus** Swainson: HOODED ORIOLE;

L. *cucallatus,* wearing the *cuculla,* "a hood." It doesn't. **I. galbula** (Linnaeus): NORTHERN ORIOLE; L. *galbula,* "a small yellow bird." The name for the species is Northern Oriole and includes both the Baltimore and Bullock Orioles. **I. galbua bullockii** (Swainson): BULLOCK'S ORIOLE for William Bullock (see Appendix). It is now considered conspecific with **I. galbula. I. graduacauda** (Lesson): BLACK-HEADED ORIOLE; L. *gradus,* "a step"; L. *cauda,* "tail"; the label "graduated tail" is not obvious nor is the tail distinctive as is the head. It would have been more helpful if the original describer of the bird had concentrated on the other end of it. **I. gularis** (Wagler): LICHTENSTEIN'S ORIOLE; L. *gula,* "throat," for the black throat, although this is a feature of all orioles. **I. parisorum** Bonaparte: SCOTT'S ORIOLE; for the Paris brothers (see Appendix). **I. pectoralis** (Wagler): SPOTTED-BREASTED ORIOLE; L. *pectoralis,* "pertaining to the breast." We now have the part of the anatomy which is distinctive in appearance, but not the reason for the name. It could not have been in the interest of brevity, as *maculata pectoralis* would be *anatis jusculum* (duck soup) to any scientist. **I. spurius** (Linnaeus): ORCHARD ORIOLE; L. *spurius,* "spurious," an undeserved name implying an inferior relationship to the Baltimore Oriole, which was also reflected in a former common name "Bastard Baltimore Oriole." Alexander Wilson pointed out that the name resulted from an error in identifying the female Baltimore Oriole as the male of this species.

ICTINIA Vieillot Gr. *iktinos,* "a kite." **I. misisippiensis** (Wilson): MISSISSIPPI KITE. The reason for Wilson's spelling is puzzling as the article on the bird in his *American Ornithology* is entitled "The Mississippi Kite." This spelling of the common name from which the scientific one is derived assures us that the schoolteacher knew how to spell the word. Why drop the double *s* and keep the double *p*? The misspelling irritated Elliott (note the double *l* and *t*) Coues who among other things was a high-handed and aggressive champion of conservative orthography. In his *Key to North American Birds*, 1872, he has *mississippiensis*, as has the first and second edition of the A.O.U. *Check-list* of whose committee Coues was a member. Coues was not on the committee for the third edition, but no change was made. Subsequent editions have gone back to Wilson's original spelling out of deference to the law of priority. Coues, by the way, may have noted the correction in spelling in Thomas H. Brewer's edition (1840) of Wilson's *American Ornithology.*

IRIDOPROCNE Coues   Gr. *iridos,* "of the rainbow," referring to the color; Gr. *Prokne,* who was changed into a "swallow." For the gruesome details, see *Pandion.* **I. bicolor** (Vieillot): TREE SWALLOW; L. *bicolor,* "two-colored."

IXOBRYCHUS Billberg   Gr. *ixos,* "the mistletoe berry, the mistletoe plant or the bird lime made from the berry"; Gr. *brycho,* "to eat, to eat noisily with a belching accompaniment and to roar or bellow." Jordan translates *ixes* as "reed." Eaton gives us Gr. *ixos,* "birdlime," and Gr. *bryxaomai,* "to bellow." MacLeod says, "Billberg who invented the name in 1828 translates *ixos* by L. *arundo,* reed and *brycho* by L. *fremo,* 'to roar or boom': with reference presumably to the old belief that the (common) bittern produced its 'boom' by plunging its bill into a reed and blowing through it." Billberg's Greek is questionable although we surmise his meaning. One wonders whether he ever heard the series of soft coos of the Least Bittern. **I. exilis** (Gmelin): LEAST BITTERN; L. *exilis,* "small."

IXOREUS Bonaparte Gr. *ixos,* "misteltoe"; Gr. *oreos,* "mountain." Although the American bird is not partial to a diet of mistletoe, the plant has been associated from the time of Aristotle with a European thrush which breeds in mountains. **I. naevius** (Gmelin): VARIED THRUSH; L. *naevius,* "spotted or varied," as its plumage is striking for a thrush.

JACANA Brisson A native Brazilian name for the bird. **J. spinosa** (Linnaeus): JACANA; L. *spina,* "thorn"; L. *osus,* "carrying"; for the spur at the bend of the wing.

JUNCO Wagler L. *juncus,* "a rush." A singularly inappropriate name for a genus whose habitat is not among the reeds. **J. aikeni, J. hyemalis,** and **J. oreganus** are now considered conspecific with consequent changes below. **J. hyemalis** (Linnaeus): DARK-EYED JUNCO; L. *hyemalis,* "winter." Linnaeus based the name on Catesby who was familiar only with the bird as a winter visitor. This is now the species name. **J. hyemalis aikeni** Ridgway: WHITE-WINGED JUNCO; for C. E. Aiken (see Appendix). **J. caniceps** (Woodhouse): GRAY-HEADED JUNCO; L. *caniceps,* "gray-headed," for the head color. **J. hyemalis hyemalis.** Formerly of species status with retention of the name SLATE-COLORED JUNCO. **J. hyemalis oreganus** (Townsend): OREGON JUNCO, a place name. **J. phaenotus** Wagler: MEXICAN JUNCO; Gr. *phaios,* "dun-colored"; Gr. notos, "back"; although the back is more reddish chestnut than gray brown. This species now includes the former **J. bairdii** and as enlarged becomes the YELLOW-EYED JUNCO.

LAGOPUS Brisson Gr. *lagopus,* "hare-footed," for the feathering on the tarsi suggesting a resemblance to a rabbit's foot. **L. lagopus** (Linnaeus): WILLOW PTARMIGAN. **L. leucurus** (Richardson): WHITE-TAILED PTARMIGAN; Gr. *leukos,* "white"; Gr.

oura, "tail"; the only ptarmigan without any black in the tail. **L. mutus** (Montini): ROCK PTARMIGAN; L. *mutus,* "silent," probably for the low call.

LAMPORNIS Swainson   Gr. *lampas,* "a lamp"; Gr. *ornis,* "a bird." **L. clemenciae** (Lesson): BLUE-THROATED HUMMINGBIRD; for Clemence Lesson (see Appendix).

LANIUS Linnaeus   L. *lanius,* "a butcher," from its hanging its prey on thorns. **L. excubitor** Linnaeus: NORTHERN SHRIKE–GREAT GREY SHRIKE; L. *excubitor,* "a sentinel," from L. *ex,* "out"; L. *cubo,* "to lie down"; literally, "one who lies down out of doors." MacLeod points out, "for once Linnaeus explains his meaning. 'Accipitres adventates observat et aviculis indicat,' 'it looks out for the approach of hawks and warns little birds.'" No comment from this side of the Atlantic which has the same species as Europe. **L. ludovicianus** Linnaeus: LOGGERHEAD SHRIKE; ML. *ludovicianus,* "of Louisiana." Linnaeus specimen probably a subspecies found in southern United States.

LARUS Linnaeus   Gr. *laros,* L. *larus,* "a gull." **L. argentatus** Pontoppidan: HERRING GULL; L. *argentatus,* "silvery," originally "plated with silver." **L. atricilla** Linnaeus: LAUGHING GULL; L. *ater,* "black"; ML. *cilla,* "tail"; rather a poor term as only the immature have a black band on the tail. **L. californicus** Lawrence: CALIFORNIA GULL; ML. *californicus,* "of California," where the first specimen was obtained. **L. canus** Linnaeus: MEW GULL; L. *canus,* "grayish-white," from the plumage. This is a subspecies of the COMMON GULL of Europe. As it is not common in America except in winter on the Pacific coast, the American Ornithologists' Union decided to bestow on it an American name. **L. delawarensis** Ord: RING-BILLED GULL; "of the

Delaware" referring to the river below Philadelphia where it was first found. **L. glaucescens** Naumann: GLAUCOUS-WINGED GULL; L. *-escens,* "somewhat like," referring to the Glaucous Gull which it resembles except for darker primaries. **L. glaucoides** Meyer: ICELAND GULL; Gr. *glaukos,* "silvery"; Gr. *-oides,* suffix meaning "like." The name means "like the Glaucous Gull" which formerly had the scientific name *L. glaucus.* Although smaller, it resembles it. **L. heermanni** Cassin: HEERMANN'S GULL; for A. L. Heermann (see Appendix). **L. hyperboreus** Gunnerus: GLAUGOUS GULL; Gr. *hyperboreos,* "beyond the north wind," the extreme north, named for Boreas, the god of the north wind. Poor Boreas met with no encouragement from the nymph, Orithyia, as his inability to breathe gently, let alone sigh, did not fit her maidenly idea of a lover. So, being a Greek god, and not overly patient, he carried her off. Things did not work out too badly as the union was blessed with two superb winged warriors, Zetes and Calais, who on the Argonautic foray did a good job on those monstrous birds, the Harpies. **L. marinus** Linnaeus: GREAT BLACK-BACKED GULL–GREATER BLACK-BACKED GULL; L. *marinus,* "marine." **L. minutus** Pallas: LITTLE GULL; L. *minutus,* "very small," and it is for a gull. **L. occidentalis,** Audubon: WESTERN GULL; L. *occidentalis,* "western." **L. philadelphia** Ord: BONAPARTE'S GULL; for Philadelphia, the city near which the type specimen was found. **L. pipixcan** Wagler: FRANKLIN'S GULL; *pipican,* an Aztec word whose meaning Wagler did not reveal if he knew it. **L. ridibundus** (Linnaeus): BLACK-HEADED GULL; L. *rid,* "laugh"; L. *abundo,* "overflow." W. H. Hudson says "his notes . . . often sound like laughter"; hence laughing gull and the species name **ribundus. L. thayeri** Brooks: THAYER'S GULL, for John Eliot Thayer (see Appendix).

LATERALLUS Gray   L. *lateo,* "lurk or hide"; ML. *rallus,* "a rail"; from F. *rale,* "a rail," which also means "a rattle in the throat" and possibly suggested the name of the bird for its rattle-like calls in the marsh, where the bird is more often heard than seen. **L. jamaicensis** (Gmelin): BLACK RAIL; ML. *jamaicensis,* "of Jamaica," first specimen possibly a winter migrant.

LEPTOTILA Swainson   Gr. *leptos,* "thin"; Gr. *ptilon,* "feather"; from the shape of the first primary for which Coues called them "pinwing doves." **L. verreauxi** (Bonaparte): WHITE-FRONTED DOVE; for the Verreaux brothers (see Appendix).

LEUCOSTICTE Swainson   Gr. *leucos,* "white"; Gr. *sticte,* "varied"; for the muted white plumage. **L. atrata** Ridgway: BLACK-ROSY FINCH; L. *atrata,* "blackened," for the dominant color of the male's plumage. **L. australis** Ridgway: BROWN-CAPPED ROSY FINCH; L. *australis,* "southern," for its range, which is to the south of the other rosy finches. **L. tephrocotis** (Swainson): GRAY-CROWNED ROSY FINCH; Gr. *tephros,* "gray"; Gr. *kotis,* "top and back of the head."

LIMNODROMUS Wied   Gr. *limne,* "marsh"; Gr. *dromos,* "running." Although not given to running, the birds are marsh feeders. **L. griseus,** (Gmelin): SHORT-BILLED DOWITCHER – RED - BREASTED SNIPE; ML. *griseus,* "gray," coined from HG. *gris* or F. *gris,* "gray." Restored to species status after 1950 explorations supplied more accurate knowledge of the breeding range. **L. scolopaceus** (Say): LONG-BILLED DOWITCHER; Gr. *scolopax,* "the woodcock," of Aristotle, from Gr. *skolops,* "anything pointed," for the bill. So "a woodcock that courses about the marsh" is apt enough.

LIMNOTHLYPIS Stone   Gr. *limne,* "a marsh"; Gr. *thlypis,* "a kind of finch." **L. swainsonii** (Audubon): SWAIN-SON'S WARBLER for William Swainson (see Appendix).

LIMOSA Brisson   L. *limosa,* "muddy," from the habitat. **L. fedoa** (Linnaeus): MARBLED GODWIT. The origin of *fedoa* is unknown. Coues says, "The word goes back to Turner (1544) 'Anglorum goduuittam, sive fedoam', and has been variously applied to godwits and some other birds before and since Linnaeus named this species, *Scolopax fedoa* in 1758." Newton regards it as a Latinized form of some English name of the European godwit, ". . . now apparently lost beyond recovery." **L. haemastica** (Linnaeus): HUDSONIAN GODWIT; Gr. *haimastidos,* "blood-red," for the color of the breast in breeding plumage. **L. lapponica** (Linnaeus): BAR-TAILED GODWIT; ML. *lapponica,* "of Lapland," one of its breeding areas and the site of the type specimen.

LOBIPES Cuvier   L. *lobus,* "lobe"; L. *pes,* "foot." **L. lobatus** (Linnaeus): NORTHERN PHALAROPE–RED-NECKED PHALAROPE; L. *lobatus,* "lobed," so we have the lobed lobe-foot.

LOPHODYTES Reichenbach   Gr. *lophos,* "crest"; Gr. *dytes,* "a diver." **L. cucullatus,** (Linnaeus): HOODED MERGANSER; L. *cucullata,* "hooded."

LOPHORTYX Bonaparte   Gr. *lophos,* "a crest"; Gr. *ortyx,* "a quail." **L. californicus** (Shaw): CALIFORNIA QUAIL; ML. *californicus,* "of California," for the range. **L. gambelii** Gambel: GAMBEL'S QUAIL; for William Gambel (see Appendix).

LOXIA Linnaeus   Gr. *loxos,* "crooked," for the shape of the bill. **L. curvirostra** Linnaeus: RED CROSSBILL–CROSSBILL. L. *curvirostra,* "curved bill," for the shape of the bill, which must have impressed Linnaeus to name it the crooked curved bill in two

languages. **L. leucoptera** (Gmelin): WHITE-
WINGED CROSSBILL–TWO-BARRED CROSS-
BILL; Gr. *leucos,* "white"; Gr. *pteron,* "wing"; for
the white wing bars.

LUNDA Pallas Scandinavian, *lunde,* "a puffin." Possibly
the island of Lundy in the Bristol Channel is named
after this bird. **L. cirrhata** (Pallas): TUFTED PUF-
FIN; *L. cirratus,* "curled," literally "curly locks."
The spelling *cirrh* is due to the mistaken notion that
there was a Greek word with such a stem.

LUSCINIA Forster L. *luscinia,* "a nightingale." **L. svecica** (Linnaeus): BLUETHROAT; L. *svecica,* "Sweden," for its breeding range.

MEGACERYLE Kaup Gr. *megas,* "great"; Gr. *kerylos,* "a
sea bird," "the kingfisher." **M. alcyon** (Linnaeus):
BELTED KINGFISHER; Gr. *alkyon,* "the
kingfisher," after Alcyon who so grieved after her
drowned husband, Ceryx, that the gods changed
them both into kingfishers. Pliny says, "They breed
in winter, at the season called the halcyon days,
wherein the sea is calm." **M. torquata** (Linnaeus):
RINGED KINGFISHER; L. *torquatus,* "wearing a
necklace," for its white collar.

MELANERPES Swainson Gr. *melas,* "black"; Gr. *herpes,*
"a creeper." **M. erythrocephalus** (Linnaeus): RED-
HEADED WOODPECKER; Gr. *erythros,* "red";
Gr. *cephale,* "head." **M. formicivorus** (Swainson):
ACORN WOODPECKER; L. *formica,* "an ant"; L.
voro, "devour." Acorn-devourer might be more appropriate although ants are also part of the bird's
diet.

MELANITTA Boie Gr. *melas,* "black"; *nitta,* appears to
be a misspelling for Gr. *netta,* "duck." **M. deglandi**
(Bonaparte): WHITE-WINGED SCOTER; for C.
D. Degland (see Appendix). **M. nigra** (Linnaeus):
BLACK SCOTER; L. *nigra,* "black," for the color of

the plumage. **M. perspicillata** (Linnaeus): SURF
SCOTER; L. *perspicillata,* "conspicuous."

MELEAGRIS Linnaeus   Gr. and L. *meleagris,* "a Guinea-
fowl," apparently from the vague resemblance of the
American turkey to the African Guinea-fowl. **M.
gallopava** (Linnaeus): TURKEY; L. *gallus,* "a
cock"; L. *pavo,* "a pea fowl"; thus we have an
American bird named for both an African and an
Asiatic bird.

MELOSPIZA Baird   Gr. *melos,* "song"; Gr. *spiza,* "a
finch." **M. georgiana** (Latham): SWAMP SPAR-
ROW; ML. *georgiana,* "of Georgia," for King
George II of England. The type specimen was
collected in Georgia in 1790. **M. lincolnii** (Audubon): LINCOLN'S SPARROW for Thomas Lincoln
(see Appendix). **M. melodia** (Wilson): SONG SPAR-
ROW; Gr. and L. *melodia,* "a pleasant song," the
taxonomists' favorite with thirty-one subspecies so
far described. California, where the aim seems to be
to have one for each county, is in the lead with
thirteen subspecies.

MERGUS Linnaeus   L. *mergus,* "a diver," name of a bird
mentioned by Pliny. **M. merganser** Linnaeus: COM-
MON MERGANSER; LL. *mergus,* "diver"; L.
anser, "goose." **M. serrator** Linnaeus: RED-
BREASTED MERGANSER; L. *serrator,* "a sawer,"
referring to the serrated bill.

MICRATHENE Coues   Gr. *micros,* "small"; Gr. *Athene,*
"the goddess of wisdom," to whom the owl was
sacred. **M. whitneyi** (Cooper): ELF OWL; for Josiah
Dwight Whitney (see Appendix).

MICROPALAMA Baird   Gr. *mikros,* "small"; Gr. *palame,*
"a web"; for small webs between front toes. **M.
himantopus** (Bonaparte): STILT SANDPIPER; Gr.
himantos, "a leather strap or thong"; Gr. *pous,*
"foot"; for the resemblance of the long legs to
thongs.

MIMUS Boie L. *mimus,* "a mimic." **M. polyglottos** (Linnaeus): MOCKINGBIRD; Gr. *poly,* "many"; Gr. *glotta,* "tongue"; alluding to the bird's varied mimicry.

MNIOTILTA Vieillot Gr. *mnion,* "moss"; Gr. *tiltos,* "plucked"; possibly due to the erroneous idea that moss is used habitually in the nest. **M. varia** (Linnaeus): BLACK-AND-WHITE WARBLER; L. *varia,* "varied," for the plumage.

MOLOTHRUS Swainson Gr. *molothrus,* an error for *molobros,* "a parasite or greedy person." **M. ater** (Boddaert): BROWN-HEADED COWBIRD; L. *ater,* "black," for the color of the plumage.

MORUS Vieillot Gr. *moros,* "stupid." SULA in B.O.U. *Check-list.* **M. bassanus** (Linnaeus): GANNET. The gannet has finally come to rest in the genus *Morus,* after sojourns in *Pelecanus* and *Sula.* Bassanus refers to the Bass Rocks, a breeding place of the birds in the Firth of Forth.

MOTACILLA Linnaeus L. *motus,* "moving"; ML. *cilla,* "tail"; see Bombycilla. **M. alba** Linnaeus: WHITE WAGTAIL; L. *alba,* "white," for the predominantly white plumage. **M. flava** Linnaeus: YELLOW WAGTAIL; L. *flavus,* "yellow," for the yellow underparts.

MUSCIVORA Lacepede L. *musca,* "a fly"; L. *voro,* "eat." **M. forficata** (Gmelin): SCISSOR-TAILED FLYCATCHER; ML. *forficata,* "forked" from L. *forfic,* "scissors." **M. tyrannus** (Linnaeus): FORK-TAILED FLYCATCHER; L. *tyrannus,* "a tyrant."

MYADESTES Swainson Gr. *myia,* Attic Gr. *mya,* "a fly"; Gr. *edestes,* "anteater." **M. townsendi** (Audubon): TOWNSEND'S SOLITAIRE; for John K. Townsend (see Appendix).

MYCTERIA Linnaeus Gr. *mykter,* "a nose." **M. americana** (Linnaeus): WOOD IBIS; ML. *americana,* "American" i.e., Western Hemisphere.

MYIARCHUS Cabanis Gr. *myia,* "a fly"; Gr. *archos,* "a

ruler." **M. cinerascens** (Lawrence): ASH-THROATED FLYCATCHER; L. *cinerascens,* "ashy." **M. crinitus** (Linnaeus): GREAT CRESTED FLYCATCHER; L. *crinitus,* "hairy," which can be stretched a bit to mean "crested." **M. tuberculifer** (Lafresnaye and D'Orbigny): OLIVACEOUS FLY-CATCHER; L. *tuberculum,* diminutive of *tuber,* "a lump" (a knob); L. *fero,* "to bear or carry." After studying the name of this bird from every side, the best we can come up with is "a carrier of little lumps." A carrier of a little knob most likely refers to the bird's small crest. **M. tyrannulus** (Muller): WIED'S CRESTED FLYCATCHER; ML. *tyrannulus,* "little tyrant."

MYIODYNASTES Bonaparte   Gr. *myia,* "a fly"; Gr. *dynastes,* "a ruler." **M. luteiventris** Sclater: SULPHUR-BELLIED FLYCATCHER; L. *luteus,* "yellow"; L. *venter,* "belly"; for the light gray-olive underparts which are heavily streaked.

MYIOPSITTA Bonaparte   Gr. *myia,* "a fly"; Gr. *psittake,* "a parrot." **M. monachus** Boddaert: MONK PARA-KEET; Gr. *monachos,* "solitary," to L. *monas, monacis,* "a monk." Originally applied to the solitary religious hermit, the word changed its meaning to apply to members of religious communities and possibly to this bird, as it flies about in small flocks and nests in colonies.

NUCIFRAGA Brisson   L. *nux, nucis,* "nut"; L. *frango,* "break." **N. columbiana,** (Wilson): CLARK'S NUT-CRACKER; ML. *columbiana,* for the Columbia River area, as the bird was first discovered along the Clearwater River which flows into the Columbia.

NUMENIUS Brisson   Gr. *neos,* "new"; Gr. *mene,* "moon"; for the resemblance of the shape of the bill to the new moon. **N. americanus** Bechstein: LONG-BILLED CURLEW; ML. *americanus,* "of America." **N. borealis** (Forster): ESKIMO CURLEW; L.

borealis, "northern." **N. phaeopus** (Linnaeus): WHIMBREL; Gr. *phaios,* "dusky"; Gr. *pous,* "foot"; for the grayish feet and legs. **N. tahitiensis** (Gmelin): BRISTLE-THIGHED CURLEW; ML. *tahitiensis,* "of Tahiti," where it was first found by Sir James Banks, a naturalist who accompanied Captain James Cook round the world (1768–1771).

NUTTALLORNIS Ridgway For Thomas Nuttall (see Appendix); Gr. *ornis,* "bird." **N. borealis** (Swainson): OLIVE-SIDED FLYCATCHER; L. *borealis,* "northern," for its breeding range in the northern coniferous woods.

NYCTANASSA Stegneger Gr. *nyctos,* "night"; Gr. *anassa,* "a lady, a queen." **N. violacea** (Linnaeus): YELLOW-CROWNED NIGHT HERON; L. *viola,* "the violet," for the color of the bird's back, which is stretching it a bit as the bird has an overall gray appearance.

NYCTEA Stephens Gr. *nycteus,* "nocturnal." Most owls are, but not this one. **N. scandiaca** (Linnaeus): SNOWY OWL; L. *scandia,* an ancient name for the southern end of Sweden, although the breeding range is in the north in both hemispheres.

NYCTICORAX Forster Gr. *nyx, nyctos,* "night"; Gr. *corax,* "a crow." **N. nycticorax** (Linnaeus): BLACK-CROWNED NIGHT HERON–NIGHT HERON. The repetition of the name is the responsibility of Forster and not Linnaeus, who first termed the bird *Ardea nycticorax.* The bird's squawk in the darkness overhead very likely suggested the name to Linnaeus.

NYCTIDROMUS Gould Gr. *nyx, nyctos,* "night"; Gr. *dromos,* "running or coursing"; i.e., a night flyer. **N. albicollis** (Gmelin): PAURAQUE; L. *albus,* "white"; L. *collum,* "neck"; for the white collar of feathers.

OCEANITES Keyserling and Blassius The Oceanides or Oceanites were, according to the Greeks, sea nymphs, the daughters of Oceanus and Tethys. According to Apollodorus they numbered three thousand, while Hesiod could count only forty-one. Both, however, agree that they spent their lives at sea, as, for the most part, do the petrels. **O. oceanicus** (Kuhl): WILSON'S PETREL; Gr. *Oceanes* (see above and *Oceanodroma*).

OCEANODROMA Reichenbach   L. *oceanus,* from Gr. *Okeanos,* "the ocean"; the name, according to Homer, of the great river that encompasses the earth and also the name of the god who rules this domain. Gr. *droma,* "running or coursing." **O. castro** (Harcourt): HARCOURT'S PETREL–MADEIRAN PETREL; from *Roque* (rook) de *castro,* the bird's name, according to Harcourt, in the Dezerta Islands, Madeira. He first described the bird in his *Sketch of Madeira,* 1851. **O. furcata** (Gmelin): FORK-TAILED PETREL; L. *furcatus,* "forked," for the shape of the tail. **O. homochroa** (Coues): ASHY PETREL; Gr. *homos,* "same"; Gr. *chroa,* "color"; for the uniform coloration. **O. leucorhoa** (Vieillot): LEACH'S PETREL; Gr. *leukos,* "white"; Gr. *orrhos,* "the rump"; for the white upper tail coverts. **O. melania** (Bonaparte): BLACK PETREL; Gr. *melania,* "black," for its plumage. **O. tethys** (Bonaparte): GALAPAGOS PETREL; Gr. *Tethys,* wife of Okeanos, who rules the sea with her husband.

OENANTHE Vieillot   Gr. *oinanthe,* "a bird," possibly the wheatear and also the name of "a kind of plant." It seems that the bird appeared at the time of the plant's blossoming. Gr. *oinas,* "wild pigeon"; Gr. *anthos,* "flower"; to the Greeks the bird seems to have been called "the flower bird." **O. oenanthe** (Linnaeus): WHEATEAR.

OLOR (CYGNUS B.O.U. *Check-list*) Wagler: L. *olor,* "swan." **O. buccinator** (Richardson): TRUMPETER SWAN; L. *bucinator,* "a trumpeter." **O. columbianus**

(Ord): WHISTLING SWAN; ML. *columbianus,* refers to the great narrows of the Columbia River where Lewis and Clark obtained the specimen described by Ord. **O. cygnus** (Linnaeus): WHOOPER SWAN; L. *cygnus,* "a swan."

OPORORNIS Baird Gr. *opera,* "end of summer"; Gr. *ornis,* "bird." **O. agilis** (Wilson): CONNECTICUT WARBLER; L. *agilis,* "active." **O. formosus** (Wilson): KENTUCKY WARBLER; L. *formosus,* "beautiful." **O. philadelphia** (Wilson): MOURNING WARBLER; for the city near which Wilson found the bird. **O. tolmiei** (Townsend): MACGILLIVRAY'S WARBLER; for W. F. Tolmie (see Appendix).

OREORTYX Baird Gr. *oros, orees,* "mountain"; Gr. *ortyx,* "quail." **O. pictus** (Douglas): MOUNTAIN QUAIL; L. *pictus,* "painted," as its plumage appears to be the work of an artist in color.

OREOSCOPTES Baird Gr. *oros,* "a mountain"; Gr. *scoptes,* "a mimic." **O. montanus** (Townsend): SAGE THRASHER; L. *montanus,* "mountain." Although found in the high plains of the Rocky Mountains, it is essentially a desert bird.

ORTALIS (Merram) Gr. *ortalis,* "a young bird." **O. vetula,** (Wagler): CHACHALACA; L. *vetula,* "a little old woman," most likely in reference to the bird's constant calling.

OTUS Pennant Gr. *otos,* "an eared owl." Let us quote Aristotle, "The Otus is like a Noctua (Night Owl), furnished with little tufts sticking out near the ears, whence it has got its name, as though one should say eared." Gr. *ous, otos,* "ear." **O. asio** (Linnaeus): SCREECH OWL; L. *asio,* "a king of horned owl." **O. flammeolus** (Kaup): FLAMMULATED OWL; L. *flammeus,* "flame-colored," plus the diminutive suffix *-eus* for its reddish color. **O. trichopsis** (Wag-

ler): WHISKERED OWL; Gr. *thrix, trichos,* "hair";
Gr. *opsis,* "appearance"; for its long whiskers.

OXYURA Bonaparte   Gr. *oxys,* "sharp"; Gr. *oura,* "tail."
O. dominica (Linnaeus): MASKED DUCK; ML.
dominica; Dominican Republic where the first specimen was found. **O. jamaicensis** (Gmelin): RUDDY
DUCK; ML. *jamaicensis,* "of Jamaica," the source
of the bird originally described by Latham as the
Jamaican Shoveler in 1785.

PAGOPHILA Kaup   Gr. *pagos,* "frost"; Gr. *phileo,*
"love"; hence frost lover for its main range in the
north. **P. eburnia** (Phipps): IVORY GULL; L.
eburneus, "ivory-colored," for the white adult plumage.

PANDION Savigny   The law of priority in nomenclature
has an embarrassing side effect, to wit, it perpetuates
not only initial errors of a minor sort as in spelling,
but also embalms errors of fact and fancy. For
example, Savigny quite justifiably moved the osprey
from the genus *Falco* where Linnaeus had placed it
to a new genus of his own creation which, in a flight
of mythological exuberance, he called *Pandion.* If he
had checked the delightful Greek myth, he would
have found birds in it but that Pandion was not
directly involved. Pandion, the king of Athens, had
two daughters, Procne and Philomel. The former
married Tereus, king of Thrace. After a son, Itylus,
was born, Tereus decided that Philomel was the
more attractive sister but was given pause by his
awareness of the Pandion family's high regard for
the sanctity of marriage and also their rather fervid
clannishness. Not wishing to go to extremes, he cut
out his wife's tongue and let it be known that she was
dead. After an appropriate interval of mourning, he
married Philomel. But he had underestimated
Procne. Although she could not speak, she, like most

of the Greek girls, could weave. So she wove the story into a web which was given to Philomel. The two sisters did not cry and mope, but went into action which they considered adequately vengeful. They served, properly roasted and seasoned, the baby, Itylus, as part of a full-course dinner to Tereus, the father and erring husband. Although the gods, given to indulge in phallic frolics themselves, were quite tolerant with human amatory escapades, they were angry with the lengths to which this family group had gone. For penance, they transformed Procne into a swallow and Philomel into a nightingale. This in itself would not have been so bad except for the fact that they had continuously to lament their sin while being pursued by Tereus in the form of a hawk. The chase was to last eternally. Thus it seems that Savigny made two errors. First, if he wished to commemorate the mythological hawk, he should have named his new genus *Tereus,* as it was he who was metamorphosed and not Pandion. Second, it is rather stretching things a bit ornithologically to have an osprey that preys on fish chasing a swallow and a nightingale. Another version of this story is that Philomel was the sister who had her tongue removed. This is obviously the wrong version as Philomel in being changed into a nightingale could not possibly be a good singer without a tongue. She could only twitter like a swallow. Having faith in the god's omniscience, which surely included a familiarity with the songs of birds, we can be certain that the first version of the myth is the authentic one. Gr. *Pandion* possibly from Gr. *pan,* "all"; Gr. *dio(n),* "god." **P. haliaetus** (Linnaeus): OSPREY; here we have the correct spelling. See *Haliaeetus.*

PARABUTEO Ridgway Gr. *para,* "beside," a prefix

meaning near or parallel, plus L. *buteo,* "a kind of hawk." The meaning here is that this genus is closely related to the genus, *Buteo.* **P. unicinctus** (Temminck): HARRIS' HAWK; L. *uni-* "once"; L. *cinctus,* "girdled"; possibly referring to the single broad band on the tail.

PARULA Bonaparte L. *parus,* "a titmouse"; L. *-ula,* "little," a diminutive suffix, hence "little titmouse." **P. americana** (Linnaeus): PARULA WARBLER; ML. *americana,* "American." **P. pitiayuma** (Vieillot): OLIVE–BACKED WARBLER; *pitiayumi,* possibly a South American word for the fiber used in the nest.

PARUS Linnaeus L. *parus,* "a titmouse." **P. atricapillus** Linnaeus: BLACK-CAPPED CHICKADEE; L. *ater,* "black"; L. *capillus,* "hair of the head." **P. atricristatus** Cassin: BLACK-CRESTED TITMOUSE; L. *ater,* "black"; L. *cristatus,* "crested." **P. bicolor** Linnaeus: TUFTED TITMOUSE; L. *bi*(s), "two"; L. *color,* "color"; because the buffy tint on the sides gives at least his underparts two colors. **P. carolinensis** Audubon: CAROLINA CHICKADEE; ML. *carolinensis,* "of Carolina," a more southern bird than the Black-capped. **P. cinctus** Boddaert: GRAY-HEADED CHICKADEE; L. *cinctus,* "girdled"; as the bird is not banded in any way, the meaning is not clear. **P. gambeli** Ridgway: MOUNTAIN CHICKADEE; for William Gambel (see Appendix). **P. hudsonicus** Forster: BOREAL CHICKADEE; ML. *hudsonicus,* of Hudson's Bay, alluding to its northern range. **P. inornatus** Gambel: PLAIN TITMOUSE; L. *inornatus,* "unadorned." In contrast to "bicolor" above, "inornatus" is a uniformly gray bird. **P. rufescens** Townsend: CHESTNUT-BACKED CHICKADEE; L. *rufescens,* "reddish" for the color of the back. **P. sclateri** Kleinschmidt: MEXICAN CHICKADEE; for P. L.

Sclater (see Appendix). **P. wollweberi** (Bonaparte): BRIDLED TITMOUSE; for Wollweber (see Appendix).

PASSER Brisson L. *passer,* "sparrow." **P. domesticus** (Linnaeus): HOUSE SPARROW; L. *domesticus,* "house." The species that the Romans called *passer.* **P. montanus** (Linnaeus): EUROPEAN TREE SPARROW; L. *montanus,* "mountain," although the bird is not partial to mountains.

PASSERCULUS Bonaparte L. *passerculus,* "little sparrow." **P. sandwichensis princeps** Maynard: IPSWICH SPARROW; L. *princeps,* "chief." As it is not so in size, color or voice, it is difficult to understand the reason for the term. However, the closely related species below *is* a small sparrow and no doubt *princeps* refers to its size as compared to its near relative. This is not too weighty a problem as the bird is now relegated to a race of the following species and may be disappearing as Sable Island on which it breeds seems to be gradually eroding into the ocean. **P. sandwichensis** (Gmelin): SAVANNAH SPARROW; ML. *sandwichensis,* "of Sandwich Bay" in the Aleutians whence the first specimen.

PASSERELLA Swainson L. *passer,* "sparrow"; L. *-ella,* "little"; hence "little sparrow" for the genus which has one of our largest sparrows. **P. iliaca** (Merrem): FOX SPARROW; L. *iliacus,* "relating to colic," from L. *ilia,* "the groin" or "lower intestine," the anatomical seat of the Roman bellyache. It is remotely possible that the taxonomist who named the bird had in mind "flanks," as this portion of the bird's anatomy is conspicuously streaked.

PASSERINA Vieillot L. *passerina,* "sparrow-like." **P. amoena** (Say): LAZULI BUNTING; L. *amoena,* "lovely." **P. ciris** (Linnaeus): PAINTED BUNTING; Gr. *ciris,* name of the bird into which Scylla, the daughter of Nisus, king of Megara, was trans-

formed. Minos, the king of Crete, had beseiged
Megara for six months to no avail. This was because
the city was unconquerable as long as a purple lock
of hair remained intact upon the head of Nisus.
Scylla, who had plenty of time on her hands, whiled
it away by looking over the enemy encampment
from one of her father's battlements. Her interest
gradually became concentrated on one individual,
King Minos, and then quite rapidly evolved into an
obsessive fixation. What would please Minos more
than conquering the city? And most surely he would
be most pleased with anyone who would make this
possible. So the lovelorn damsel clipped the purple
lock from her father's sleeping head and in the dead
of night made her way to Minos' tent and demanded
an audience. Was Minos gratified? Enough to con-
quer the city, yes, but to reward Scylla? No. He was
overcome with moral revulsion, spurned the maiden
and took off in his fleet in high dudgeon for Crete.
Scylla, being a girl of spirit and now having no place
to go, followed the fleet into the sea and grabbed
hold of a rudder. Her father, who had now been
changed into a sea eagle, spied her and beset her
with bill and claw. She lost her hold and was just
about to disappear beneath the waves when the gods
who had all the time been watching the drama got
into the act. They changed Scylla into a ciris, a bird
which has not been identified, although it is still
pursued upon sight by the sea eagle. The reason
Linnaeus decided to name the painted bunting after
the heroine is no doubt because of its purple head,
but, if so, he seems to have been confused about who
had the purple lock. As for the gods getting into the
act, it shows their understanding of the strength of
passionate love. **P. cyanea** (Linnaeus): INDIGO
BUNTING; Gr. *cyaneos,* "dark blue," for the male's
plumage. **P. versicolor** (Bonaparte): VARIED

BUNTING; L. *versus,* "change"; L. *color,* "hue," "tint."

PEDIOECETES Baird   Gr. *pedion,* "a plain"; Gr. *oiketes,* "inhabiting." **P. phasianellus** (Linnaeus): SHARP-TAILED GROUSE; Gr. *phasianos,* "a pheasant," from the river Phasis in Colchis, which flows into the Black Sea. Thus we see that naming a bird for its range was done by the ancient Greeks. L. *-ellus,* "little"; the grouse is somewhat like a small pheasant.

PELAGODROMA Reichenbach   Gr. *pelagos,* "the sea"; Gr. *dromos,* "running." **P. marina** (Latham): WHITE-FACED PETREL; L. *marinus,* "of the sea."

PELECANUS Linnaeus   L. *pelicanus,* from Gr. *pelekan,* "woodpecker," referring to the bird's pecking habits and also "pelican." The name applied to birds notable for their bills, as W. Turner writing in 1544 used Pelicanus as a synonym for the Shovelard or Spoonbill. **P. erythrorhyncos** Gmelin: WHITE PELICAN; Gr. *erythros,* "red"; Gr. *rhyncos,* "beak." At least it is of an orange color. **P. occidentalis** Linnaeus: BROWN PELICAN; L. *occidentalis,* "western." As it is a New World species.

PERDIX Brisson   L. *perdix,* "a partridge," mentioned by Pliny. **P. perdix** (Linnaeus): GRAY PARTRIDGE. Perdix was apprenticed to his uncle, Daedalus, an exceptionally skilled craftsman. After contemplating the spine of a fish, Perdix proved himself to be an apt pupil by inventing the saw. When he followed this by inventing the compass, Daedalus, overcome with envy, seized the opportunity to push his talented nephew from a high tower. Minerva, who was partial to inventiveness, happened to witness this episode. Before Perdix could touch the ground, she changed him into a perdix and now, clothed in feathers but still retaining his name, he flew away unscathed. In spite of the fact that this is recorded in Ovid's *Metamorphoses*, MacLeod suggests that the youth may have been named for the bird rather than vice versa.

PERISOREUS Bonaparte Gr. *perisoreuo*, "to heap up," alluding to the bird's acquisitive habits. **P. canadensis** (Linnaeus): GRAY JAY; ML. *canadensis*, "Canadian," for the range.

PETROCHELIDON Cabanis Gr. *petra*, "a rock"; Gr. *chelidon*, "a swallow"; nesting sites are often on rocky cliffs. **P. fulva** (Vieillot): CAVE SWALLOW; L. *fulvus*, "tawny," for the buffy breast. **P. pyrrhonota** (Vieillot): CLIFF SWALLOW; Gr. *pyrrhos*, "flame-colored"; Gr. *notos*, "back"; for the orange rump.

PEUCEDRAMUS Henshaw Gr. *peuce*, "pine"; Gr. *dram*(ema), "a running"; for the habitat in the pine woods. **P. taeniatus** (DuBus): OLIVE WARBLER; ML. *taeniatus*, "striped," referring to the black eye stripe of the male.

PHAETON Linnaeus Gr. *Phaeton*, "Phaeton," the son of Phoebus, was allowed by his father, whom he wore down by his whining begging, to drive the chariot of the sun. His incapacity to control the flight of the horses almost resulted in the burning of both heaven and earth. Just why such superb flyers as the tropic birds should have to bear the name of one most noted for ineptness in the air can be explained by giving credit to Linnaeus for a wry sense of humor. **P. aethereus** Linnaeus: RED-BILLED TROPIC BIRD; Gr. *aether*, "the upper air." **P. lepturus** Daudin: WHITE-TAILED TROPIC BIRD; Gr. *leptos*, "thin"; Gr. *oura*, "tail." **P. rubicauda** Boddaert: RED-TAILED TROPIC BIRD; L. *ruber*, "red"; L. *cauda*, "tail."

PHAINOPEPLA Baird Gr. *phainos*, "shining"; Gr. *peplos*, "robe"; for the glitter of the plumage. **P. nitens** (Swainson): PHAINOPEPLA; L. *nitens,* "shining," emphasizing the bright reflecting plumage.

PHALACROCORAX Brisson L. *phalacrorax,* "cormorant." The word was used by Pliny and means "bald crow." Gr. *phalakros,* "bald"; Gr. *korax,* "crow or raven." "Bald" probably refers to the white-headed appearance of the common European subspecies, P. *carbo sinensis,* which probably acquired its name in the same way our bald eagle did. To those familiar with land birds, it looked like a balding, white-headed, ocean-going crow. **P. auritus** (Lesson): DOUBLE-CRESTED CORMORANT; L. *auritus,* "eared," for the inconspicuous crest above the eyes. **P. carbo** (Linnaeus): GREAT CORMORANT–CORMO-RANT; L. *carbo,* "charcoal," for the color of the bird. **P. olivaceus** (Humbolt): OLIVACEOUS COR-MORANT; L. *oliva,* "an olive," for the color. **P. pelagicus** Pallas: PELAGIC CORMORANT; Gr. *pelagos,* "the sea." **P. pencillatus** (Brandt): BRANDT'S CORMORANT; L. *pencillus,* "a painter's brush" (a pencil of hairs), hence *pencillatus,* "pencil-like," i.e., ending in a tuft for the crest of feathers. **P. urile** (Gmelin): RED-FACED CORMO-RANT; *urile,* possibly a Russian place name of or in the area of the Kurile Islands.

PHALAENOPTILUS Ridgway Gr. *phalaina,* "a moth"; Gr. *ptilon,* "a feather"; for the light texture of the wing feathers. **P. nuttalli** (Audubon): POOR-WILL; for Thomas Nuttall (see Appendix).

PHALAROPUS Brisson Gr. *phalaris,* "a coot"; Gr. *pous,* "foot"; hence "coot-footed" for the lobes on the toes like those of a coot. **P. fulicarius** (Linnaeus): RED PHALAROPE–GRAY PHALAROPE; L. *fuliga,* "a coot," as the bird's feet are coot-like.

PHASIANUS Linnaeus Gr. *phasianos,* "a pheasant," for the river Phasis in Colchis, the area where the bird ranged. **P. colchicus** Linnaeus: RING-NECKED PHEASANT; ML. *colchicus;* a double locality name.

PHEUCTICUS Reichenbach Probably Gr. *phycticos,* "painted with cosmetics," as if the male's breast was rouged. **P. ludovicianus** (Linnaeus): ROSE-BREASTED GROSBEAK; ML. *ludovicianus,* "of Louisiana," the locality of the original specimen. **P. melanocephalus** (Swainson): BLACK-HEADED GROSBEAK; Gr. *melanos,* "black"; Gr. *cephale,* "head"; for the color of the male's head.

PHILACTE Bannister Gr. *philos,* "loving"; Gr. *akte,* "sea coast." **P. canagica** (Sewastianov): EMPEROR GOOSE; ML. *canagica,* "Kanaga Island," one of the Aleutians where the original specimen was obtained.

PHILOHELA Gray Gr. *philos,* "loving"; Gr. *helos,* "a bog." **P. minor** (Gmelin): AMERICAN WOOD-COCK; L. *minor,* "smaller," in comparison with the European Woodcock.

PHILOMACHUS Merrem Gr. *philos,* "loving"; Gr. *mache,* "combat"; for the aggressive dance of the males in the breeding season. **P. pugnax** (Linnaeus): RUFF; L. *pugnax,* "quarrelsome," from L. *pugnus,* "first"; repeating the idea that the bird is addicted to violence although it has sublimated this inclination into a dance.

PHOENICOPTERUS Linnaeus Gr. *phoinix,* "crimson"; Gr. *pteron,* "wing." **P. ruber** (Linnaeus): AMERI-CAN FLAMINGO; L. *ruber,* "red," for its reddish plumage.

PHYLLOSCOPUS Boie Gr. *phyllon,* "leaf"; Gr. *scopos,* "one that looks about, a watchman." **P. borealis** (Blasius): ARCTIC WARBLER; L. *borealis,* "north-ern," for the breeding range.

PICA Brisson L. *pica,* "magpie." **P. nuttalli** (Audubon): YELLOW-BILLED MAGPIE; ML. *nuttalli* for Thomas Nuttall (see Appendix). **P. pica** (Linnaeus):

BLACK-BILLED MAGPIE–MAGPIE; L. *pica,* "magpie."

PICOIDES Lacepede L. *picus,* "a woodpecker"; Gr. *oides,* a contraction of *o,* "the," and *eidos,* "like," to mean "resembling." **P. arcticus** (Swainson): BLACK-BACKED THREE-TOED WOOD-PECKER; L. *arcticus,* "northern" (see *Gavia,* G. *arctica*). **P. tridactylus** (Linnaeus): NORTHERN THREE-TOED WOODPECKER; Gr. *trias,* "three"; Gr. *daktylos,* "toe."

PINGUINUS Bonnaterre ML. *pinquinus.* Bonnaterre chose this name in 1790 when he placed the Great Auk in a genus of its own. He most likely derived it from F. *pingouin* which in an earlier form was *penguyn* which may have come from Breton *pengouin* (white head) or E. *penguin.* The latter is from Welsh *pen* (white), *gwyn* (head), Breton and Welsh being closely related Celtic languages. The name was used by the fishermen of both countries for the Great Auk which had a large white patch in front of its eye. It was also probably used for more than one bird, and sailors are probably responsible for its initial be-stowal on the birds of the Southern Hemisphere now commonly known as penguins. Skeat points out that "Sir F. Drake gave a certain island the name of Penguin Island in 1587 from the penguins he found there." Weekley quotes Richard Hawkins, c. 1600, "Pengwyns, which in Welsh, as I have been en-formed, signifieth white head. From which deriva-tion . . . some doe inferre that America was first peopled with Welshmen." This "inferres" that the Welsh and the Breton fishermen named the bird through their acquaintance with it about the fishing banks of New Foundland and not from the days when it wintered on the coasts of their homeland. If the above stretches into a credibility gap, one may opt for L. *pinguis,* "fat," "stout"; L. *-inus,* "-like," hence; "fat-looking." **P. impennis** (Linnaeus): GREAT AUK; L. ' *-im,* "without"; L. *penna,* "feather," in the singular, and L. *pennae,* "wing" in the plural. Linnaeus gets no accolade here, as the bird had feathers, although short and tough, and wings, although it did not fly in the air, which reminds us of Coues who lamented "HIS GRACE, THE AUK, or GAREFOWL, who lost the use of his wings, and perished off the face of the earth in consequence."

PINICOLA Vieillot L. *pinus,* "pine"; L. *colere,* "inhabit." **P. enucleator** (Linnaeus): PINE GROSBEAK; L. *enucleator,* "one who 'shells out,'" from the bird's way of husking the pine seeds.

PIPILO Vieillot ML. *pipilo,* from L. *pipo,* "to chirp or peep." **P. aberti** Baird: ABERT'S TOWHEE for James W. Abert (see Appendix). **P. erythrophthalmus** (Linnaeus): RUFOUS-SIDED TOWHEE; Gr. *erythros,* "red"; Gr. *opthalmos,* "eye." For the color of the iris of the adult in most of North America, although it is white or orange in the southeastern United States. **P. fuscus** (Swainson): BROWN TOWHEE; L. *fuscus,* "dark brown," for the color of the plumage.

PIRANGA Vieillot *Piranga,* a native name for some kind of South American bird. **P. flava** (Vieillot): HEPATIC TANAGER; L. *flava,* "yellow," referring to the color of the female, which possibly was found and described before the male. **P. ludoviciana** (Wilson): WESTERN TANAGER; ML. *ludoviciana,* "of Louisiana." Wilson in naming the bird for its locality was not referring to the state but to the Louisiana Territory from which the bird described by him was brought back by Lewis and Clark who collected it in Idaho. **P. olivacea** (Gmelin): SCARLET TANAGER; L. *oliva,* "olive." We again have the color of the female, which seems to have been settled upon due to possible confusion with the Summer Tanager which already had preempted the term for the color red. **P. rubra** (Linnaeus): SUMMER TANAGER; L. *rubra,* "red," for the entirely red plumage of the male.

PITANGUS Swainson   *Pitangus,* a native Brazilian name for the bird. **P. sulphuratus** (Linnaeus): KISKADEE FLYCATCHER; L. *sulphur,* "sulphur"; L. *-atus,* "having"; for the bright yellow underparts.

PLATYPSARIS Sclater   Gr. *platys,* "broad"; Gr. *psar,* "a starling." In poor light from the rear without binoculars, at a distance it might look like a fat starling. **P. aglaiae** (Lafresnaye): ROSE-THROATED BE-CARD; Gr. *Aglais,* "one of the three graces," as it is a dainty little bird.

PLECTROPHENAX Stejneger   Gr. *plectron,* "something to hit with, a cock's claw"; Gr. *phenax,* "a cheat." According to MacLeod the word was originally *Plectophanes,* the latter stem from Gr. *phaino,* "to display." So the whole word meant "showy claw" for the bird's long hind claw. MacLeod goes on to say that Stejneger changed *Plectophanes* to *Plectophenax* for technical reasons. From here it seems that Stejneger for taxonomic "technical reasons" moved the Snow Bunting from the genus *Emberiza* where Linnaeus had placed it into a new genus of his own designation, which he misspelled. Coues placed the bird in the *Passerina* which neither the B.O.U. or the A.O.U. *Check-list* mentions. In its present permanently embalmed state the term may roughly be translated to mean "something to hit a cheat with." **P. hyperboreus** (Ridgway): MCKAY'S BUNTING; L. *hyperboreus,* "beyond the north wind," for the birds far-northern range (see *Larus hyperboreus).* **P. nivalis** (Linnaeus): SNOW BUNTING; L. *nivalis,* "snowy," for its white plumage and its appearance during the season of snow.

PLEGADIS Kaup   Gr. *plegadis,* "a sickle or scythe." **P. chihi** (Vieillot): WHITE-FACED IBIS. Chihi is possibly a South American native name for the bird. **P. falcinellus** (Linnaeus): GLOSSY IBIS; L. *falx,* "sickle," for the shape of the bill; L. *-ellus,* "little"; this gives us the little sickle sickle.

PLUVIALIS Brisson   L. *pluvialis,* "rainy" (see Plover). **P. dominica** (Muller): AMERICAN GOLDEN PLOVER; ML. *dominica,* for St. Domingo on Hispaniola where the first specimen was obtained in 1776. **P. squatarola** (Linnaeus): BLACK-BELLIED PLOVER; squatarola is a Venetian name for the bird.

PODICEPS Latham   A contraction of the ML. *podicipes* from L. *podex, podicis,* "rump"; L. *pes,* "foot." **P. auritus** (Linnaeus): HORNED GREBE–SLAVONIAN GREBE; L. *auritus,* "eared," for the tufts on the head. **P. dominicus** (Linnaeus): LEAST GREBE; ML. *dominicus,* "of St. Domingo," on Hispaniola, the site of the first specimen. **P. grisigena** (Boddaert): RED-NECKED GREBE; L. *griseus,* "gray"; L. *gena,* "cheek"; for the color of the cheek in breeding plumage. **P. nigricollis** Brehm: EARED GREBE–BLACK-NECKED GREBE; L. *niger,* "black"; L. *collis,* "neck," which it has in its breeding plumage.

PODILYMBUS Lesson   Lesson coined the word by combining the first syllable of ML. *podiceps,* a generic name for grebes; and the last part of *Colymbus,* a generic name for loons and grebes, from Gr. *kolumbos,* "a diving bird," mentioned by Aristotle. Colymbus was formerly used as a generic term for some of our grebes. It is at present used as a generic term for the loons (divers in Britain) in the B.O.U. *Check-list.* **P. podiceps** (Linnaeus) PIED-BILLED GREBE.

POLIOPTILA Sclater   Gr. *polios,* "gray"; Gr. *ptilon,* "feather"; as the primaries are edged with gray. **P. caerulea** (Linnaeus): BLUE-GRAY GNAT-

CATCHER; L. *caerulea,* "blue," for the blue back.
P. melanura (Lawrence): BLACK-TAILED GNAT-
CATCHER; Gr. *melas,* "black"; Gr. *oura,* "tail"; as
it has more black in the tail than the former.

POLYSTICTA Eyton Gr. *poly stictos,* "many-spotted,"
despite the fact that it is not, although the birds are
curiously marked. **P. stelleri** (Pallas): STELLER'S
EIDER for George W. Steller (see Appendix).

POOECETES Baird Gr. *poe,* "grass"; Gr. *oiketes (oecetes)*
"dweller." **P. gramineus** (Gmelin): VESPER SPAR-
ROW; L. *gramineus,* "of the grasses," for the habitat.

PORPHYRULA Blyth Gr. *porphyrion,* "the purple gallin-
ule" of southern Europe, a different species from the
American bird with the same common name. From
Gr. *porphyreos,* "purple"; L. *-ula,* "little," added to
differentiate this genus from the larger one of
Europe. **P. martinica** (Linnaeus): PURPLE GAL-
LINULE; ML. *martinica,* "of Martinique," where
the bird was first found.

PORZANA Vieillot I. *porzana,* "the crake." **P. carolina**
(Linnaeus): SORA; ML. *carolina,* "of Carolina."

PROGNE Boie Gr. *progne,* who was changed into a
swallow (see *Pandion*). **P. subis** (Linnaeus): PURPLE
MARTIN; L. *subis,* "name of an unknown bird."

PROTONOTARIA Baird L. *protonotarius,* "an authorized
scribe," from Gr. *protos,* "first"; L. *notarius,* "a note
taker." As Coues puts it, "Why?" **P. citrea** (Boddaert): PROTHONOTARY WARBLER; L. *citrus,*
"the citrus tree," hence to the fruit of the tree and its
color, which is a roundabout way of getting to
yellow, the bird's color.

PSALTRIPARUS Bonaparte Gr. *psaltria,* "a harpist"; L.
parus, "a titmouse." **P. minimus** (Townsend): BUSH-
TIT; L. *minimus,* "least." Coues calls them "dwarfs
among pygmies."

PTERODROMA Bonaparte Gr. *pteron,* "wing"; Gr. *dromos,* "running." **P. cahow** (Nichols and Mowbray):

BERMUDA PETREL; *cahow* in imitation of its call.
P. hasitata (Kuhl): BLACK-CAPPED PETREL. As
there is no such word as *hasitatus* in Latin, MacLeod
speculates, "It first appears in Forster's unpublished
plates as the name of a species of *Procellaria,* and
was adopted by Kuhl in 1820. In 1863, however,
Schlegel (in his account of *Procellaria neglecta*) refers
to Kuhl's *Procellaria haesitata* which suggests that
hasitata is a mistake for *haesitata.* If so, *haesitata*
appears to be coined from L. *haesito,* hesitate, and
having the meaning of 'uncertain,' the idea being
that it was uncertain whether the bird belongs to a
distinct species." Now it is so classified with the past
uncertainty carried in the uncertain spelling. **P.
inexpectata** (Forster): SCALED PETREL; L. *inex-
pecta,* "unexpected," evidently to the describer, as it
is a Western Pacific bird only casual in the Alaskan
Gulf.

PTYCHORAMPHUS Brandt   Gr. *ptyk,* "a fold"; Gr. *ramphos,* "beak"; alluding to the ridges across the bill
which are evident only when the bird is in the hand.
P. aleuticus (Pallas): CASSIN'S AUKLET; ML.
aleutica, "Aleutian Islands," one of the breeding
sites.

PUFFINUS–PROCELLARIA Brisson ML. *puffinus,* E.
puffin. The use of the word puffin as the generic term
for shearwaters is attributed to Ray, "the father of
English natural history," 1628–1705. He should not
be criticized for contributing to confusion as in his
day "puffin" was used indiscriminately for the puffin,
the razorbill and the shearwater. He had no way of
knowing which bird would eventually take over the
word "puffin" for its exclusive use. Then, too,
Linneaus and his successors generally adapted terms
already in use rather than invent new ones for the
binomial nomenclature. Once given a binomial
name, the law of priority decrees that no change be

made despite seeming inappropriateness or original error. The original name is maintained to avoid confusion, at least, among taxonomists. **P. assimilis** Gould: LITTLE SHEARWATER; L. *assimilis,* "similar," so called on account of its resemblance to the Madeiran Little Shearwater which at the time was *Puffinus obscurus* (a species) but is now *P. assimilis baroli* (a subspecies) for the Marchese Farloti di Barol of Turin. As the species *P. assimilis* cannot look like a species that does not exist, its name has to mean that it "looks like itself" which is probably less ridiculous than having the bird look like the Marchese. Thus a valid revision of classification makes the original name meaningless. **P. bulleri** (Salvin): NEW ZEALAND SHEARWATER; for Sir Walter L. Buller (see Appendix). **P. carneipes** (Gould): PALE-FOOTED SHEARWATER; L. *carnis,* "flesh"; L. *pes,* "foot"; for the color of the feet. **P. creatopus** (Coues): PINK-FOOTED SHEAR-WATER; Gr. *kreatos,* "flesh"; Gr. *pous,* "foot"; for the color of the feet, a repetition using Greek roots. **P. diomedea** (Scopoli): CORY'S SHEARWATER; for Diomedes whose companions were changed into birds after the ship returning them from the Trojan War was lost. **P. gravis** (O'Reilly): GREATER SHEARWATER; L. *gravis,* "heavy," for its large size. **P. griseus** (Gmelin): SOOTY SHEARWATER; ML. *griseus,* "gray," which is not as appropriate as the common name for this sooty black bird. **P. l'herminieri** Lesson: AUDUBON'S SHEAR-WATER; for F. J. L'Herminier (see Appendix). **P. puffinus** (Brunnich): MANX SHEARWATER (see *Puffinus*). **P. tenuirostris** (Temminck): SLENDER-BILLED SHEARWATER; L. *tennis,* "thin"; L. *rostrum,* "beak."

PYCNONOTUS Boie Gr. *pycnos,* "solid, strong"; Gr. *notos,* "back." **P. jocosus** (Linnaeus): RED-WHISK-

ERED BULBUL; L. *jocosus,* "full of fun," possibly for its liveliness. Given authentic status as a North American bird in the *Auk* (vol. 85, no. 1, 1968), it is locally common in South Miami, Florida, where it has been "free" since 1955.

PYROCEPHALUS Gould   Gr. *pyros,* "fire"; Gr. *cephale,* "head." **P. rubinus** (Boddaert): VERMILION FLY-CATCHER; L. *rubinus,* "ruby," for the red plumage of the male.

PYRRHULOXIA Bonaparte   Gr. *pyrrhoulis,* "the bullfinch," of Aristotle, from Gr. *pyrrhos,* "flame-colored"; Gr. *loxias,* "crooked." **P. sinuata** (Bonaparte): PYRRHULOXIA; L. *sinuata,* "bent," for the bill, from L. *sinus,* "a fold, bosom, or bay." A look at the profile of the bill may suggest what Bonaparte had in mind.

QUISCALIS Vieillot   ML. *quiscalis,* "quail." There are several spellings of the Modern Latin term. See Quail, another form of the word, in the list of common names. The use of a word meaning "quail" seems out of place for a genus in the family Icteridae. **Q. quiscula** (Linnaeus): COMMON GRACKLE; ML. *quiscula,* another spelling for the generic term adding to the variety by changing the gender. We have been unable to determine why *quisquilla, quaquila, quaquara,* and *quaquadra* were passed by as they are all equally inappropriate.

RALLUS Linnaeus   ML. *rallus,* "a rail"; F. *rale,* "a rail"; OF. *raale,* "to make a scraping noise"; L. *raelare,* "to scrape." **R. elegans** Audubon: KING RAIL; L. *elegans,* "elegant." **R. limicola** Vieillot: VIRGINIA RAIL; L. *limus,* "mud"; L. *colo,* "to inhabit." **R. longirostris** Boddaert: CLAPPER RAIL; L. *longus,* "long"; L. *rostrum,* "bill."

RECURVIROSTRA Linnaeus   L. *recurvo,* "to bend backward"; L. *rostrum,* "bill." **R. americana** Gmelin:

AMERICAN AVOCET; ML. *americana,* "American," to distinguish it from the European.

REGULUS Cuvier   L. *regulus,* "little king." **R. calendula** (Linnaeus): RUBY-CROWNED KINGLET; ML. *calendula* from L. *caliendrum,* "false hair or a wig," for the ruby crown. **R. satrapa** Lichtenstein: GOLDEN-CROWNED KINGLET; Gr. *satrapes,* "a ruler" who wears a golden crown.

RHODOSTETHIA MacGillivray   Gr. *rhodon,* "rose"; Gr. *stethos,* "breast." **R. rosea** (MacGillivray): ROSS' GULL; L. *roseus,* "rosy," hence the rosy rose-breasted.

RHYNCHOPSITTA Bonaparte   Gr. *rhynchos,* "beak"; Gr. *psittake,* "parrot." **R. pachyrhyncha** (Swainson): THICK-BILLED PARROT; Gr. *pachys,* "thick," and *rhyncha* repeated for good measure. Here we find the scientific term means the same as the common name.

RIPARIA Forster   L. *riparia,* "bank of a stream," for the nesting site. **R. riparia** (Linnaeus): BANK SWALLOW-SAND MARTIN; L. *riparia,* see above.

RISSA Stephens   Ic. *rissa,* "kittiwake." **R. brevirostris** (Bruch): RED-LEGGED KITTIWAKE; L. *brevis,* "short"; L. *rostrum,* "bill," for its small bill. **R. tridactyla** (Linnaeus): BLACK-LEGGED KITTIWAKE; Gr. *treis,* L. *tris,* "three"; Gr. *daktylos,* "finger or toe." Not so named for the three front toes which are like those in other gulls, but because the rear toe is abnormally small, making the three normal ones stand out in contrast.

ROSTRHAMUS Lesson   L. *rostrum,* "beak"; L. *hamus,* "a hook." **R. sociabilis** (Vieillot): EVERGLADE KITE; L. *sociabilis,* "gregarious," for its nesting in loose colonies.

RYNCHOPS Linnaeus   Gr. *rhynchos,* "a beak"; Gr. *ops,*

"face." **R. nigra** Linnaeus: BLACK SKIMMER; L. *niger,* "black," for the color of the upper parts.

SALPINCTES Cabanis Gr. *salpinctes,* "a trumpeter." **S. obsoletus** (Say): ROCK WREN; L. *obsoletus,* "indistinct," for the dull coloration.

SAYORNIS Bonaparte For Thomas Say (see Appendix). Gr. *ornis,* "bird." **S. nigricans** (Swainson): BLACK PHOEBE; L. *nigricans,* "blackening." **S. phoebe** (Latham): EASTERN PHOEBE; Gr. *Phoebe,* "one of the twelve Titans"; imitative of the bird's call. **S. saya** (Bonaparte): SAY'S PHOEBE; doubly honoring Thomas Say (see Appendix).

SCARDAFELLA Bonaparte I. *scardafella,* "scaley appearance." **S. inca** (Lesson): INCA DOVE. This dove is not a native of Peru, the home of the Incas. It is a native of Mexico, home of the Aztecs. If Lesson thought he was using a place name, it might have been more accurate to have used the name of the country where the bird lives.

SCOLOPAX Linnaeus Gr. *scolopax,* "the woodcock." **S. rusticola** Linnaeus: WOODCOCK (the European one); ML. *rusticola,* "a country dweller."

SEIURUS Swainson Gr. *seio,* "to wave"; Gr. *oura,* "tail." **S. aurocapillus** (Linnaeus): OVENBIRD; L. *aurum,* "gold"; L. *capillus,* "hair"; for the gold crown. **S. motacilla** (Vieillot): LOUISIANA WATERTHRUSH; L. *metacilla,* "wagtail" (see *Bombycilla*). **S. novaboracensis** (Gmelin): NORTHERN WATERTHRUSH; ML. *Novaboracensis,* "of New York," where the bird was first found.

SELAPHORUS Swainson Gr. *selas,* "light"; Gr. *phoros,* "carrying." **S. platycercus** (Swainson): BROAD-TAILED HUMMINGBIRD; Gr. *platys,* "broad"; Gr. *kerkos,* "tail." **S. rufus** (Gmelin): RUFOUS HUMMINGBIRD; L. *rufus,* "reddish." **S. sasin** (Lesson): ALLEN'S HUMMINGBIRD; of *sasin,*

Alexander Wetmore says, "Lesson in his original description of Allen's hummingbird called it the Sasin, from 'Sasime' or 'Sasin,' from a French edition of Cook's third voyage. I do not know what the word means."

SETOPHAGA Swainson   Gr. *setos,* "a moth"; Gr. *phago,* "to eat." **S. picta** Swainson: PAINTED RED-START; L. *picta,* "painted." **S. ruticilla** (Linnaeus): AMERICAN REDSTART; L. *ruticilla,* "red tail."

SIALIA Swainson   Gr. *sialis,* "a kind of bird." **S. curru-coides** (Bechstein): MOUNTAIN BLUEBIRD; Sp. *curruca,* "the linnet"; Gr. *oides,* "like." **S. mexicana** (Swainson): WESTERN BLUEBIRD; ML. *mexicana,* "Mexican," as the first specimen came from Mexico. **S. sialis** (Linnaeus): EASTERN BLUE-BIRD; Gr. *sialis,* see above.

SITTA Linnaeus   Gr. *sitte,* "nuthatch." **S. canadensis** (Linnaeus): RED-BREASTED NUTHATCH; ML. *canadensis,* "Canadian," for its breeding range although this is only partially in Canada. **S. carolin-ensis** (Latham): WHITE-BREASTED NUT-HATCH; ML. *carolinensis,* "of Carolina," although it breeds wherever there are deciduous trees in the United States. **S. pusilla** (Latham): BROWN-HEADED NUTHATCH; L. *pusilla,* "very small." **S. pygmaea** (Vigors): PYGMY NUTHATCH; L. *pygmaeus,* "a pigmy," "dwarfish" from Gr. *pygme,* "the fist," which was a measure of length from the elbow to the closed fist. It refers to the bird's small size.

SOMATERIA Leach   Gr. *soma,* "body"; Gr. *erion,* "wool"; for the thick down on the body. **S. fischeri** (Brandt): SPECTACLED EIDER; for Gotthelf Fischer (see Appendix). **S. mollissima** (Linnaeus): COMMON EIDER; L. *mollissima,* "softest," for the down. **S. spectabilis** (Linnaeus): KING EIDER; L.

spectabilis, "showy," referring to the conspicuous orange knob on the front of the head of the male bird in the breeding season which makes it a "spect"acular bird.

SPEOTYTO Gloger Gr. *speos,* "a cave"; Gr. *tyto,* "a night owl." **S. cunicularia** (Molina): BURROWING OWL; L. *cunicularius,* "a miner or burrower," from L. *cuniculus,* "a rabbit."

SPHYRAPICUS Baird Gr. *sphyra,* "a hammer"; L. *picus,* "a woodpecker." Picus loved Pomona and spurned the importunities of Circe. Lacking the guile of Ulysses and possibly ignorant of the proclivity of the one he disdained for turning those she found indifferent into some specimen of the animal kingdom, he ended up as a woodpecker. MacLeod disagrees with Ovid, stating that it is his belief that the woodpecker had a name before the youth's transformation. **S. thyroideus** (Cassin): WILLIAMSON'S SAPSUCKER: Gr. *thyreos,* "a shield"; Gr. *oidos,* "like"; as the black breast of the male resembles a breastplate. **S. varius** (Linnaeus): YELLOW-BELLIED SAPSUCKER; L. *varius,* "variegated," for the mixed plumage.

SPINUS Koch Gr. *spinos,* "a linnet" or a similar bird. **S. lawrencei** (Cassin): LAWRENCE'S GOLDFINCH; for George N. Lawrence (see Appendix). **S. pinus** (Wilson): PINE SISKIN; L. *pinus,* "pine," as the bird favors conifers for breeding. **S. psaltria** (Say): LESSER GOLDFINCH; Gr. *psaltria,* "a lutist," for the bird's musical song. **S. tristris** (Linnaeus): AMERICAN GOLDFINCH; L. *tristis,* "sad." Coues says the term is for the bird's note. Linnaeus in naming the bird changed it from the one given by Catesby which did not suggest sadness. As the call is not mournful it is difficult to understand the reason for Linnaeus' choice.

SPIZA Bonaparte Gr. *spiza,* "a finch." **S. americana** (Gmelin): DICKCISSEL; ML. *americana,* "American," to distinguish it from others in the genus where it was originally placed, as they were European.

SPIZELLA Bonaparte I. *spizella,* "a finch," diminutive from L. *spiza,* "a finch," from the same in Greek. **S. arborea** (Wilson): TREE SPARROW; L. *arbor,* "a tree." **S. atrogularis** (Cabanis): BLACK-CHINNED SPARROW; L. *atrogularis,* "black-throated." **S. breweri** (Cassin): BREWER'S SPARROW; for Thomas M. Brewer (see Appendix). **S. pallida** (Swainson): CLAY-COLORED SPARROW; L. *pallida,* "pale." **S. passerina** (Bechstein): CHIPPING SPARROW; L. *passer,* "sparrow"; L. *-ina,* "like." **S. pusilla** (Wilson): FIELD SPARROW; L. *pusillus,* "smallest," although three spizella's are smaller.

SPOROPHILA Cabanis Gr. *sporos,* "seed"; Gr. *philos,* "loving." **S. torqueola** (Bonaparte): WHITE-COLLARED SEEDEATER; L. *torquis,* "a twisted neck chain," for the white neck band.

STEGANOPUS Vieillot Gr. *steganos,* "closed or watertight"; Gr. *pous,* "foot"; for the partially webbed feet. **S. tricolor** (Vieillot): WILSON'S PHALAROPE; L. *tricolor,* "three-colored," as it is gray, black, and red in summer.

STELGIDOPTERYX Baird Gr. *stelgis,* "a scraper"; Gr. *pteryx,* "wing"; for the stiff recurved hooks on the first primary. **S. ruficollis** (Vieillot): ROUGH-WINGED SWALLOW; L. *rufus,* "reddish"; L. *collum,* "neck." As there is no red in the neck or in the plumage at all, this term is evidently an error.

STELLULA Gould L. *stellula,* "little star." **S. calliope** (Gould): CALLIOPE HUMMINGBIRD; Gr. *Calliope,* "the muse responsible for epic poetry." So one of the smallest birds is named for the sponsor of the greatest form of poem.

STERCORARIUS Brisson L. *stercorarius,* "having to do

with dung," alluding to the scavenging habits of
the bird which at times feeds on offal. **S. longi-
caudus** Vieillot: LONG-TAILED JAEGER–LONG-
TAILED SKUA; L. *longus*, "long"; L. *caudas*,
"tail"; for the extensive central tail feathers. **S.
parasiticus** (Linnaeus): PARASITIC JAEGER–
ARCTIC SKUA; for its pursuit of other sea birds till
they disgorge. **S. pomarinus** (Temminck): POMAR-
INE JAEGER–POMATORHINE SKUA; Gr.
poma, "a lid"; Gr. *rhynchos*, "beak"; for the rim over
the base of the bill in the breeding season. Erratic
spelling.

STERNA Linnaeus ML. *sterna*, Latinized by Turner in
1544 from OE. *stern, starn*, or *tern* from AS. *stearn*,
"a tern." **S. albifrons** Pallas: LEAST TERN; L.
albus, "white"; L. *frons*, "forehead"; for the white
feathering above the bill. **S. aleutica** Baird: ALEU-
TIAN TERN; ML. *aleutica*, "Aleutian Islands,"
where it breeds. **S. anaethetus** Scopoldi: BRIDLED
TERN; a mistake for Gr. *anaisthetos*, "stupid,"
"without sense," as the bird was supposed to let itself
be approached without taking alarm. **S. dougallii**
Montagu: ROSEATE TERN; for Dr. MacDougall
of Scotland who provided the first specimen in 1812
(see Appendix). It seems rather singular to leave out
the first syllable of the name of the man who is
supposed to be honored in perpetuity. **S. forsteri**
Nuttall: FORSTER'S TERN; for John R. Forster
(see Appendix). **S. fuscata** Linnaeus: SOOTY
TERN; L. *fuscus*, "dark," for the color of the
plumage. **S. hirundo** Linnaeus: COMMON TERN;
L. *hirundo*, "a swallow," for its resemblance in shape
and flight to a swallow. **S. paradisaea** Pontoppidan:
ARCTIC TERN; LL. *paradisus* from Zend (old
Persian), *pairidaeza*, "an enclosure, a park," from
Zend, *pairi*, "around"; Zend, *diz*, "to mold"; hence
"form a wall of mud around," which was the way the

old Persians made a park. The word was first used in Greek in the Septuagint for the 'Garden of Eden' which translated the Old Testament from Hebrew into Greek. Tradition says the Septuagint is so called because it was translated by seventy-two Jews in seventy-two days for Ptolemy II of Egypt in the third century B.C. It is the biblical version used by the Greek Church. Erik Pontoppidan (1698–1764) attained eminence as a theologian, bishop of Bergen, and as a scientist, author of *A Natural History of Norway*. Possibly his dual career influenced his naming of the bird in the hope that he could convey the idea that so beautiful a creature belonged in that perfect home beyond the sky. **S. trudeaui** Audubon: TRUDEAU'S TERN; for J. Trudeau (see Appendix).

STREPTOPELIA Bonaparte Gr. *streptos,* "twisted"; Gr. *pel(e)ia,* "a kind of dove"; in reference to the black and white patch on the side of the neck in the European species. **S. chinensis** (Scopoli): SPOTTED DOVE; ML. *chinensis,* "of China," where it is native, having been introduced into the United States. **S. risoria** (Linnaeus): RINGED TURTLE DOVE; L. *risor,* "a laugher," for the bird's call.

STRIX Linnaeus L. *strix,* Gr. *strigx,* "a screech owl," which members of this genus are not. **S. nebulosa** Forster: GREAT GRAY OWL; L. *nebulosa,* "clouded," as it has the color of a dark cloud. **S. occidentalis** (Xantus): SPOTTED OWL; L. *occidentalis,* "western," for its range in western United States. **S. varia** Barton: BARRED OWL; L. *varia,* "variegated," for the plumage.

STURNELLA Vieillot L. *sturnus,* "a starling"; L. *-ella,* "little"; hence "little starling," although both members of this genus are about two inches larger than the starling proper, *sturnus,* in the following genus. **S. magna** (Linnaeus): EASTERN MEADOWLARK; L. *magna,* "large," so we end up with "large little

starling," which is about as confusing as a scientific
term can be. **S. neglecta** Audubon: WESTERN
MEADOWLARK; L. *neglecta,* "neglected." So
named by Audubon in 1844 as a word of censure for
the ornithologists who had named *magna* in 1758
and who he felt were guilty of inordinate procrasti-
nation in identifying this bird.

STURNUS Linnaeus L. *sturnus,* "a starling." **S. vulgaris**
Linnaeus: STARLING; L. *vulgaris,* "common," for
its ubiquity.

SULA Brisson Ic. *sulan,* "gannet." Originally the term
meant "an awkward fellow" and possibly was applied to the bird because of its awkward gait. Cf.
Nor. *sula,* "gannet." **S. dactylatra** Lesson: BLUE-
FACED BOOBY; Gr. *dactyl,* "finger or toe"; L.
atra, "black." This looks like an error as the webbed
feet are yellow. **S. leucogaster** Boddaert: BROWN
BOOBY; Gr. *leukos,* "white"; Gr. *gaster,* "the belly."
S. nebouxii Milne-Edwards: BLUE-FOOTED
BOOBY; for Adolphe S. Neboux (see Appendix). **S.
sula** Linnaeus: RED-FOOTED BOOBY; for *sula*
(see above).

SURNIA Dumeril May be an arbitrary word invented
by Dumeril in 1806. Coues suggests it is modern
Greek for "owl." **S. ulula** (Linnaeus): HAWK-OWL;
L. *ulula,* "screech owl," imitative of the bird's cry.
Cf. L. *ululare,* "to cry or howl"; Gr. *alala,* "an
outcry."

SYNTHLIBORAMPHUS Brandt Gr. *synthlibo,* "compress,
small"; Gr. *ramphos,* "beak." **S. antiquum** (Gmelin):
ANCIENT MURRELET; L. *antiquus,* "old," hence
gray-headed for the hoary appearance of the head.

TACHYCINETA Cabanis Gr. *tachys,* "swift"; Gr. *kineo,*
"to move"; hence swift mover. **T. thalassina** (Swainson): VIOLET-GREEN SWALLOW; Gr. *thal-
assina,* "like the sea," for the sea-green color of the
plumage.

TANGAVIUS Lesson ML. *tangavius,* probably a combination of a Tuni South American native word, *tanger*, and L. *avis*, "bird." **T. aeneus** (Wagler): BRONZED COWBIRD; L. *aeneus*, "brassy," for the sheen of the plumage.

TELMATODYTES Cabanis Gr. *telma*, "a swamp"; Gr. *dytes*, "an inhabitant." **T. palustria** (Wilson): LONG-BILLED MARSH WREN; L. *palustris*, "marshy."

THALASSEUS Boie Gr. *thalassa*, "the sea." **T. elegans** (Gambel): ELEGANT TERN; L. *elegans*, "elegant." **T. maximus** (Boddaert): ROYAL TERN; L. *maximus*, "largest." If Boddaert, who described this tern in 1783, had looked up the measurements of the Caspian tern described in 1770, he would probably not have used the term *maximus*. **T. sandvicensis** (Latham): SANDWICH TERN; ML. *sandvicensis*, "of Sandwich," Kent, England, whence came the first specimen.

THRYOMANES Sclater Gr. *thryon*, "a reed"; Gr. *manes*, "a cup," for the nest. **T. bewickii** (Audubon): BEWICK'S WREN; for Thomas Bewick (see Appendix).

THRYOTHORUS Vieillot Gr. *thryon*, "a reed"; Gr. *thouros*, "rushing." **T. ludovicianus** (Latham): CAROLINA WREN; ML. *ludovicianus*, "of Louisiana," the site of the original specimen.

TOXOSTOMA Wagler Gr. *toxon*, "a bow"; Gr. *stoma*, "a mouth"; literally "bow mouth" for the curved beak. **T. bendirei** (Coues): BENDIRE'S THRASHER; for Charles E. Bendire (see Appendix). **T. curvirostre** (Swainson): CURVE-BILLED THRASHER; L. *curvus*, "curved"; L. *rostrum*, "beak." **T. dorsale** Henry: CRISSAL THRASHER; ML. *dorsalis*, "of the back," which does not appear distinctive. **T. lecontei** Lawrence: LECONTE'S THRASHER; for John L. LeConte (see Appendix). **T. longirostre** (Lefresnaye): LONG-BILLED THRASHER; L. *longus*, "long"; L. *rostrum*, "bill." **T. redivivum**

(Gambel): CALIFORNIA THRASHER; L. *redivi-vus,* "revived," as the bird was rediscovered after a lapse of time. **T. rufum** (Linnaeus): BROWN THRASHER; L. *rufum,* "reddish."

TRINGA Linnaeus Gr. *tryngas,* "a sandpiper." **T. flavipes** (Gmelin): LESSER YELLOWLEGS; L. *flavus,* "yellow"; L. *pes,* "foot," for the color of the feet and legs. **T. melanoleucus** (Gmelin): GREATER YELLOWLEGS; Gr. *melanos,* "black"; Gr. *leucos,* "white"; as black and white approximate the contrasting color of the upper parts. **T. solitaria** Wilson: SOLITARY SANDPIPER; L. *solitarius,* "solitary."

TROGLODYTES Vieillot Gr. *troglodytes,* "cave dweller," from Gr. *trogle,* "hole"; Gr. *dytes,* "a diver"; for the bird's diving into cover. **T. aedon** (Vieillot): HOUSE WREN; Gr. *aedon,* "a songstress" from Aedon, the daughter of Pandereus, who was changed into a nightingale by the gods but into a wren by Vieillot. **T. brunneicollis** (Sclater): BROWN-THROATED WREN; ML. *brunneus,* "dark brown"; L. *collum,* "neck," for the light brown on the front of the neck. **T. troglodytes** (Linnaeus): WINTER WREN–WREN.

TROGON Brisson Gr. *trogon,* "a gnawer," for the tooth-like edge of the bill. **T. elegans** Gould: COPPERY-TAILED TROGON; L. *elegans,* "elegant."

TRYNGITES Cabanis Gr. *tryngas,* "a sandpiper"; Gr. *-tes,* "having to do with." **T. subruficollis** (Vieillot): BUFF-BREASTED SANDPIPER; ML. *subruficollis,* "reddish below the neck." As all the underparts are the same buff color, it is difficult to see the need for the word "neck."

TURDUS Linnaeus L. *turdus,* "a thrush." **T. migratorius** (Linnaeus): ROBIN; LL. *migrator,* "wanderer."

TYMPANUCHUS Gloger Gr. *tympanon,* "a drum"; ML. *nucha,* "neck"; for the exposed skin on the bird's neck. **T. cupido** (Linnaeus): GREATER PRAIRIE

CHICKEN; so named for the tufts of feathers on the neck which are supposed to resemble the wings of Cupid; not for the bare skin of the air sacs, as the nakedness of Cupid was not so circumscribed. **T. pallidicinctus** (Ridgway): LESSER PRAIRIE CHICKEN; L. *pallidus,* "pale"; L. *cinctus,* "banded"; as it is more lightly barred than T. *cupido.*

TYRANNUS Lacepede L. *tyrannus,* "a tyrant." **T. dominicensis** (Gmelin): GRAY KINGBIRD; ML. *dominicensis,* "of Hispaniola," site of original specimen. **T. melancholicus** (Vieillot): TROPICAL KINGBIRD; L. *melancholicus,* "melancholy"; from Gr. *melangkolia,* from Gr. *melan,* "black"; *khole,* "bile." When there was too much of this in a body, the one afflicted with ML. *melancholia,* showed symptoms of ill temper, sadness and depression. As the bird is lively and has a rather loud two-syllable call, we can only infer that *melancholicus* indicates Vieillot's disposition rather than the birds. **T. tyrannus** (Linnaeus): EASTERN KINGBIRD; see above for *tyrannus.* **T. verticalis** (Say): WESTERN KINGBIRD; L. *verticalis,* relating to the L. *vertex,* "the top of the head" which has a bright red patch. **T. vociferans** (Swainson): CASSIN'S KINGBIRD; L. *vociferans,* "voice carrying," for its loud call.

TYTO Billberg Gr. *tyto,* "a night owl." **T. alba** (Scopoli): BARN OWL; L. *alba,* "white."

URIA Brisson Gr. *ouria,* one of the most overworked words in the Greek language, which in various contexts might mean "a fair wind," "a guardian," "a boundary," "a trench for hauling up ships," "a buffalo," or (as we take it to mean here) "a dark water bird with a long and narrow bill." **U. aalge** (Pontoppidan): COMMON MURRE–GUILLE-MOT; D. *aalge,* "the murre." **U. lomvia** (Linnaeus): THICK-BILLED MURRE–BRUNNICH'S GUIL-

LEMOT; Faroese, *lomvia,* "some kind of small diving bird."

VANELLUS Brisson ML. *vanellus,* "a little fan," for the way the broad wings beat the air, from L. *vannus,* "a fan" (note misspelling). **V. vanellus** (Linnaeus): LAPWING; a repetition.

VERMIVORA Swainson L. *vermis,* "worm": L. *voro,* "to eat." **V. bachmanii** (Audubon): BACHMAN'S WARBLER for John Bachman, its discoverer (see Appendix). **V. celata** (Say): ORANGE-CROWNED WARBLER; L. *celata,* "concealed," for the orange crown which is not easy to see. **V. chrysoptera** (Linnaeus): GOLDEN-WINGED WARBLER; Gr. *chrysos,* "gold"; Gr. *pteron,* "wing." **V. crissalis** (Salvin and Godman): COLIMA WARBLER; ML. *crissalis,* "pertaining to the crissum, the undertail coverts, which are yellow." **V. luciae** (Cooper): LUCY'S WARBLER for Lucy Baird, daughter of Spencer Baird (see Appendix under Lucy). **V. peregrina** (Wilson): TENNESSEE WARBLER; L. *peregrina,* "wandering," hence migratory. So named by Wilson who, having obtained only two specimens in his lifetime, considered it a very rare bird. **V. pinus** (Linnaeus): BLUE-WINGED WARBLER; L. *pinus,* "a pine tree." Wilson says that William Bartram discovered the bird and sent it to Edwards who confused it with the Pine Creeper of Catesby and gave it an inappropriate name. Linnaeus copied the error. **V. ruficapilla** (Wilson): NASHVILLE WARBLER; L. *rufus,* "reddish"; L. *capillus,* "hair"; for the dull reddish crown of the male. **V. virginiae** (Baird): VIRGINIA'S WARBLER; for Mrs. Virginia Anderson, wife of Dr. W. W. Anderson, a collector, who first found the bird (see Appendix under Virginia).

VIREO Vieillot L. *vireo,* "a small bird, possibly the

greenfinch. **V. altiloquus** (Vieillot): BLACK-WHISKERED VIREO; L. *altus,* "high"; ML. *loquus,* "chatterer," as the bird calls constantly from the high trees. **V. atricapilla** (Woodhouse): BLACK-CAPPED VIREO; L. *atri,* "black"; L. *capilla,* "hair"; for the black cap. **V. bellii** (Audubon): BELL'S VIREO; for J. G. Bell (see Appendix). **V. flavifrons** (Vieillot): YELLOW-THROATED VIREO; L. *flavus,* "yellow"; L. *frons,* in this case "front" for the yellow throat. **V. flavoviridis** (Cassin): YELLOW-GREEN VIREO; L. *flavus,* "yellow"; L. *viridis,* "green"; for the color of the plumage. **V. gilvus** (Vieillot): WARBLING VIREO; L. *gilvus,* "yellowish." **V. griseus** (Boddaert): WHITE-EYED VIREO; ML. *griseus,* "gray," not too apt. **V. huttoni** (Cassin): HUTTON'S VIREO; for William Hutton (see Appendix). **V. olivaceus** (Linnaeus): RED-EYED VIREO; L. *olivaceus,* "olive-colored." **V. philadelphicus** (Cassin): PHILADELPHIA VIREO; ML. *philadelphicus,* for the city within whose boundaries the first specimen was found. **V. solitarius** (Wilson): SOLITARY VIREO; L. *solitarius,* "solitary." Wilson, who first described the bird from one collected in Bartram's Woods in Philadelphia, was familiar with the bird as a migrant under which circumstances it is generally seen alone. Noting this fact most likely suggested the name to him. **V. vicinior** (Coues): GRAY VIREO; L. *vicinior,* "more neighborly." Coues who named the bird said, "It is unnecessary to compare *vicinior* with any other species, it is so very dissimilar from them all." This rules out the supposition that it was named for its close similarity to other vireos. So it is possible that the name was suggested by the bird's constant, pleasant and far-reaching song making it an easily recognized neighbor.

WILSONIA Bonaparte For Alexander Wilson (see Appendix). **W. canadensis** (Linnaeus): CANADA WARBLER; ML. *canadensis,* "Canadian," for most of the breeding range. **W. citrina** (Boddaert): HOODED WARBLER; LL. *citrina,* "lemon-colored." **W. pusilla** (Wilson): WILSON'S WARBLER; L. *pusilla,* "very small," though it is not noticeably so. There are twenty-four warblers that are larger, most of them by one quarter of an inch; seventeen the same size and four smaller.

XANTHOCEPHALUS Bonaparte Gr. *xanthos,* "yellow"; Gr. *cephalos,* "head." **X. xanthocephalus** (Bonaparte): YELLOW-HEADED BLACKBIRD; a repetition.

XEMA Leach NL. *xema.,* "name of an unknown bird." **X. sabini** (Sabine): SABINE'S GULL for Edward Sabine, named by his brother, Joseph (see Appendix).

ZENAIDA Bonaparte For his wife, Zenaida (see Appendix under Zenaide). **Z. asiatica** (Linnaeus): WHITE-WINGED DOVE; L. *asiatica,* "Asian." Linnaeus based this bird on "the Brown Indian Dove" of Edwards whose specimen came, according to him, from "Indiis," though he should have indicated it was Jamaica in the West Indies. This unclear identification of the place possibly confused Linnaeus. **Z. aurita** (Temminck): ZENAIDA DOVE; L. *auritus,* "eared," for the dark line of feathers above and below the ear coverts which suggests an ear's outline. **Z. macroura** (Linnaeus): MOURNING DOVE; Gr. *macros,* "long"; Gr. *oura,* "tail." We suggest that the literal meaning "Zenaida's long tail" be taken to refer to the rear end of the bird as this is its outstanding characteristic.

ZONOTRICHIA Swainson Gr. *zone,* "a band"; Gr. *trichias,* "a thrush." **Z. albicollis** (Gmelin): WHITE-THROATED SPARROW; L. *albus,* "white"; L. *collum,* "neck." Close but missed again as the bird has a white throat and not a white neck. Possibly

Gmelin should not be blamed as he had to depend on the sometimes erratic Edwards who recorded that the specimen came from "Pensilvania." **Z. atricapilla** (Gmelin): GOLDEN-CROWNED SPARROW; L. *atrus,* "black"; L. *capilla,* "hair"; for the black band around the golden crown. **Z. leucophrys** (Forster): WHITE-CROWNED SPARROW; Gr. *leucos,* "white"; Gr. *ophrys,* "eyebrow"; for the white line that goes back over the eye. **Z. querula** (Nuttall): HARRIS' SPARROW; L. *querula,* "plaintive," for the whistle-like song.

Biographical Appendix

Abert, James William (1820–1897). Served in the United States Army as an officer, rising from lieutenant to major. While on duty in the southwestern part of the United States he collected birds, among which was the towhee named in his honor by Baird.

Adams, Edward (1824–1856). G. R. Gray in 1859 named the Yellow-billed Loon for "the late Mr. Adams, Surgeon of H.M.S. Enterprise, commanded by Capt. Collinson, in the voyage made by him through the Behring Straits." "Dr. Adams is reported to have died on the coast of Africa," says a note from Alexander Wetmore.

Aiken, Charles E. H. (1850–1936). A taxidermist who lived in Colorado Springs. He made contributions to ornithological publications.

Alexandre, Dr. We know only that he discovered the Black-chinned Hummingbird in the Sierra Madre of Mexico. Boucier and Mulsant named the species in his honor in 1846.

Allen, Charles Andrew (1841–1930). A collector in California who secured several new species. Henshaw described what he thought was a new species collected by Allen in 1877 and named it for him. When it was found that the hummingbird had been described in 1830, Allen's name was dropped from the scientific term but retained in the common one.

Anna, Duchess of Rivoli (1806–1896). Wife of Prince Victor Massena, son of Marshal Andre Massena, Duc de Rivoli and Prince d'Essling, a marshal of France under Napoleon. The type specimen of Anna's Hummingbird was in Prince Victor's collection. It was acquired by the Academy of Natural Sciences of Philadelphia in 1846. Lesson named the bird in her honor in 1829. Audubon who met her in Paris in 1828 was impressed by her beauty and charm.

Audubon, John James (1785–1851). Audubon was born in Haiti, brought to France where he was legally adopted by his father, John Audubon, and educated. He came to America when eighteen years of age to manage his father's estate at Mill Grove on the outskirts of Philadelphia. Although remaining here only about a year, the two most important events in his life took place; he met his future wife, Lucy Bakewell, and developed his lifelong preoccupation with American birds. For forty years he roamed the country east of the Rocky Mountains making notes and drawing the birds. He visited England to raise funds and get help for publishing *Birds of America* (1827–1838). The illustrations and descriptions of birds were a monumental achievement and inspiration of lasting influence. His *Ornithological Biography* (1839) and *Synopsis of the Birds of North America* (1839) with MacGillivray established his reputation. In order to include in his work the birds west of the Rockies, he worked out an amicable arrangement with John Townsend to use his collection of western birds. Audubon described thirty-four birds for the first time, which are included in the fourth edition of the A.O.U. *Check-list.* This number includes both

species and subspecies, as in Audubon's time there
was no distinction made between the two. Of the
thirty-four birds listed, twenty-three were named
for people. In the fifth edition of the A.O.U.
Check-list (1957), twenty-one species were named
by Audubon, fourteen of them for people. Nuttall
was so honored twice with a magpie and a poorwill,
as was Bachman with a warbler and an oystercatcher. Townsend was commemorated three times
with a solitaire, a bunting and a fox sparrow. All
were named for men who had befriended him or
whom he admired. No bird bears the name of the
one who did the most for him, his wife, Lucy.
Northwood suggests that she may have arrived
surreptitiously as Baird's daughter, was most likely
named for Lucy Audubon, and a warbler was
named for her.

Bachman, Dr. John (1790–1874).   Dr. Bachman was a
minister of Charleston, South Carolina, and a close
friend of Audubon whose two sons married Bachman's daughters. Audubon named the warbler
which Bachman discovered after him as well as the
Black Oystercatcher and a sparrow. Audubon says,
"My friend Bachman has the merit of having
discovered this pretty little species of warbler, and
to him I have the pleasure of acknowledging my
obligations for the pair which you will find pre-
sented in the plate,—I myself have never had the
good fortune to meet with any individuals of this
interesting Sylvia."

Baird, Spencer Fullerton (1823–1887).   Baird was se-
cretary of the Smithsonian Institution, First United
States Fish Commissioner, and organizer of the
zoological work of the Pacific Railroad Surveys.
Author of *Catalogue of North American Mammals*,
Catalogue of North American Birds; co-author with
Brewer and Ridgway of *Land Birds* and *Water*

Birds. He described and named several genera and many species of birds. This was done in the ninth volume of the *Pacific Railroad Reports.* Coues says, "This . . . volume, published in 1858, represents the most important and decided single step ever taken in North American ornithology in all that related to the technicalities of the science. It affected a revolution in classification and nomenclature, nearly all the names of our birds being changed in accordance with more modern usages in generic and specific determinations." Northwood relates, "As a boy of seventeen Baird wrote to Audubon about a new bird he had discovered, the Yellow-bellied Flycatcher. Audubon answered, offering to name it and asking for help in collecting species of small mammals for the "Quadrupeds." So started a friendship that lasted for the rest of Audubon's career. Baird visited Audubon in New York two years later and became a great friend of the family. Audubon wanted Baird to come with him on the Missouri expedition, but the boy could not get permission from his family. Concerning Baird's Sparrow, Audubon says, "I have named this species after my young friend, Spencer F. Baird, of Carlisle, Pennsylvania." Coues also named a sandpiper for him.

Barrow, Sir John (1764–1848). A native of England, Secretary of the Admiralty, founder of the Royal Geographical Society and a promoter of Arctic exploration. He was the author of "Historic Arctic Voyages" (1818) and other works. We find his name in Point Barrow and Barrow's Straits. Swainson named Barrow's Goldeneye for him, but the scientific name was preempted although the popular name has been retained. His name is still valid in the scientific name of a subspecies of the Glaucous Gull.

Bartram, William (1739–1823). Called the "Grandfather of American Ornithology" mainly because of his influence on Alexander Wilson. His book of travels as a naturalist was his chief work. His father, John, was world famous as a botanist.

Bell, John Graham (1812–1889). A famous taxidermist of New York who accompanied Audubon on his Missouri River trip in 1843. Later in California he collected several new species of birds described by Cassin. Bell's Vireo and the Sage Sparrow were named for him.

Bendire, Charles Emil (1836–1897). While an officer in the United States Army, he collected in the west. He was Curator of Oology in the United States National Museum. He was the author of *Life Histories of North American Birds.* Coues named a thrasher in his honor.

Bewick, Thomas (1754–1828). English author and wood engraver, wrote and illustrated *A History of British Birds.* Audubon says, "I honored this species (Bewick's Wren) with the name of Bewick, a person too well known for his admirable talents as an engraver on wood, and for his beautiful work on the *Birds of Great Britain,* to need any eulogy of mine. I have enjoyed the pleasure of a personal acquaintance with him, and found him at all times a most agreeable, kind and benevolent friend."

Blackburn, Anna (1740–1793). "Mrs." according to both Coues and Bent, which raises a question as her brother was Ashton Blackburn. Possibly she married a cousin or retained her maiden name for business purposes. She was a patron of ornithology and had a museum in Fairfield, Lancashire, England. Her brother Ashton collected in the United States before his death in 1780. Possibly he sent the specimen to England which for some time bore her name. She did, nevertheless, achieve scientific ornithological immortality by having her name attached to a type of rail in 1789, which so far the law of priority has not displaced.

Bonaparte, Charles Lucien Jules Laurent, Prince of Canino and Musignano (1803–1857). Naturalist. He was one of eleven children of Lucien, a younger brother of Napoleon. His wife Zenaida q.v., was the daughter of Joseph, Napoleon's older brother. With the decline in the family fortunes after Waterloo, Charles, Zenaida, and uncle, father-in-law, Joseph, came to America where they lived in Bordentown, New Jersey, and Philadelphia, Pennsylvania. Here the first of the couple's eight children was born. While residing in the United States from 1822 until 1828, he re-edited a volume with the longest title in American ornithology even without appending the full names of the author, *American Ornithology, or History of Birds Inhabiting the United States not given by Wilson.* He is considered to be the father of systematic ornithology in America. His name is commemorated in Bonaparte's Gull.

Botteri, Matteo (1808–1877). Born in Yugoslavia, he lived in Mexico from 1854 until his death. The sparrow named for him by Sclater was presumably collected by him near Orizaba in Southern Mexico.

Brandt, Johaan Friedrich (1802–1879). An eminent German zoologist who became head of the Zoological Museum at St. Petersburg. He described several birds and mammals from western United States and the Pacific coast. The common name of a west coast cormorant commemorates him.

Brewer, Thomas Mayo (1814–1880). Boston publisher and editor. He was well known for his work on *North American Oology* (1857) and was a champion of the House Sparrow upon its introduction in the United States.

Buller, Sir Walter Lawry (1838–1906). A native of New Zealand and a lawyer by profession who became one of the leading authorities on New Zealand birds. He spent the latter part of his life in England. Although Buller never visited America, the New Zealand Shearwater, named for him, appears on the west coast of the United States.

Bullock, William (1775–1840). English traveler and mine owner, proprietor of Bullock's Museum in London. While visiting a mine near Mexico City, he collected a number of birds new to science. Swainson described these and named in his honor Bullock's Oriole, *Icterus galbula bullockii*, now a subspecies.

Cabot, Dr. Samuel (1815–1885). He was Curator of the Department of Ornithology at the Boston Society of Natural History. On expedition to Yucatan in the 1840s, he made important ornithological collections and discovered several new species. He described Cabot's Tern as a new species, but it has since been relegated to subspecific status. Most of his work was published in the "Proceedings" and "Journal" of the Boston Society of Natural History. His ornithological collection is in the Harvard Museum of Comparative Zoology.

Cassin, John (1813–1869). Curator of Ornithology at the Academy of Natural Sciences of Philadelphia, the institution with which he was connected for twenty-six years. He was one of the leading systematists of his time, possessing what was then rather unusual in this country, a broad knowledge of foreign birds. In all he described 193 species of birds. Many of these were done in connection with the ornithological reports of government expeditions including the Wilkes Exploring Expedition around the World, the Gillis Astronomical Expedition to Peru and the Perry Expedition to Japan which he accompanied. Several birds have been named in his honor. *Cassinia,* the journal of the Delaware Valley Ornithological Club, also commemorates him.

Clark, Captain William (1770–1838). With his fellow captain in the United States Army he led the famous expedition which crossed the country in 1804–1806. Shortly after the return of the expedition, he resigned from the army and became the governor of the Missouri Territory. He was a brother of George Rogers Clark, the famous Indian fighter. The dairy of Lewis and Clark, *History of the Expedition under the Commands of Captain Lewis and Clark*, was published in 1814. Clark's Nutcracker was named for him.

Cooper, William C. (1798–1864). One of the founders of the New York Lyceum of Natural History. He described the Evening Grosbeak. Cooper's Hawk was named in his honor. He was the father of Dr. James C. Cooper, a noted California ornithologist.

Cory, Charles Barney (1857–1921). American ornithologist who was with the Field Museum in Chicago after 1906. He described the shearwater whose common name commemorates him. The vernacular name used in Britain according to the *Check-list of the Birds of Britain and Ireland* published by the British Ornithologists' Union is North Atlantic Shearwater. They, however, list the vernacular name used in the United States as a second vernacular name whenever there is a difference. Hence Cory is listed overseas.

Costa, Louis Marie Pantaleon, Marquis de Beau-Regard (1806–1864). This French nobleman began to collect birds and minerals in his boyhood. He later specialized in hummingbirds gathering together an imposing collection. In recognition of this interest, Bourcier in 1839 named a species *Calypte costae* in his honor.

Coues, Dr. Elliott (1842–1899). Served as a surgeon in the United States Army (1864–1881). He was the author of *Birds of the Colorado Valley, Birds of the Northwest, Key to North American Birds* and many papers. He served on the committee that prepared the first and second editions of the A.O.U. *Checklist of North American Birds.* Coues' Flycatcher bears his name.

Craveri, Frederico (1815–1890). An Italian scientist of wide interests (chemistry, meteorology, mineralogy, zoology). In 1840 he went to Mexico where he assisted in the school of chemistry in the University in Mexico City. During his twenty years in the country he traveled widely collecting minerals and animals. While on a trip with his brother to examine the guano deposits on islands off the west coast of Lower California he collected a murrelet which twenty years later Sclater named in his honor. His last thirty years were spent teaching in Turin, Italy.

Degland, Dr. Come Damien (1787–1856). Director of the Museum d'Histoire Naturelle in Lille, France. He was the author of several publications on European birds. Bonaparte in 1850 named the White-winged Scoter in his honor.

Diaz, Augustin (1829–1893). Director of the Geographical and Exploring Commission of Mexico which made extensive natural history collections in that country. Ridgway who described the birds collected in 1886 named the Mexican Duck *Anas diazi* in his honor.

Fischer, Gotthelf (1771–1853). German naturalist and chemist who was professor of Natural History at

Moscow about 1804. He was the author of works on natural history and anatomy. The Spectacled Eider bears his name.

Forster, Johann Reinhold (1729–1798). Accompanied Captain Cook on his voyage around the world in 1772. He wrote *Observations made during a Voyage Around the World* in 1778. His ornithological fame rests on a treatise on the birds of Hudson Bay for which Nuttall commemorated him by naming a tern in his honor. His son, Johann Georg Adam Forster, was on the voyage with Captain Cook and also published a book, *A Voyage Around the World.*

Franklin, Sir John (1786–1847). British navigator and explorer who perished on his fourth Arctic expedition. He served at Trafalgar and New Orleans. His wife fitted out several ships to search for him. It was finally determined his ship was abandoned and his whole party lost. Franklin's Gull bears his name.

Gambel, William (1819–1849). A protégé of Nuttall who crossed the continent first in 1841. He was the first ornithologist to spend several years in California collecting and describing birds. The Mountain Chickadee and a quail bear his name. He died of typhoid fever while attempting to cross the Sierra in mid-winter.

Grace Darlington Coues (1847–1939). Dr. Elliott Coues, while stationed at Fort Whipple near Prescott, Arizona, in 1865 collected a new warbler. He requested his friend Spencer Baird to name it in honor of his sister and this was done. Miss Coues married Charles Albert Page, one time United States Minister to Switzerland, and after his death, Dana Estes, a publisher.

Hammond, William Alexander (1828–1900). He was Surgeon-General of the United States Army from 1862 until 1864, when he was court-martialed and dismissed, but reinstated in 1878. Through him John Xantus met Spencer Baird and was given an opportunity to do zoological field work in the West. He repaid Hammond by naming a flycatcher for him that was collected at Fort Tejon in California.

Harcourt, Edwin Vernon (1825–1891). An English naturalist who discovered and described in his book, *Sketch of Madeira* the petrel *Thallassidroma castro* in 1851. "In recognition of his work, the bird was given its common name," according to Alexander Wetmore.

Harlan, Dr. Richard (1796–1843). A prominent physician and naturalist. He was the author of *Fauna Americana*, published in 1825. Audubon says, "Long before I discovered this fine hawk, I was anxious to have an opportunity of honoring some new species of the feathered tribe with the name of my excellent friend Dr. Richard Harlan of Philadelphia. This I might have done sooner, had I not waited until a species should occur, which in size and importance should bear some proportion to my gratitude toward that learned and accomplished friend." And so we have Harlan's Hawk.

Harris, Edward (1799–1863). A companion of Audubon on his Missouri trip in 1843 whom Audubon called "one of the best friends I have in the world." Audubon named a sparrow, a woodpecker and a hawk for him. Although the birds are now classified as subspecies, Harris' name is used for the common name of Harris' Hawk. The woodpecker is a subspecies of the Hairy Woodpecker. In naming this bird Audubon says, "Having been left at liberty to give names to whatever species might occur among the birds transmitted to me by that zealous naturalist, (John Townsend) I have honored the present woodpecker with the name of my friend Edward Harris, Esq., a gentleman to whom I am most deeply indebted for many acts of kindness and generosity, and in particular for his efficient aid at a time when, like my predecessor Wilson, I was reduced to the lowest degree of indigence and removed from any individuals to whom I could make known my wants. But, independently of his claim to scientific recognition as the friend and supporter of one who has devoted his life to the study of birds, he merits this tribute as an ardent and successful cultivator of ornithology. . . ."

Heermann, Dr. Adolphus L. (1818–1865). He was an active collector in the western part of the United States and a surgeon naturalist on one of the Pacific Railroad surveys in 1853–1854. Interested particularly in bird eggs, he is credited with introducing the term, "oology." A gull and a song sparrow commemorate him.

Henslow, John Stevens (1796–1861). English botanist, compiler of *Catalogue of British Plants* and *Dictionary of Botanical Terms.* Audubon, in naming the sparrow, says, "In naming it after the Rev. Professor Henslow of Cambridge, a gentleman so well-known in the scientific world, and has permitted me to so designate it, my object has been to manifest my gratitude for the many kind attentions which he has shown towards me." Henslow was Professor of Botany at the University of Cambridge and helped Audubon obtain the subscription of the University to the "Birds." He recommended Charles Darwin as a naturalist and introduced him to Captain Fitz Roy of the Beagle.

Holboell, Carl Peter (1795–1856). An officer in the Danish Royal Navy, he served as Royal Inspector of Colonies and Whaling and Governor of South Greenland. While in this post he became interested in natural history. He described the Hoary Redpoll, which he named for Hornemann. At one time the Gryfalcon and the Red-necked Grebe bore his name. Reclassification necessitated changes in nomenclature, causing Holboell's name to be pushed aside as a species name. His name continued to be used as the common name for the grebe until Red-necked, approved by the A.O.U. *Check-list* Committee gradually took over.

Hornemann, Jens Wilken (1770–1841). Danish scientist, professor in the University of Copenhagen.

Hutton, William. A little known field collector who obtained birds about Washington, D.C. in 1844, 1845 and 1857. He collected in California in 1847 and 1848, where he obtained the vireo that John Cassin named for him.

Kirtland, Dr. Jared Potter (1793–1877). A prominent physician and naturalist of Cleveland, Ohio, who founded the Cleveland Medical College. Spencer Baird named the warbler first found near Cleveland in his honor.

Kittlitz, Friedrich Heinrich (1779–1874). A German Naval Officer and explorer whose account of his work in Kamchatka and Alaska was published in 1858. The last twenty-five years of his life were spent at Mainz, where he was probably connected with the university there. Kittlitz Murrelet was first collected by him.

Lawrence, George Newbold (1806–1895). Lawrence worked with Baird and Cassin describing the birds collected on the Pacific Railroad Surveys, mainly the water birds. Cassin named in his honor the goldfinch which bears his name.

Leach, William Elford (1790–1836). An English naturalist who developed a system of arrangement in conchology and entomology. He acquired the specimen of petrel which was named for him in a sale of a collection of Bullock's specimens.

LeConte, Dr. John (1818–1891). A native of Georgia,

he turned from the practice of medicine to teaching physics and chemistry, mainly in southern colleges from which he took a respite to operate a gunpowder factory in South Carolina during the Civil War. He resumed his academic career teaching physics at the University of California at Berkeley of which he was president from 1875 till 1881. Coues refers to him as Major LeConte, a rank he probably held while supervising the production of anti-Yankee detonation chemicals. The common name of a sparrow commemorates him. He and John L. LeConte were first cousins.

LeConte, Dr. John Lawrence (1825–1883). A leading entomologist in the United States, who specialized in Coleoptera. He was also interested in birds and had a thrasher named for him. Independently wealthy he never practiced medicine. He was president of the American Association for the Advancement of Science.

Lesson, Clemence, wife of Rene P. Lesson (1794–1849). A French naturalist who originally described the Blue-throated Hummingbird, *Lanpornis clemenciae*, and named it for "notre épouse," his wife.

Lewis, Captain Meriwether (1774–1809). One of the leaders of the Lewis and Clark Expedition which crossed the West in 1804–1806 but paused long enough on Saturday, July 20, 1805, near Helena, Montana, to collect a woodpecker. Wilson in describing it named it in honor of Lewis. Although the original name has been changed somewhat, the "Lewis" has been maintained.

L'Herminier, Dr. Ford J. (1802–1866) and Felix L. (1779–1833). Son and father who lived on Guadeloupe in the West Indies. Audubon's Shearwater was named either for one or both of them.

Lichtenstein, Martin Henrich (1780–1857). German zoologist and traveler, and founder of the Berlin

Zoo. An oriole was named for him by Wagler, another German zoologist.

Lincoln, Thomas (1812–1883). When twenty-one years old he accompanied Audubon on his trip to the coast of Labrador. A new sparrow was found and as this was discovered by Lincoln, Audubon named it for him.

Lucy Hunter Baird (1848–1913). Daughter of Spencer F. Baird, q.v. When she was thirteen years old, Dr. J. G. Cooper named a warbler for her. She collected bibliographical material for her father which formed the basis for the book authored by Dr. W. H. Dall.

McCown, John P. (1815–1879). The following is from *Life Histories of North American Cardinals, Grosbeaks, Buntings, Towhees, Finches, Sparrows and Their Allies* by Bent, p. 1564: " 'I fired at a flock of Shore Larks,' writes Captain John P. McCown, U.S.A. (1851), 'and found this bird among those killed.' For this, in the first published description of the bird, George N. Lawrence (1851) announced, 'It gives me pleasure to bestow upon this species the name of my friend, Capt. J. P. McCown, U.S.A.' " He served in the U.S. Army, 1840–1869.

MacDougall, Dr. Patrick (1770–1817). Dr. MacDougall of Glasgow, Scotland, obtained the first specimen of the Roseate Tern in the Cumbrey Islands in the Firth of Clyde in 1812. For this he is honored by having the last part of his name "Dougall" given to the bird.

MacGillivray, William (1796–1852). Author of *A History of British Birds*, (five volumes). Of him, Northwood says, "He agreed to revise and correct Audubon's proof for two guineas for each sheet of sixteen pages, about six dollars today. He was well grounded in the anatomy of birds, and Audubon was fortunate to have obtained the services of so able and diligent a worker, who originated modern classification based on anatomy. When the work was well in hand Audubon and his family toured the lowlands of Scotland with MacGillivray as guide."

McGregor, Richard Crittenden (1871–1936). Came to America from Australia in the eighties, and after collecting birds in California, he was appointed ornithologist in the Bureau of Science at Manila in the Philippines. He published numerous papers on the birds of the Philippines when editor of the *Philippine Journal of Science.* In 1920 he published a condensed *Index to the Genera of Birds* of the world. In 1897 A. W. Anthony named the House Finch, *Carpodacus McGregori*, in his honor.

McKay, Charles Leslie (?–1883). The following paragraph is from *Birds of Alaska* by Ira N. Gabrielson and Frederick C. Lincoln, p. 12: "Charles Leslie McKay, another Signal Corps man who was stationed at Bristol Bay, also was active in collecting birds. He arrived at Nushagak, then known as Fort Alexander, in the spring of 1881. He continued active until April 19, 1883, when he was drowned in Bristol Bay after a small boat, in which he was traveling, capsized. During this period he collected about 400 specimens which were sent to the National Museum where many are still available. Among others, he secured the first specimens of the bird now known as McKay's Snow Bunting." The common name of this species, but not the scientific one, bears his name.

Mauri, Prof. Ernesto (1791–1836). An Italian naturalist connected with the Botanical Gardens in Rome. Cabanis named the Western Sandpiper in his honor in 1858.

Neboux, Dr. Adolphe Simon. "Little is known about

Neboux except that he was Surgeon Major on the French exploring vessel 'Venus,' which visited the coast of California in the course of a cruise extending from 1836 to 1839." The Blue-footed Booby named in his honor in 1882 by Milne-Edwards, the eminent French zoologist, was possibly based on a specimen collected on the "Venus" expedition.

Nuttall, Thomas (1786–1859). Born in England, he came to the United States in 1808. He was first interested in botany and was Curator of the Botanical Gardens at Harvard (1822–1832). Later devoting himself to ornithology, he authored *A Manual of the Ornithology of the United States and Canada*, of which Coues says, "Nuttall like good wine does not deteriorate with age." On a trip to California by boat he may be identified as the naturalist, Old Curious, in Richard Henry Dana's *Two Years before the Mast*. His name appears in a genus, *Nuttallornis*, and three species; a woodpecker, a poorwill and a magpie as well as a subspecies of sparrow. Audubon, in naming the Yellow-billed Magpie in his honor, says, "I have conferred on this beautiful bird the name of a most zealous, learned and enterprising naturalist, my friend Thomas Nuttall, Esq., to whom the scientific world is deeply indebted for many additions to our zoological and botanical knowledge which have resulted from his labors." Succeeding to an inheritance, he returned to England.

Oberholser, Dr. Harry Church (1870–1963). A leading American systematist who revised some groups and described a number of new species and subspecies. His name was commemorated by Phillips when he described the Dusky Flycatcher. After his retirement from the Fish and Wildlife Service, he was

Curator of Ornithology at the Cleveland Museum
of Natural History.

Paris brothers. They were dealers in natural history
specimens in Paris in 1837 when Bonaparte named
Scott's Oriole for them. They quite likely financed
scientific collecting expeditions as part of their
business.

Ridgway, Robert (1850–1929). He was on the staff of
the Smithsonian Institution in charge of bird
collections from 1869 till 1880 and Curator of Birds
of the United States National Museum from 1880
till 1929. He served on the committees that published the first, second and third editions of the
American Ornithologists' Union's *Check-list of
North American Birds*. He also served as president
of that organization. With Spencer F. Baird and
Thomas M. Brewer he wrote *A History of North
American Birds* (5 vols., I–III,1874; IV–V,1884). He
was sole author of *Color Standards and Nomenclature* (1886), *The Birds of North and Middle America*
(8 vols., 1901–1919) and many papers. A whip-
poor-will bears his name.

Rivoli, Victor Massena, Duc de (1798–1863). Son of
one of Napoleon's marshals and owner of an
extensive collection of hummingbirds. Lesson
named one for him but it was preempted by the
name given by Swainson two years earlier, so the
scientific name did not stand although the common
name has done so. See Anna for another hummingbird, honoring Rivoli's wife.

Ross, Bernard Rogan (1827–1874). Chief factor of the
Hudson Bay Company and a correspondent of the
Smithsonian Institution. Cassin named the Little
Snow Goose for him.

Ross, Sir James Clark (1800–1862). This Scottish polar
explorer made several Arctic expeditions and one
Antarctic one. With his uncle, Sir John Ross, he

determined the position of the north Magnetic Pole. He published *Voyage of Discovery* (1847). Ross' Gull was named in his honor.

Sabine, Sir Edward (1788–1883). An eminent English astronomer and physicist, president of the British Association for the Advancement of Science and of the Royal Society. On a voyage to the Arctic in 1819 with the Ross and Perry expedition as astronomer, a fork-tailed gull was obtained near Melville Bay on the west coast of Greenland. This bird was named in his honor by his brother, Joseph, who in turn is commemorated by having his name attached to one of the ten subspecies of the Ruffed Grouse.

Say, Thomas (1787–1843). He accompanied Major Stephen H. Long's expedition to the Rocky Mountains in 1819–1820 as a naturalist and prepared its report on the birds. He was a pioneer in the field of entomology and the author of *American Entomology*, a three-volume work describing the insects of North America, published 1824–1828. The genus *Sayornis* and Say's Phoebe commemorate him.

Sclater, Dr. P. L. (1829–1913). A fellow of the Royal Society, Secretary of Zoological Society of London (1859–1903). He contributed several volumes to the *Catalogue of Birds of the British Museum.* The scientific name of the Mexican Chickadee commemorates him.

Scott, Winfield (1786–1866). Commander of the American forces in the Mexican War. Couch, one of his lieutenants, thought he found (1854) a new bird and described it under the name *Icterus scottii,* but Bonaparte had named it *parisorum* seventeen years previously. The common name, however, has been kept.

Smith, Gideon B. (1793–1867). Audubon, a friend of Smith, gave the common name to Smith's Longspur in honor of his Baltimore friend and editor.

Sprague, Isaac (1811–1895). An artist who accompanied Audubon on his Missouri River trip. Audubon named a pipit for him, saying, "The first specimen of this truly interesting lark, was procured by Mr. Isaac Sprague, another of my companions."

Steller, George Wilhelm (1709–1746). A German naturalist who accompanied Vitus Bering, the Danish navigator who was employed by Russia to determine whether or not the coasts of Siberia and Alaska were contiguous. Bering died when the expedition was wintering on Bering Island in 1741–1742. Steller wrote an account of his travels and described birds and animals, among them Steller's sea cow (extinct) and Steller's sea lion. An eider and jay bear his name. He died in Tiumen, Siberia.

Swainson, William (Liverpool, England, 1789–New Zealand, 1855). Widely traveled and versatile naturalist. Visited the shores of the Mediterranean and South America. He collected, illustrated, and wrote. Among his principal works are *Zoological Illustrations or Original Figures and Descriptions of New, Rare or Interesting Animals* (six volumes); eleven volumes in Lardner's *Cabinet Encyclopedia*; three volumes in Jardiner's *Naturalist's Library*; and other works. He wrote on molluscs, fish and animals. Audubon met him in England and was helped by his favorable reviews. They traveled to Paris together and met Cuvier and other French scientists. Audubon failed to obtain Swainson's services as joint author in describing birds. Swainson emigrated to New Zealand in 1841 where he became attorney general. Audubon named a warbler for him and Bonaparte a hawk. We also have his name in the common name for a thrush.

Thayer, John Eliot (1862–1933). An outstanding ornithologist who assembled a large collection of birds
and a comprehensive ornithological library. The
gull named for him has been restored to specific
status.

Tolmie, Dr. William Fraser (1818–1886). A physician,
educated in Scotland, he was assigned by the
Hudson Bay Company to Fort Vancouver in 1833.
He was the first to describe a climb to the summit
of Mount Ranier. In 1836 he met Townsend, q.v.,
who discovered a new warbler which he named in
Tolmie's honor. Audubon, thinking he was making
an initial description, named the bird for MacGillivray. As Townsend's publication preceded Audubon's the scientific name reverted although the
common name has been retained. Tolmie became
chief factor in Vancouver for the Hudson Bay
Company in 1856 and retired in 1860.

Townsend, John Kirk (1809–1851). Much admired by
contemporary ornithologists, he is best known for
his *Narrative of a Journey across the Rocky Mountains.* In this he described some of the new birds he
found and sent them as specimens, along with
some he did not describe, to Audubon, who states
he was given "the liberty to name whatever new
specimens might occur." This caused confusion in
naming MacGillivray's Warbler (see Tolmie, Dr.
William Fraser). Audubon wrote of another bird,
the Solitaire, "Transmitted to me by my friend, Mr.
Townsend, after whom, not finding any description
of it, I have named it." This seems to indicate not
only that Audubon became a bit more wary in
naming birds, but also that the "Tolmie" episode
caused no animosity, especially as Audubon also
named a bunting for him. It seems that when
Townsend was about to publish a description of a
new warbler, he found out that Nuttall was about

to do the same thing, and had named the warbler for him. Townsend decided that Nuttall's manuscript had priority and that the name should stand. Thus, although he is recorded as its describer, Townsend cannot be charged with naming a bird in his own honor, even if he worked the law of priority a bit overtime.

Traill, Dr. Thomas Stewart (1781–1862). A founder of the Royal Institution of Liverpool, where Audubon visited him and in return for his support said, "I have named this species (Traill's Flycatcher) after my learned friend, Dr. Thomas Stewart Traill, of Edinburgh, in evidence of the gratitude which I cherish toward that gentleman for all his kind attention to me." He became professor of medical jurisprudence at the University of Edinburgh and edited the eighth edition of the *Encyclopedia Britannica*. By exposing the neglect of the Natural History Museum when it was part of the British Museum, he was instrumental in the independent establishment of the Museum of Natural History in South Kensington.

Trudeau, James deBertz (1817–1887). A physician and friend of Audubon, with whom he became acquainted during Audubon's stay in Louisiana. Audubon named the White-winged Dove for him, but his name has been dropped for this bird. It remains, however, in Trudeau's Tern, the type specimen of which he procured for Audubon.

Vallisnieri, Antonio (1661–1730). Italian naturalist, professor of medicine at the University of Padua. Wilson named the Canvasback after one of its main foods, the wild celery *Vallisnieri americana* which was named in honor of the Italian naturalist.

Vaux, William S. (1811–1882). A member of the Academy of Natural Sciences of Philadelphia and a friend of John K. Townsend, who named a swift he had discovered on the Columbia River in his honor.

Verreaux, J. B. Edouard (1810–1868). A French naturalist who worked in South Africa (1828–1830) and in China (1832–1837).

Verreaux, Jules P. (1807–1873). Brother of J. B. Edouard. Worked in South Africa (1818–1820), China (1825–1830), the Philippines (1832–1839), and Australia (1842–1847). Bonaparte honored the brothers by naming the White-fronted Dove for them.

Virginia, for Mrs. William W. Anderson, nee Mary Virginia Childs. Her husband, Dr. William Wallace Anderson (1824–1911), a native of South Carolina, served as a surgeon in the United States Army from 1849 until his registration in 1861, and in the Confederate Army until 1865 when the whole army resigned. While stationed in New Mexico in 1860, he discovered a new warbler named by Baird for Mrs. Anderson, which seems a roundabout way of honoring the bird's discoverer, although it was most likely done at her husband's request.

Whitney, Josiah Dwight (1819–1896). An eminent American geologist. While he was director of the Geographical Survey of California, a member of his staff, Dr. James G. Cooper, whose father already had a hawk named for him, found a new Elf Owl which he named for the head of the survey, Dr. Whitney.

Wied, Prince Maximilian zu (1782–1867). A German naturalist and traveler who wrote *Journey to Brazil* (1815–1817) and *Journey to Interior of North America* (1832–1834). His name was given to Wied's Crested Flycatcher.

Williamson, Robert Stockton (1824–1882). A lieutenant in the United States Army in charge of the

Pacific Railroad Survey in northern California and
Oregon. Dr. Newberry, the surgeon on the survey,
collected what he thought to be specimens of a new
woodpecker, which he named in honor of the
leader of the expedition. These specimens, which
happen to be all males, were collected in 1857. Six
years before this Cassin collected specimens of a
new woodpecker which he named *thyroideus*. These
specimens happened to be all females, a fact that
became evident when *thyroideus* and *williamsonii*
were found to be connubially cooperative. So the
williamsonii was dropped, not in deference to the
fair sex, but to the rule of priority. The common
name knowing no such restriction has been retained in Williamson's Sapsucker.

Wilson, Alexander (1766–1813).   Born in Scotland, the
"Father of American Ornithology" came to the
United States in 1794. While teaching school in
Philadelphia, his interest in birds was encouraged
by William Bartram. Traveling throughout the
eastern United States collecting birds he meticu-
lously noted range, habitat and behavior. His
observations were published in his nine-volume
American Ornithology (1808–1814) which was com-
pleted by George Ord. Twenty-three specimens
originally described by him in this classic still
retain their validity in the latest (1957) A.O.U.
Check-list. He was prone to name birds for the
places where he found them. A petrel, a plover, a
warbler and a genus of warblers bear his name. It
has been said that his contemporary Audubon was
a great artist with a talent for ornithology, but that
Wilson was a great ornithologist with artistic talent.

Wollweber.   An obscure German naturalist who collected the first specimen of the Bridled Titmouse in
Zacatecas, Mexico, which Bonaparte described and
named for him.

Wright, Charles (1811–1855). A self-taught botanist who collected plants for Asa Gray of Harvard in Texas, Cuba, Africa, China and Japan. He accompanied the Exploratory Team for the Pacific Railroad as a botanist. When Baird described the new birds found on the railroad survey he named the Gray Flycatcher in Wright's honor. Possibly Wright collected the original specimen.

Xantus de Vescy, Louis Jonas (commonly known as John Xantus) (1825–1894). Born in Hungary, he came to the United States as a young man and enlisted in the army. Stationed as a hospital steward at Fort Tejon, California, he described two new species of birds from his large collection in that area. Later he collected on the lower California coast and about Colira, Mexico, where he was the United States Consul. He returned to Hungary as custodian of the museum in Budapest, traveled to the East Indies and was active in the International Ornithological Congress in Vienna in 1884. Although three birds from Lower California bear his name, a murrelet is the only one on the A.O.U. *Check-list* that does so.

Zenaide, Princess Zenaide Charlotte Julie Bonaparte (1804–1854). Cousin and wife of Charles Lucien Jules Laurent Bonaparte, Prince of Canino and Musignano, whom she married in 1822 on the eve of their departure for the United States. Here they lived in Bordentown, New Jersey, and Philadelphia, Pennsylvania, with her father, Joseph, king of Spain (1808–1813) till 1828, when they returned to Europe. The close association of mated pairs that gave rise to the old common name of "love bird" for the dove may be the reason Bonaparte wished to link the name of his wife to this ornithological symbol of conjugal bliss. Her name is preserved in the generic name Zenaida.

Bibliography

American Ornithologists' Union. *Check-list of North American Birds*. Washington, D.C.: Smithsonian Institution, 1957.

Audubon, John James. *American Ornithological Biography*. Edinburgh: Adam Black, 1831.

Auk, The. Journal of the American Ornithologists' Union. Washington, D.C. Particularly the Thirty-second Supplement to the *Check-list of North American Birds,* vol. 90, no. 2 (April 1957), pp. 411–419.

Bent, Arthur Cleveland. *Life Histories of North American Birds*. 26 volumes. New York: Dover Publications, Inc., 1961–1968.

British Ornithologists' Union. *Check-list of the Birds of Great Britain and Ireland*. London, 1952.

Bullfinch, Thomas. *The Age of Fable*. Philadelphia: David McKay, 1898.

Catesby, Mark. *Natural History of Carolina, Florida and the Bahama Islands,* 1731.

Chaucer, Geoffrey. *The Works of Chaucer*. Globe edition. New York: Macmillan Co., 1919.

Coble, Mary F. *Introduction to Ornithological Nomenclature*. Los Angeles: American Book Institute, 1964.

Coues, Elliott. *Key to North American Birds*. 6th edition. Boston: The Page Company, 1927.

Darwin, Charles. *The Origin of Species and the Descent of Man,* 1859. New York: Modern Library, new edition.

Driver, Samuel Rolles. *The International Critical Commentary,* section on Deuteronomy. New York: Scribner, 1902.

Eaton, Elon Howard. *Birds of New York.* Albany: New York State Museum, Memoir 12, 1914.

Eisenman, E., and H. H. Poor. *Suggested Principles of Vernacular Nomenclature.* Wilson Bulletin 58 (1946), pp. 2,100–2,115.

Ellis, Edward S. *Classical Dictionary.* Philadelphia: Penn Publishing Co., 1895.

Evans, A. H. *Turner on Birds.* Cambridge: Cambridge University Press, 1903.

Fisher, James. *The Shell Bird Book.* London: George Rainbind, Ltd., 1966.

Fisher, James A. "Systematics." *A History of Birds.* Boston: Houghton Mifflin Co., 1954.

Francis, W. Nelson. "Revolution in Grammar." *Quarterly Journal of Speech,* October 1954.

Greenough, James B., and George L. Kittredge. *Words and Their Ways in English Speech.* New York: Macmillan Co., 1920.

Grossman, Mary Louise, and John Hamley. *Birds of Prey of the World.* New York: Clarkson N. Potter, Inc., 1964.

Harting, James Edmund, and Grundy Steiner, ed. *The Birds of Shakespeare.* Chicago: Argonaut, 1965.

Ingersoll, Ernest. "An Adventure in Etymology." *The Scientific Monthly,* vol. 45, no. 3 (1937), pp. 233–249.

Innes, Mary M. *The Metamorphoses of Ovid.* Baltimore: The Penguin Classics, 1955.

Jaeger, Edmund O. *A Source Book of Biological Names and Terms.* 2nd edition. Springfield, Illinois: Charles C Thomas, 1950.

Jordan, David Starr. *Manual of the Vertebrate Animals of the Northeastern United States.* 13th edition. Yonkers on Hudson, New York: World Book Company, 1929.

MacLeod, R. D. *Key to the Names of British Birds.* London and New York: Sir Isaac Piman & Sons, 1954.

Mayr, Ernst. *Systematics and the Origin of Species.* New York: Columbia University Press, 1942.

Newton, Alfred, assisted by Hans Gaslow. *A Dictionary of Birds.* London: Adam Black, 1896.

Northwood, J. d'Arcy. "Audubon's Firsts." *The Atlantic Naturalist,* vol. 2, no. 5. Washington, D.C.: Audubon Society of the District of Columbia, 1956.

Nybakken, Oscar E. *Greek and Latin Scientific Terminology.* Ames, Iowa: Iowa State College Press, 1959.

Oxford Dictionary of English Etymology. New York: Oxford University Press, 1966.

Oxford English Dictionary. New York: Oxford University Press, 1933.

Palmer, T. S. "Notes on Persons Whose Names Appear in the Nomenclature of California Birds." *The Condor,* vol. 30, no. 5 (1928).

Peterson, Roger Tory. *A Field Guide to the Birds.* Boston: Houghton Mifflin Co., 1947.

———. *A Field Guide to Western Birds.* Boston: Houghton Mifflin Co., 1941.

———. *A Field Guide to Birds of Texas.* Boston: Houghton Mifflin Co., 1960.

Peterson, Roger Tory, Guy Mountfort, and P. A. D. Hollom. *A Field Guide to the Birds of Britain and Europe.* Boston: Houghton Mifflin Co., 1954.

Proceedings XII. International Ornithological Congress. Helsinki, 1958: 30–43.

Robbins, Chandler S., Bertel Braun, and Herbert S.

Zim. *Birds of North America.* New York: Golden Press, 1966.

Salomonsen, F. Report of the Standing Committee on Ornithological Nomenclature, 1960.

Skeat, Walter W. *A Concise Etymological Dictionary of the English Language.* Oxford: Oxford University Press, 1882.

Stout, Gardner D., ed. *The Shorebirds of North America.* New York: The Viking Press, 1967.

Swann, H. Kirke. *A Dictionary of English and Folk Names of British Birds.* London: Witherby & Co., 1913.

Thompson, A. Landsborough. *A New Dictionary of Birds.* London: Thomas Nelson, Ltd., and New York: McGraw-Hill, 1964.

Thomson, Helen. *Murder at Harvard.* Boston: Houghton Mifflin Co., 1971.

Wakefield, John. "Birds in Legend." *The Strange World of Birds.* Philadelphia: MacRae Smith Co., 1964.

Wallace, George W. *An Introduction ot Ornithology.* New York: Macmillan Co., 1955.

Weekly, Ernest. *An Etymological Dictionary of Modern English.* Reprint. New York: Dover Publications, 1921.

Wilson, Alexander. *American Ornithology,* vols. 1–9. Philadelphia, 1808–1814.

Woods, Robert S. *An English Classical Dictionary for the Use of Taxonomists.* Pomona, California: Pomona College.

Wynne, Col. Owen E. *Biographical Key—Names of the Birds of the World—to Authors and Those Commemorated,* 1969. O. E. Wynne, Courtwood, Sandleheath, Fordinbridge, Hants, England.

English/Latin Glossary

Accentor	*Seiurus aurocapillus*
Albatross	*Diomedia*
Black-browed	*melanophris*
Black-footed	*nigripes*
Laysan	*immutabilis*
Short-tailed	*albatrus*
White-capped	*cauta*
Yellow-nosed	*chlororhynchos*
Alta Mira	*Icterus gularis*
Anhinga	*Anhinga anhinga*
Ani	*Crotophaga*
Groove-billed	*sulcirostris*
Smooth-billed	*ani*
Auk	
Great	*Pinguinus impennis*
Little	*Alle alle*
Auklet	
Cassin's	*Ptychoramphus aleuticus*
Crested	*Aethia cristatella*
Least	*pusilla*

Parakeet	*Cyclorrhynchus psittacula*
Rhinoceros	*Cerorhinca monocerata*
Whiskered	*Aethia pygmaea*
Avocet, American	*Recurvirostra americana*
Baldpate	*Anas americana*
Bananaquit	*Coereba flaveola*
Basketbird	*Icterus galbula* or *spurius*
Becard, Rose-throated	*Platypsaris aglaiae*
Bee-bird	*Tyrannus tyrannus*
Bee-martin	*Tyrannus tyrannus*
Bellbird	*Hylocichla mustelina*
Big Cranky	*Ardea herodias*
Bill-willie	*Catoptrophorus semipalmatus*
Bittern	
American	*Botaurus lentiginosus*
Least	*Ixobrychus exilis*
Blackbird	
Brewer's	*Euphagus cyanocephalus*
Red-winged	*Agelaius phoeniceus*
Rusty	*Euphagus carolinus*
Tricolored	*Agelaius tricolor*
Yellow-headed	*Xanthocephalus xanthocephalus*
Bluebill for either	
Greater Scaup or	*Aythya marila*
Lesser Scaup or	*affinis*

Ring-necked Duck or	*collaris*
Ruddy Duck	*Oxyura jamaicensis*
Bluebird	*Sialia*
Eastern	*sialis*
Mountain	*currucoides*
Western	*mexicana*
Blue Crane	*Ardea herodias*
Blue Darter for either	
Cooper's Hawk or	*Accipiter cooperii*
Sharp-shinned Hawk	*striatus*
Blue Peter for either	
American Coot or	*Fulica americana*
Purple Gallinule	*Porphyrula martinica*
Bobolink	*Dolichonyx oryzivorus*
Bobwhite	*Colinus virginianus*
Bogbumper	*Botaurus lentiginosus*
Bonxie	*Catharacta skua*
Booby	*Sula*
Blue-faced or Masked	*dactylatra*
Blue-footed	*nebouxii*
Brown or White-bellied	*leucogaster*
Bottle-head	*Pluvialis squatarola*
Brant	*Branta bernicla*
Black	*nigricans*
Bristle Tail	*Oxyura jamaicensis*
Broad-bill for either	
Greater Scaup or	*Aythya marila*
Lesser Scaup or	*affinis*

Redhead or	*americana*
Ruddy Duck or	*Oxyura jamaicensis*
Shoveler	*Anas clypeata*
Buffalo-bird	*Molothrus ater*
Bufflehead	*Bucephala albeola*
Bulbul	
Red-whiskered	*Pycnonotus jocosus*
Bunting	
Indigo	*Passerina cyanea*
Lark	*Calamospiza melanocorys*
Lazuli	*Passerina amoena*
McKay's	*Plectrophenax hyperboreus*
Painted	*Passerina ciris*
Snow	*Plectrophenax nivalis*
Varied	*Passerina versicolor*
Burgomaster	
Glaucous Gull or	*Larus hyperboreus*
Great Black-backed Gull	*marinus*
Bushtit	*Psaltriparus minimus*
Butcher-bird for either	*Lanius*
Loggerhead Shrike or	*ludovicianus*
Northern Shrike	*excubitor*
Buzzard	
Black	*Coragyps atratus*
Mexican	*Caracara cheriway*
Turkey	*Cathartes aura*

Calico-back	*Arenaria interpres*
Camp Robber	*Perisoreus canadensis*
Canary	
Blue	*Passerina cyanea*
Wild for either	
Goldfinch or	*Spinus tristis*
Yellow Warbler	*Dendroica petechia*
Canvasback	*Aythya valisineria*
Caracara	*Caracara cheriway*
Cardinal	*Cardinalis cardinalis*
Catbird	*Dumetella carolinensis*
Cedar Bird	*Bombycilla cedrorum*
Chachalaca	*Ortalus vetula*
Chaparral Cock	*Geococcyx californianus*
Chat	
Yellow-breasted and	
Long-tailed	*Icteria virens*
Chebec	*Empidonax minimus*
Cherry Bird	*Bombycilla cedrorum*
Chewink	*Pipilo erythrophthalmus*
Chickadee	*Parus*
Black-capped	*atricapillus*
Boreal	*hudsonicus*
Carolina	*carolinensis*
Chestnut-backed	*rufescens*
Gray-headed	*cinctus*
Mexican	*sclateri*
Mountain	*gambeli*

Chicken	*Tympanuchus*
Greater Prairie	*cupido*
Lesser Prairie	*pallidicinctus*
Chippy	*Spizella passerina*
Chuck-will's-widow	*Caprimulgus carolinensis*
Chukar	*Alectoris chukar*
Clam Bird	*Haemotopus palliatus*
Cock of the Woods	*Dryocopus pileatus*
Coffin-bearer	*Larus marinus*
Condor, California	*Gymnogyps californianus*
Coot, American	*Fulica americana*
Cormorant	*Phalacrocorax*
Brandt's	*penicillatus*
Double-crested	*auritus*
Great	*carbo*
Olivaceous	*olivaceus*
Pelagic	*pelagicus*
Red-faced	*urile*
Corn Crake	*Crex crex*
Cowbird	
Brown-headed or Common	*Molothus ater*
Bronzed or Red-eyed	*Tangavius aeneus*
Cowcow	*Coccyzus*
Crane	*Grus*
Sandhill	*canadensis*
Whooping	*americana*
Creeper, Brown or Tree	*Certhia familiaris*

Crossbill	*Loxia*
Red	*curvirostra*
White-winged	*leucoptera*
Crow	
Carrion	*Coragyps atratus*
Common	*Corvus brachyrhynchos*
Fish	*ossifragus*
Northwestern	*caurinus*
Cuckoo	*Coccyzus*
Black-billed	*erythropthalmus*
Black-eared or Mangrove	*minor*
Yellow-billed	*americanus*
Ground	*Geococcyx californianus*
Curlew	*Numenius*
Bristle-thighed	*tahitiensis*
Eskimo	*borealis*
Hudsonian	*phaeopus*
Long-billed	*americanus*
Spanish	*Eudocimus albus*
Cutwater	*Rynchops nigra*
Dabchick	*Podilymbus podiceps*
Daddy-long-legs	*Himantopus mexicanus*
Darter	*Accipiter*
Blue	*cooperii*
Little Blue	*striatus*
Devil-down-head	*Sitta*
Dickcissel	*Spiza americana*
Dipper	*Cinclus mexicanus*

Dotterel	*Eudromias morinellus*
Dove	
Ground	*Columbina passerina*
Inca	*Scardafella inca*
Mourning	*Zenaida macroura*
Ringed Turtle	*Streptopelia risoria*
Rock	*Columba livia*
Spotted	*Streptopelia chinensis*
White-fronted	*Leptotila verreauxi*
White-winged	*Zenaida asiatica*
Zenaida	*aurita*
Dovekie	*Alle alle*
Dowitcher	*Limnodromus*
Long-billed	*scolopaceus*
Short-billed	*griseus*
Duck	
Black	*Anas rubripes*
Black-bellied Tree	*Dendrocygna autumnalis*
Fulvous Tree	*bicolor*
Dusky	*Anas fulvigula*
Gray	*strepera*
Harlequin	*Histrionicus histrionicus*
Labrador	*Camptorhynchus labradorius*
Masked	*Oxyura dominica*
Mexican	*Anas diazi*
Mottled	*fulvigula*
Ring-necked	*Aythya collaris*

Rock	*Histrionicus histrionicus*
Ruddy	*Oxyura jamaicensis*
Whistling	*Bucephala clangula*
American Wigeon	*Anas americana*
European Wigeon	*penelope*
Wood	*Aix sponsa*
Dunlin	*Calidris alpina*
Eagle	
Bald	*Haliaeetus leucocephalus*
Golden	*Aquila chrysaetos*
Egret	
Cattle	*Bubulcus ibis*
Common or Great	*Casmerodius albus*
Reddish	*Dichromanassa rufescens*
Snowy	*Egretta thula*
Eider	
Common	*Somateria mollissima*
King	*spectabilis*
Spectacled	*fischeri*
Steller's	*Polysticta stelleri*
Falcon	*Falco*
Aplomado	*femoralis*
Peregrine	*peregrinus*
Prairie	*mexicanus*
Finch	
Black Rosy	*Leucosticte atrata*
Brown-capped Rosy	*australis*

Cassin's	*Carpodacus cassinii*
Gray-crowned Rosy	*Leucosticte tephrocotis*
House	*Carpodacus mexicanus*
McGregor's House	*mexicanus*
Purple	*purpureus*
Flamecrest	*Regulus satrapa*
Flamingo, American	*Phoenicopterus ruber*
Flicker, Common	*Colaptes auratus*
Gilded	*auratus*
Red-shafted	*auratus*
Yellow-shafted	*auratus*
Flinthead	*Mycteria americana*
Flycatcher	
Alder	*Empidonax alnorum*
Ash-throated	*Myiarchus cinerascens*
Beardless	*Camptostoma imberbe*
Buff-breasted	*Empidonax fulvifrons*
Coues'	*Contopus pertinax*
Dusky	*Empidonax oberholseri*
Fork-tailed	*Muscivora tyrannus*
Gray	*Empidonax wrightii*
Great Crested	*Myiarchus crinitus*
Hammond's	*Empidonax hammondii*
Kiskadee	*Pitangus sulphuratus*
Least	*Empidonax minimus*
Olivaceous	*Myiarchus tuberculifer*
Olive-sided	*Nuttallornis borealis*
Scissor-tailed	*Muscivora forficata*

Sulphur-bellied	*Myiodynastes luteiventris*
Traill's (now divided into Alder and Willow)	
Vermillion	*Pyrocephalus rubinus*
Western	*Empidonax difficilis*
Wied's Crested	*Myiarchus tyrannulus*
Willow	*Empidonax traillii*
Yellow-bellied	*flaviventris*
Fly-up-the-creek	*Butorides virescens*
Forest Chippy	*Helmitheros vermivorus*
Frigate Bird	*Fregata magnificens*
Fulmar	*Fulmarus glacialis*
Gadwal	*Anas strepera*
Gallinule	
Common	*Gallinula chloropus*
Purple	*Porphyrula martinica*
Gannet	*Morus bassanus*
Gnatcatcher	
Black-tailed	*Polioptila melanura*
Blue-gray	*caerulea*
Goatsucker	*Caprimulgus*
Gobbler	*Meleagris gallopavo*
Godwit	
Bar-tailed	*Limosa lapponica*
Hudsonian	*haemastica*
Marbled	*fedoa*
Goldcrest	*Regulus satrapa*

Goldeneye

    Barrow's   *Bucephala islandica*

    Common   *clangula*

Goldfinch

    American   *Spinus tristis*

    Lawrence's   *lawrencei*

    Lesser   *psaltria*

Goosander   *Mergus merganser*

Goose

    Barnacle   *Branta leucopsis*

    Blue   *Chen caerulescens*

    Cackling   *Branta canadensis minima*

    Canada   *Branta canadensis*

    Emperor   *Philacte canagica*

    Ross'   *Chen rossii*

    Snow   *Chen caerulescens hyperborea*

    Tule   *Anser albifrons*

    White-fronted   *Anser albifrons*

Goshawk   *Accipiter gentilis*

    Mexican   *Buteo nitidus*

Gosling

Grackle

    Boat-tailed   *Cassidix major*

    Bronzed   *Quiscalus quiscula*

    Common   *quiscula*

    Great-tailed   *Cassidix mexicanus*

    Purple   *Quiscalus quiscula*

Grebe

Eared	*Podiceps nigricollis*
Holboell's	*grisigena*
Horned	*auritus*
Least	*dominicus*
Mexican	*dominicus*
Pied-billed	*Podilymbus podiceps*
Red-necked	*Podiceps grisegena*
Western	*Aechmophorus occidentalis*

Greenlet

Grosbeak

Black-headed	*Pheucticus melanocephalus*
Blue	*Guiraca caerulea*
Evening	*Hesperiphona vespertina*
Pine	*Pinicola enucleator*
Rose-breasted	*Pheucticus ludovicianus*

Ground-chat   *Geothlypis poliocephala*

Grouse

Blue	*Dendragapus obscurus*
Ruffed	*Bonasa umbellus*
Sage	*Centrocercus urophasianus*
Sharp-tailed	*Pedioecetes phasianellus*
Spruce	*Canachites canadensis*

Guillemot

Black	*Cepphus grylle*
Pigeon	*columba*

Gull

Black-headed	*Larus ridibundus*
Bonaparte's	*philadelphia*
California	*californicus*
Franklin's	*pipixcan*
Glaucous	*hyperboreus*
Glaucous-winged	*glaucescens*
Great Black-backed	*marinus*
Heermann's	*heermanni*
Herring	*argentatus*
Iceland	*glaucoides*
Laughing	*atricilla*
Little	*minutus*
Mew	*canus*
Ring-billed	*delawarensis*
Ross'	*Rhodostethia rosea*
Sabine's	*Xema sabini*
Thayer's	*Larus thayeri*
Western	*occidentalis*

Gyrfalcon	*Falco rusticolus*
Hag, Hagdon, Hagdown, Haglet	*Puffinus gravis*
Handsaw	*Ardea*
Hangnest	*Icterus*
Harrier, Marsh	*Circus cyaneus*

Hawk

Black	*Buteogallus anthracinus*
Broad-winged	*Buteo platypterus*

Cooper's	*Accipiter cooperii*
Duck	*Falco peregrinus*
Ferruginous	*Buteo regalis*
Fish	*Pandion haliaetus*
Gray	*Buteo nitidus*
Harlan's	*jamaicensis*
Harris'	*Parabuteo unicinctus*
Marsh	*Circus cyaneus*
Red-shouldered	*Buteo lineatus*
Red-tailed	*jamaicensis*
Rough-legged	*lagopus*
Sharp-shinned	*Accipiter striatus*
Short-tailed	*Buteo brachyurus*
Sparrow	*Falco sparverius*
Swainson's	*Buteo swainsoni*
White-tailed	*albicaudatus*
Zone-tailed	*albonotatus*
Heath Hen	*Tympanuchus cupido*
Hell-diver	*Podiceps*
Heron	
Black-crowned Night	*Nycticorax nycticorax*
Great Blue	*Ardea herodias*
Great White	*herodias*
Green	*Butorides virescens*
Little Blue	*Florida caerulea*
Louisiana	*Hydranassa tricolor*
Tricolored	*tricolor*
Yellow-crowned Night	*Nyctanassa violacea*

High-hole	*Colaptes auratus*
Honeycreeper, Bahama	*Coereba flaveola*
Hummingbird	
Allen's	*Selasphorus sasin*
Anna's	*Calypte anna*
Black-chinned	*Archilochus alexandri*
Blue-throated	*Lampornis clemenciae*
Broad-billed	*Cyanthus latirostris*
Broad-tailed	*Selasphorus platycercus*
Buff-bellied	*Amazilia yucatanensis*
Calliope	*Stellula calliope*
Costa's	*Calypte costae*
Lucifer	*Calothorax lucifer*
Rivoli's	*Eugenes fulgens*
Ruby-throated	*Archilochus colubris*
Rufous	*Selasphorus rufus*
Violet-crowned	*Amazilia verticalis*
White-eared	*Hylocharis leucotis*
Ibis	
Glossy	*Plegadis falcinellus*
Scarlet	*Eudocimus ruber*
White	*albus*
White-faced	*Plegadis chihi*
Wood	*Mycteria americana*
Jacana	*Jacana spinosa*
Jaeger	
Long-tailed	*Stercorarius longicaudus*
Parasitic	*parasiticus*
Pomarine	*pomarinus*

Jay

Arizona	*Aphelocoma ultramarina*
Blue	*Cyanocitta cristata*
California	*Aphelocoma coerulescens*
Canada	*Perisoreus canadensis*
Florida	*Aphelocoma coerulescens*
Gray	*Perisoreus canadensis*
Green	*Cyanocorax yncas*
Mexican	*Aphelocoma ultramarina*
Pinon	*Gymnorhinus cyanocephalus*
Santa Cruz	*Aphelocoma coerulescens*
Scrub	*coerulescens*
Steller's	*Cyanocitta stelleri*

Junco

Dark-eyed	*Junco hyemalis*
Gray-headed	*caniceps*
Mexican	*phaeonotus*
Oregon	*hyemalis oreganus*
Pink-sided	*hyemalis oreganus*
Red-backed	*phaeonotus*
Slate-colored	*hyemalis*
White-winged	*hyemalis*
Yellow-eyed	*phaeonotus*

Kestrel, American	*Falco sparverius*
Killdeer	*Charadrius vociferus*

Kingbird

Arkansas	*Tyrannus verticalis*
Cassin's	*vociferans*
Eastern	*tyrannus*
Gray	*dominicensis*
Tropical	*melancholicus*
Western	*verticalis*

Kingfisher

Belted	*Megaceryle alcyon*
Green	*Chloroceryle americana*
Ringed	*Megaceryle torquata*
Texas	*torquata*

Kinglet

Golden-crowned	*Regulus satrapa*
Ruby-crowned	*calendula*

Kite

Everglade	*Rostrhamus sociabilis*
Mississippi	*Ictinia misisippiensis*
Snail	*Rostrhamus sociabilis*
Swallow-tailed	*Elanoides forficatus*
White-tailed	*Elanus leucurus*

Kittiwake

Black-legged	*Rissa tridactyla*
Red-legged	*brevirostris*
Knot	*Calidris canutus*
Lanner	*Falco peregrinus*
Lapwing	*Vanellus vanellus*

Lark

Horned	*Eremophila alpestris*
Shore	*alpestris*

Limpkin	*Aramus guarauna*
Linnet	*Carduelis cannabina*
Log-cock	*Dryocopus pileatus*

Longspur

Chestnut-collared	*Calcarius ornatus*
Lapland	*lapponicus*
McCown's	*mccownii*
Smith's	*pictus*

Loon

Arctic	*Gavia arctica*
Common	*immer*
Pacific	*arctica*
Red-throated	*stellata*
Yellow-billed	*adamsii*

Magnificent Frigatebird	*Fregata magnificens*

Magpie

Black-billed	*Pica pica*
Yellow-billed	*nuttalli*

Mallard	*Anas platyrhynchos*
Man-o'-war Bird	*Fregata magnificens*
Marsh Hen	*Fulica americana* or *Rallus longirostris*
Martin, Purple	*Progne subis*

Meadowlark

Eastern	*Sturnella magna*
Western	*neglecta*

Merganser
  Common   *Mergus merganser*
  Hooded   *Lophodytes cucullatus*
  Red-breasted   *Mergus serrator*
Merlin   *Falco columbarius*
Mockingbird   *Mimus polyglottos*
Mother Carey's Chicken *Oceanodroma*
Mud-hen   *Fulica americana*
Murre
  Common   *Uria aalge*
  Thick-billed   *lomvia*
Murrelet
  Ancient   *Synthliboramphus
                    antiquum*
  Craveri's   *Endomychura craveri*
  Kittlitz's   *Brachyramphus
                    brevirostris*
  Marbled   *marmoratus*
  Xantus'   *Endomychura hypoleuca*
Nighthawk
  Common   *Chordeiles minor*
  Lesser   *acutipennis*
Nightjar   *Caprimulgus vociferus*
  Buff-collared   *ridgwayi*
Noddy   *Anous stolidus*
Nonpareil   *Passerina ciris*
Nutcracker, Clark's *Nucifraga columbiana*
Nuthatch
  Brown-headed   *Sitta pusilla*
  Pigmy   *pygmaea*

Red-breasted	*canadensis*
White-breasted	*carolinensis*
Oldsquaw	*Clangula hyemalis*
Oriole	
Baltimore	*Icterus galbula*
Black-headed	*graduacauda*
Bullock's	*galbula bullockii*
Hooded	*cucullatus*
Lichtenstein's	*gularis*
Northern	*galbula*
Orchard	*spurius*
Scott's	*parisorum*
Spotted-breasted	*pectoralis*
Osprey	*Pandion haliaetus*
Ouzel, ousel	*Cinclus mexicanus*
Ovenbird	*Seiurus aurocapillus*
Owl	
Barn	*Tyto alba*
Barred	*Strix varia*
Bog	*Asio flammeus*
Boreal	*Aegolius funereus*
Burrowing	*Speotyto cunicularia*
Elf	*Micrathene whitneyi*
Ferruginous	*Glaucidium brasilianum*
Flammulated	*Otus flammeolus*
Great Gray	*Strix nebulosa*
Great Horned	*Bubo virginianus*
Hawk	*Surnia ulula*
Hoot	*Bubo virginianus* or *Strix varia*

Long-eared	*Asio otus*
Monkey and Monkey-faced	*Tyto alba*
Pygmy	*Glaucidium gnoma*
Saw-whet	*Aegolius acadicus*
Screech	*Otus asio*
Short-eared	*Asio flammeus*
Snowy	*Nyctea scandiaca*
Spotted	*Strix occidentalis*
Whiskered	*Otus trichopsis*
Oystercatcher	
American	*Haematopus palliatus*
Black	*bachmani*
Parakeet, Paroquet	
Carolina	*Conuropsis carolinensis*
Monk	*Myiopsitta monachus*
Parrot	
Sea	*Fratercula arctica*
Thick-billed	*Rhynchopsitta pachyrhyncha*
Partridge, Gray	*Perdix perdix*
Pauraque	*Nyctidromus albicollis*
Peabody Bird	*Zonotrichia albicollis*
Pelican	
Brown	*Pelecanus occidentalis*
White	*erythrorhynchos*
Peter Bird	*Parus bicolor*

Petrel

Ashy	*Oceanodroma homochroa*
Black	*melania*
Black-bellied	*Fregetta tropica*
Black-capped	*Pterodroma hasitata*
Cape	*Daption capense*
Fork-tailed	*Oceanodroma furcata*
Galapagos	*tethys*
Harcourt's	*castro*
Leach's	*leucorhoa*
Least	*Halocyptena microsoma*
Scaled	*Pterodroma inexpectata*
White-faced	*Pelagodroma marina*
Wilson's	*Oceanites oceanicus*

Pewee

Eastern Wood	*Contopus virens*
Western Wood	*sordidulus*

Phainopepla	*Phainopepla nitens*

Phalarope

Grey	*Phalaropus fulicarius*
Northern	*Lobipes lobatus*
Red	*Phalaropus fulicarius*
Red-necked	*Lobipes lobatus*
Wilson's	*Steganopus tricolor*

Pheasant, Ring-necked	*Phasianus colchicus*

Phoebe

Black	*Sayornis nigricans*
Eastern	*phoebe*
Say's	*saya*

Pigeon

Band-tailed	*Columba fasciata*
Passenger	*Ectopistes migratorius*
Red-billed	*Columba flavirostris*
White-crowned	*leucocephala*

Pintail	*Anas acuta*

Pipit

American	*Anthus spinoletta*
Sprague's	*spragueii*
Water	*spinoletta*

Plover

American Golden	*Pluvialis dominica*
Barnyard	*Tringa solitaria*
Black-bellied	*Pluvialis squatarola*
Grey	*squatarola*
Mountain	*Charadrius montanus*
Piping	*melodus*
Ringed	*hiaticula*
Semipalmated	*semipalmatus*
Snowy	*alexandrinus*
Thick-billed	*wilsonia*
Upland	*Bartramia longicauda*
Wilson's	*Charadrius wilsonia*

Poor Joe	*Ardea herodias*
Poor-will	*Phalaenoptilus nuttallii*
Popinjay	
Prairie Chicken	*Tympanuchus*
Preacher Bird	*Vireo olivaceus*

Ptarmigan
    Rock   *Lagopus mutus*
    White-tailed   *leucurus*
    Willow   *lagopus*

Puffin
    Common   *Fratercula arctica*
    Horned   *corniculata*
    Tufted   *Lunda cirrhata*

Pyrrhuloxia   *Pyrrhuloxia sinuata*

Quail
    California   *Lophortyx californicus*
    Gambel's   *gambelii*
    Harlequin   *Cyrtonyx montezumae*
    Mountain   *Oreortyx pictus*
    Scaled   *Callipepla squamata*

Rail
    Black   *Laterallus jamaicensis*
    Clapper   *Rallus longirostris*
    King   *elegans*
    Virginia   *limicola*
    Yellow   *Coturnicops*
                    noveboracensis

Rain Bird   *Coccyzus*

Raven
    Common   *Corvus corax*
    White-necked   *cryptoleucus*

Razorbill   *Alca torda* or
                    Cepphus grylle

Redbird   *Cardinalis cardinalis*

Redbreast	*Turdus migratorius*
Redhammer	*Colaptes auritus cafer*
Redhead	*Aythya americana*
Redpoll	
Common	*Acanthis flammea*
Hoary	*hornemanni*
Redstart	
American	*Setophaga ruticilla*
Painted	*picta*
Reed-bird	*Dolichonyx oryzivorus*
Rice-bird	*Dolichonyx oryzivorus*
Roadrunner	*Geococcyx californianus*
Robert o' Lincoln	*Dolichonyx oryzivorus*
Robin	*Turdus migratorius*
Rubythroat	*Archilochus colubris*
Ruff, Reeve	*Philomachus pugnax*
Sanderling	*Calidris alba*
Sandpiper	
Bartramian	*Bartramia longicauda*
Buff-breasted	*Tryngites subruficollis*
Curlew	*Calidris ferruginea*
Least	*minutilla*
Pectoral	*melanotos*
Purple	*maritima*
Red-backed	*alpina*
Rock	*ptilocnemis*
Semipalmated	*pusillus*
Sharp-tailed	*acuminata*

Solitary	*Tringa solitaria*
Spoon-bill	*Eurynorhynchus pygmeum*
Spotted	*Actitis macularia*
Stilt	*Micropalama himantopus*
Upland	*Bartamia longicauda*
Western	*Calidris mauri*
White-rumped	*fuscicollis*
Sapsucker	
Yellow-bellied	*Sphyrapicus varius*
Williamson's	*thyroideus*
Sawbill	*Mergus*
Saw-filer	*Aegolius acadicus*
Scaup	
Greater	*Aythya marila*
Lesser	*affinis*
Scoter	
Black	*Melanitta nigra*
Common	*nigra*
Surf	*perspicillata*
Velvet	*fusca*
White-winged	*deglandi*
Sea Pigeon	*Cepphus grylle*
Seedeater, White-collared	*Sporophila torqueola*
Sewick	*Empidonax minimus*
Shag	*Phalacrocorax auritus*
Shearwater	
Audubon's	*Puffinus lherminieri*
Black-tailed	*Adamastor cinereus*

Cory's	*Puffinus diomedea*
Flesh-footed	*carneipes*
Greater	*gravis*
Little	*assimilis*
Manx	*puffinus*
New Zealand	*bulleri*
Pale-footed	*carneipes*
Pink-footed	*creatopus*
Short-tailed	*tenuirostris*
Slender-billed	*tenuirostris*
Sooty	*griseus*
Sheldrake, Sheld Duck	*Mergus*
Shite Pote or Poke	*Botaurus lentiginosus* or *Nycticorax nycticorax* or *violacea* or *Butorides virescens*
Shore Lark	*Eremophila alpestris*
Shoveler	*Anas clypeata*
Shrike	
Loggerhead	*Lanius ludovicianus*
Northern	*excubitor*
Sickle Bill	*Numenius americanus*
Siskin, Pine	*Spinus pinus*
Skimmer, Black	*Rynchops nigra*
Skua	*Catharacta skua*
Skylark	*Alauda arvensis*
Snake Bird, Snake Killer	*Anhinga anhinga* or *Geococcyx californicus*
Snipe	
Common	*Capella gallinago*

Grass	*Calidris melanotos*
Great	*Galligano media*
Jack	*Lymnocryptes minimus*
Robin	*Calidris canutus*
Rock	*maritima*
Sea	*Lobipes lobatus* or *Phalaropus fulicarius*
Wilson's	*Capella gallinago*
Telltale	*Tringa flavipes* or *melanoleucus*
Snow Bird	*Junco hyemalis*
Snowflake	*Plectrophenax nivalis*
Solitaire, Townsend's	*Myadestes townsendi*
Sora	*Porzana carolina*

Sparrow

Bachman's	*Aimophila aestivalis*
Baird's	*Ammodramus bairdii*
Black-chinned	*Spizella atrogularis*
Black-throated	*Amphispiza bilineata*
Botteri's	*Aimophila botterii*
Brewer's	*Spizella breweri*
Cape Sable	*Ammospiza maritima mirabilis*
Cassin's	*Aimophila cassinii*
Chipping	*Spizella passerina*
Clay-colored	*pallida*
Dusky Seaside	*Ammospiza maritima nigrescens*

English	*Passer domesticus*
European Tree	*montanus*
Field	*Spizella pusilla*
Fox	*Passerella iliaca*
Golden-crowned	*Zonotrichia atricapilla*
Grasshopper	*Ammodramus savannarum*
Harris'	*Zonotrichia querula*
Henslow's	*Ammodramus henslowii*
House	*Passer domesticus*
Ipswich	*Passerculus sandwichensis princeps*
Lark	*Chondestes grammacus*
LeConte's	*Ammospiza leconteii*
Lincoln's	*Melospiza lincolnii*
Olive	*Arremonops rufivirgata*
Pinewoods	*Aimophila aestivalis*
Rufous-crowned	*ruficeps*
Rufous-winged	*carpalis*
Sage	*Amphispiza belli*
Savannah	*Passerculus sandwichensis*
Seaside	*Ammospiza maritima*
Sharp-tailed	*caudacuta*
Song	*Melospiza melodia*
Swamp	*georgiana*
Tree	*Spizella arborea*
Vesper	*Pooecetes gramineus*
White-crowned	*Zonotrichia leucophrys*
White-throated	*albicollis*

Spoonbill, Roseate	*Ajaja ajaja*
Sprig	*Anas acuta*
Stake Driver	*Botaurus lentiginosus*
Starling	*Sturnus vulgaris*
Stilt	
Black-necked	*Himantopus mexicanus*
Black-winged	*himantopus*
Stork, Wood	*Mycteria americana*
Sugarbird	*Coereba flaveola*
Summer Redbird	*Piranga rubra*
Surfbird	*Aphriza virgata*
Swallow	
Bank	*Riparia riparia*
Barn	*Hirundo rustica*
Cave	*Petrochelidon fulva*
Cliff	*pyrrhonota*
Rough-winged	*Stelgidopteryx ruficollis*
Tree	*Iridoprocne bicolor*
Violet-green	*Tachycineta thalassina*
Swan	
Mute	*Cygnus olor*
Trumpeter	*Olor buccinator*
Whistling	*columbianus*
Swift	
Black	*Cypseloides niger*
Chimney	*Chaetura pelagica*
Vaux's	*vauxi*
White-throated	*Aeronautes saxatalis*

Tanager
Hepatic	*Piranga flava*
Scarlet	*olivacea*
Summer	*rubra*
Western	*ludoviciana*

Tattler, Wandering	*Heteroscelus incanus*
Teacher Bird	*Seiurus aurocapillus*

Teal
American Green-winged	*Anas crecca carolinensis*
Baikal	*formosa*
Blue-winged	*discors*
Cinnamon	*cyanoptera*
Common	*crecca*
Eurasian Green-winged	*crecca (?)*
European	*crecca (?)*
Green-winged	*crecca*

Teeter Bird	*Actitis macularia* or *Tringa solitaria*

Tern
Aleutian	*Sterna aleutica*
Arctic	*paradisaea*
Black	*Chlidonias niger*
Black Noddy	*Anous tenuirostris*
Bridled	*Sterna anaethetus*
Cabot's	*Thalasseus sandvicensis*
Caspian	*Hydroprogne caspia*
Common	*Sterna hirundo*

Elegant	*Thalasseus elegans*
Forster's	*Sterna forsteri*
Gull-billed	*Gelochelidon nilotica*
Least	*Sterna albifrons*
Noddy	*Anous stolidus*
Roseate	*Sterna dougallii*
Royal	*Thalasseus maximus*
Sandwich	*sandvicensis*
Sooty	*Sterna fuscata*
Trudeau's	*trudeaui*
Wilson's	*hirundo*
Thrasher	
Bendire's	*Toxostoma bendirei*
Brown	*rufum*
California	*redivivum*
Crissal	*dorsale*
Curve-billed	*curvirostre*
Le Conte's	*lecontei*
Long-billed	*longirostre*
Sage	*Oreoscoptes montanus*
Thrush	
Gray-cheeked	*Catharus minimus*
Hermit	*guttata*
Olive-backed	*ustulata*
Swainson's	*ustulata*
Varied	*Ixoreus naevius*
Wilson's	*Catharus fuscescens*
Wood	*Hylocichla mustelina*
Thunder Pumper	*Botaurus lentiginosus*

Tiercel	*Accipiter gentilis* or *Falco peregrinus*
Timber Doodle	*Philohela minor*
Tip-up	*Actitis macularia* or *Tringa solitaria*
Titlark	*Anthus spinoletta*
Titmouse	
Black-crested	*Parus atricristatus*
Bridled	*wollweberi*
Plain	*inornatus*
Tufted	*bicolor*
Tomtit	*Parus bicolor*
Towhee	
Abert's	*Pipilo aberti*
Brown	*fuscus*
Green-tailed	*Chlorura chlorura*
Rufous-sided	*Pipilo erythrophthalmus*
Trogon, Coppery-tailed	*Trogon elegans*
Tropicbird	
Red-billed	*Phaethon aethereus*
Red-tailed	*rubicauda*
White-tailed	*lepturus*
Turkey	*Meleagris gallopavo*
Turnstone	
Black	*Arenaria melanocephala*
Ruddy	*interpres*
Veery	*Catharus fuscescens*
Verdin	*Auriparus flaviceps*

Vireo

Bell's	*Vireo bellii*
Black-capped	*atricapilla*
Black-whiskered	*altiloquus*
Gray	*vicinior*
Hutton's	*huttoni*
Philadelphia	*philadelphicus*
Red-eyed	*olivaceus*
Solitary	*solitarius*
Warbling	*gilvus*
White-eyed	*griseus*
Yellow-green	*flavoviridis*
Yellow-throated	*flavifrons*

Vulture

Black	*Coragyps atratus*
Turkey	*Cathartes aura*

Wagtail

Yellow	*Motacilla flava*
White	*alba*

Wake Up	*Colaptes auratus*
Wandering Tatler	*Heteroscelus incanus*

Warbler

Arctic	*Phylloscopus borealis*
Audubon's	*Dendroica coronata*
Bachman's	*Vermivora bachmanii*
Bay-breasted	*Dendroica castanea*
Black-and-white	*Mniotilta varia*
Blackburnian	*Dendroica fusca*
Blackpoll	*striata*

Black-throated Blue	*caerulescens*
Black-throated Gray	*nigrescens*
Black-throated Green	*virens*
Blue-winged	*Vermivora pinus*
Canada	*Wilsonia canadensis*
Cape May	*Dendroica tigrina*
Cerulean	*cerulea*
Chestnut-sided	*pensylvanica*
Colima	*Vermivora crissalis*
Connecticut	*Oporornis agilis*
Golden-cheeked	*Dendroica chrysoparia*
Golden-winged	*Vermivora chrysoptera*
Grace's	*Dendroica graciae*
Hermit	*occidentalis*
Hooded	*Wilsonia citrina*
Kentucky	*Oporornis formosus*
Kirtland's	*Dendroica kirtlandii*
Lucy's	*Vermivora luciae*
MacGillivray's	*Oporornis tolmiei*
Magnolia	*Dendroica magnolia*
Mourning	*Oporornis philadelphia*
Myrtle	*Dendroica coronata*
Nashville	*Vermivora ruficapilla*
Necklace	*Wilsonia canadensis*
Olive	*Peucedramus taeniatus*
Olive-backed	*Parula pitiayumi*
Orange-crowned	*Vermivora celata*
Palm	*Dendroica palmarum*
Parula, Northern	*Parula americana*

Parula, Tropical	*pitiayumi*
Pine	*Dendroica pinus*
Prairie	*discolor*
Prothonotary	*Protonotaria citrea*
Red-faced	*Cardellina rubrifrons*
Swainson's	*Limnothlypis swainsonii*
Tennessee	*Vermivora peregrina*
Townsend's	*Dendroica townsendi*
Virginia's	*Vermivora virginiae*
Wilson's	*Wilsonia pusilla*
Worm-eating	*Helmitheros vermivorus*
Yellow	*Dendroica petechia*
Yellow-rumped	*coronata*
Yellow-throated	*dominica*
Water Belcher	*Botaurus lentiginosus*
Water Ouzel	*Cinclus mexicanus*
Waterthrush	
Louisiana	*Seiurus motacilla*
Northern	*Seiurus noveboracensis*
Waterturkey	*Anhinga anhinga*
Wavy	*Chen caerulescens hyperborea*
Waxwing	
Bohemian	*Bombycilla garrulus*
Cedar	*cedrorum*
Wheatear	*Oenanthe oenanthe*
Whimbrel	*Numenius phaeopus*
Whip-poor-will	*Caprimulgus vociferus*
Ridgway's	*ridgwayi*

Whiskey Jack, Whiskey Jay	*Perisoreus canadensis*
Wigeon	
American	*Anas americana*
European	*penelope*
Willet	*Catoptrophorus semipalmatus*
Woodcock	
American	*Philohela minor*
European	*Scolopax rusticola*
Woodpecker	
Acorn	*Melanerpes formicivorus*
American Three-toed	*Picoides tridactylus*
Ant	*Colaptes auratus*
Arctic Three-toed	*Picoides arcticus*
Arizona	*Dendrocopos arizonae*
Black-backed Three-toed	*Picoides arcticus*
Downy	*Dendrocopos pubescens*
Gila	*Centurus uropygialis*
Golden-fronted	*aurifrons*
Golden-winged	*Colaptes auratus*
Hairy	*Dendrocopos villosus*
Ivory-billed	*Campephilus principalis*
Ladder-backed	*Dendrocopos scalaris*
Lewis'	*Asyndesmus lewis*
Northern Three-toed	*Picoides tridactylus*
Nuttall's	*Dendrocopos nuttallii*
Pileated	*Dryocopus pileatus*

Red-bellied	*Centurus carolinus*
Red-cockaded	*Dendrocopos borealis*
Red-headed	*Melanerpes erythrocephalus*
White-headed	*Dendrocopos albolarvatus*

Wren

Bewick's	*Thryomanes bewickii*
Brown-throated	*Troglodytes brunneicollis*
Cactus	*Campylorhynchus brunneicapillus*
Canyon	*Catherpes mexicanus*
Carolina	*Thryothorus ludovicianus*
House	*Troglodytes aedon*
Long-billed Marsh	*Telmatodytes palustris*
Rock	*Salpinctes obsoletus*
Short-billed Marsh	*Cistothorus platensis*
Winter	*Troglodytes troglodytes*

Wrentit	*Chamaea fasciata*
Yellowhammer	*Colaptes auratus*

Yellowlegs

Greater	*Tringa melanoleucus*
Lesser	*Tringa flavipes*
Yellowthroat	*Geothlypis trichas*